Hospitality Management

AN INTRODUCTION

Kevin Baker
and
Jeremy Huyton

HOSPITALITY
PRESS
MELBOURNE

Hospitality Press Pty Ltd
38 Riddell Parade
PO Box 426
Elsternwick Victoria 3185
Australia
Telephone (+61 3) 9528 5021 Fax (+61 3) 9528 2645
Email hosppress@access.net.au

Hospitality Management: an Introduction

First published 2001

National Library of Australia
Cataloguing-in-publication data:

Baker, Kevin, 1949– .

   Hospitality management: an introduction.

   Bibliography.
   Includes index.
   ISBN 1 86250 500 4.

   1. Hospitality industry—Management. I. Huyton, Jeremy,
   1946– . II. Title.

647.068

Edited by Ross Gilham (Ginross Editorial Services)
Designed by Lauren Statham (Alice Graphics)
Printed in Australia by Openbook Publishers, Adelaide
Published by Hospitality Press Pty Ltd (ABN 69 935 151 798)

Contents

PART I

Functional Areas of Hospitality Management

PART II

Specialised Areas of Hospitality Management

Acknowledgments

The authors acknowledge the comments and advice of our editor, Dr Ross Gilham, who is experienced in the production of silk purses.

We also gratefully acknowledge Jamal Feerasta, Assistant Professor, Hospitality Management Program, University of Akron, Ohio, USA, for contributing the text on performance appraisal (in Chapter 9), and particularly for his development of the 'diary method' of appraisal discussed in that chapter.

Thanks also to Judy Lundy, and to colleagues and notables whose views have left subliminal imprints.

We are also grateful to the people who reviewed and corrected the various languages in Appendix 1, the Multilingual Manager—Bev Robinson, Dee Martin, Marie Hamacher, Angeline Baker, Penny Baker, Joanna Pickles, and Marcello Napoli.

The authors also acknowledge the Parkroyal Canberra, Hotel Kurrajong, and Casino Canberra Ltd for their photographs, and for giving permission for their use.

Finally, special thanks to David Cunningham, publisher of Hospitality Press, for the faith he continues to place in the authors.

About the Authors

Dr Kevin Baker is professor of hospitality management at the International University College, Bad Honnef, Germany. Dr Jeremy Huyton is assistant dean (academic) at the Australian International Hotel School, Canberra, Australia. Between them they have more than forty years' experience in hospitality industry management and teaching in Australia, the United Kingdom, Europe, the Caribbean, Africa, and China. The authors have published seven textbooks on various aspects of hospitality management and teaching.

Preface

Why write a book introducing hospitality management?

First, the hospitality sector has become a major part of a modern economy and looks set to expand still further in the twenty-first century.

Secondly, because hospitality is centred around service, good management is crucial. Surveys reveal that guests tend to judge the quality of a hospitality enterprise not so much by the quality of the physical fabric, but by the quality of the personal service that they receive. But hospitality staff might have only a few moments when checking guests in, or when taking an order, to impress guests with their friendliness and competence. First impressions are crucial. Good operational management is crucial to ensure that these first impressions are positive ones. These constant but fleeting interactions are termed 'moments of truth' by hospitality operators. They are the few short minutes in which each of us has to establish a rapport that says: 'We care'. Top-quality management of operations is perhaps even more important in a service-orientated enterprise than it is a goods-based operation—because the personal experience *is* the product.

Thirdly, hospitality management is a profession, and an important one. It requires a range of diverse skills. Hospitality is much more than the traditional role of the congenial host. Today's manager must understand the globalisation of the world's commerce, must have organisational and financial skills, and must possess a flair for dealing with people of many different cultures. The hotel manager needs some knowledge of the various aspects of hotel operations, including food & beverage, housekeeping, and the rooms division in general. The specialised areas of management require specific skills. In larger hotels or motels, these roles will be filled by qualified professionals, but a successful hotel manager will have at least some knowledge of these functions.

For these reasons—the growing economic importance of the hospitality industry, the centrality of service, and the multi-faceted nature of modern hospitality management—the authors feel that a comprehensive introductory text on hospitality management is timely.

This book introduces the industry and the skills of the hospitality manager. The book is arranged in two parts—functional areas of hospitality management, and specialised areas of hospitality management.

The first part—functional areas of hospitality management—is divided into five chapters.

- Chapter 1 is an overview placing hospitality management within an overall context of hospitality, including its history and development, the current status of the world industry, and the importance of hospitality in Australia and the Asia–Pacific region.

- Chapter 2 considers the role of management in general, and the role of the general manager in particular.
- Chapter 3 discusses the front office.
- Chapter 4 moves on to housekeeping, laundry, and maintenance.
- Chapter 5 covers food & beverage services.

Part II—specialised areas of hospitality management—is also divided into five chapters.

- Chapter 6 is a consideration of hospitality law.
- Chapter 7 is concerned with a discussion of marketing.
- Chapter 8 moves on to a discussion of hospital accounting.
- Chapter 9 is a consideration of personnel management.
- Chapter 10 covers casinos and gambling operations from a management perspective.

The book concludes with two appendices. The first provides useful foreign language phrases for hospitality managers and staff, and Appendix 2 provides a useful list of sources of data on the hospitality industry.

The volume concludes with chapter notes, a useful bibliography, a glossary, and an index.

Part I

Functional Areas of Hospitality Management

The Context of Hospitality Management

Education, technology and entrepreneurship are the three great creators of wealth in the modern community.

Brian Quinn
quoted by Tom Peters in *The Pursuit of Wow*

Synopsis of chapter

This chapter sets up the backdrop for the study of hotel management. The history and development of tourism is considered, and then the current status of the world tourism and hospitality industry is outlined. The chapter then describes the importance of the industry in Australia and the Asia–Pacific region.

Definitions of hospitality

'Hospitality' is a word that has come into common commercial use—for example, when economists speak of the 'hospitality industry', or the 'hospitality sector'. The word as it used now seems to imply no more than the exchange of a commercial service. However, in earlier common usage, 'hospitality' had a far wider meaning, conveying the bestowal of friendship and trust, and even bearing within it hints of a sacred duty.

The *Concise Oxford Dictionary* defines 'hospitality' as 'the friendly and generous reception and entertainment of guests or strangers'.[1] In the dictionary, the word comes just after 'hospitalism' which is defined as 'the adverse effects of a prolonged stay in hospital'. Sometimes it might be feared that guests who stay at a hospitality facility that is not professionally managed could emerge suffering more from 'hospitalism'—rather than the pleasant memory of 'hospitality'!

To be 'hospitable' is to 'give welcome and entertainment to strangers or guests'.[2] 'Welcome' is a word derived from an Old English word 'wilcuma', which translates into modern English as 'a person whose coming is pleasing'.[3] The *Oxford Thesaurus* offers several words that are similar to 'hospitality': they include 'graciousness', 'courtesy', 'friendliness', 'cordiality', 'sociability', and 'generosity'.[4]

It is therefore evident that 'hospitality' is a word that implies more than simply giving shelter, or allowing the occupation of a space or room. Commercial practice might have reduced the transaction to a strictly legal arrangement governed by contract law, but hospitality involves a host of other implications apart from a minimal legal contract. This is why hospitality is a profession.

There are ethical and sociological aspects to the transaction of hospitality, and there are complex psychological flavours at work as well. The guests of a hospitality establishment are in a relationship of trust with the host— while asleep, the guests are vulnerable and at risk. Similarly, the host is at risk—for he or she has admitted a stranger into the building.

Taking all of these factors into account, the authors of this book put forward the following definition of hospitality.

> A commercial contract to enter into a service relationship that involves supplying the amenities, comforts, conveniences, social interactions, and experiences of shelter and entertainment that a guest or customer values.

Note that hospitality is a 'service relationship'—which means that it is an interaction between one individual and another. It is also based upon providing a service that is *valued* by the guest or customer—which means that it has to meet the paying customer's subjective expectations. This involves far more than providing superficial inducements—such as putting a complimentary chocolate on the guest's pillow each night, or providing a lukewarm half-bottle of cheap wine as a 'welcome'. Hospitality involves *consideration and service of each guest as an individual*—an individual whose presence is welcomed and valued, whether in a hotel, a restaurant, a resort, a cruise ship, or any other of the wide range of hospitality enterprises. Hospitality is thus the art of providing a valued intangible service. 'Intangible' literally means something that cannot be touched. There is no assembly line for mass-producing hospitality services, as there can be for a physical manufactured product. This is why hospitality is a 'people skill' that must be learnt and perfected.

Tourism is linked with hospitality. A definition of 'tourism' is:[5]

. . . the science, art and business of attracting and transporting visitors, accommodating them, and graciously catering to their needs and wants.

Butkarat & Meddlik

Thus *tourism* as a concept includes *hospitality*. In some cases, *tourism* can include some functions not included within a basic understanding of hospitality—for example, the provision of transport and travel. Conversely, *hospitality* can include some services not necessarily associated with tourism— for example, food & beverage services for non-visitors, some types of business convention, gaming facilities, and some aspects of accommodation (such as long-stay accommodation). However, the concepts of hospitality and tourism are so closely intertwined that one could not exist without the other. This book does not attempt to split the two by fine distinctions. Different sectors of the industry (considered as a whole) will be considered in detail in later chapters.

A pioneer of tourism and hospitality— Thomas Cook

One of the first tourism and hospitality professionals in Europe was Thomas Cook. He was born in England in 1808 and was very religious. When in his twenties, he became involved with the Total Abstinence League and organised their meetings, which involved booking train trips and lunch for more than a hundred people at a time.

In 1845, Cook hit upon the idea of booking special trains for the meetings, and he then had the further idea of linking this train travel (and steamship travel as well) with hotel bookings. In the next year, he branched out from Total Abstinence League meetings and organised a group tour of Scotland in 1847. He followed this with trips to London in 1851, to Dublin in 1853, to Paris in 1855 and, eventually, trips to Mecca.

When he died in 1892, Cook's business had grown into the largest tour operator of the day. He had intuitively grasped the opportunity offered by improved railways and steamships to make travel popular and affordable to ordinary people.

Investigate package tours in your region.

QUESTIONS

- List the companies that operate 'package tours' in your region.
- Itemise the different packages and create a matrix of the various companies and what they offer.
- Compare prices and explain why there is a difference.
- Compare such packages with international tours.

A short history of hospitality

In ancient times

Tourism and hospitality go back a long way. In 879 BCE,[6] when the Assyrian emperor, Assurnasirpal II, completed his new capital city, called Nimrud, he invited guests from every corner of his empire to come to the capital for the inaugural celebrations. A stone tablet records that 69 574 tourists responded to the emperor's invitation and spent ten days on an all-inclusive 'group tour' of Nimrud and its attractions.

The Olympic Games first took place around 770 BCE. It could be said that the competitors and spectators who undertook journeys on foot of fifty or a hundred kilometres (or more) to attend the Games were some of the world's first tourists. The hospitality venues available to them amounted to the houses of family or friends, communal buildings or tents in a barracks style, or the shelter of trees and handy caves. The Games had a religious significance to the ancient Greeks, and the Games included festivities to honour Zeus, first among the gods. Much of the travel in these ages had religious motives. People travelled to a holy place or to meet a holy person whose message was spread by word of mouth by these travellers. They found hospitality with strangers on the road, and this shelter was often given as a religious duty, such that the host would share the merit of the pilgrim. Besides the Games at Olympia, other popular travel destinations were the Pythian Games at Delphi (featuring chariot races) and the homes of the gods at Argos and Corinth.

Travel was not easy anywhere around the world at that time, but doughty individuals still set off, most often on foot, motivated by the desire to trade, to pray, or simply to satisfy curiosity. In Australia, it was common for Aborigines to travel throughout the country and there were extensive trading routes across the continent. It was a part of tribal custom to offer sanctuary and hospitality to the peaceful visitor.

The earliest surviving map to guide world travellers was compiled by Anaximander of Miletus in approximately 570 BCE. The first road maps

Figure 1.1 *Despite the hardships, people still had a hankering to travel in ancient times*

Kevin Baker

should probably be attributed to the Romans, who built an extensive road network to make possible the military and administrative rule of their empire and, in so doing, created a means for reasonably free and economic travel around the Mediterranean and parts of Europe. The Romans might also have invented the 'business lunch'—when the keeper of an inn on the River Tiber offered special lunch deals for shipowners who did not have the opportunity to go back to their villas in Rome for a meal.

Herodotus was a Greek historian and geographer who lived from approximately 480 to 421 BCE. He travelled for curiosity and the desire to see strange and different lands—which makes him one of the world's first

Plato's view

The ancient Greek philosopher Plato wrote:[7]

'A great many different countries go to make up our world . . . It is an enormous place, and we, whose civilisation stretches from the river Phasis to the pillars of Hercules, occupy only a small part of it. In other places, there are men living in countries similar to ours.'

tourists. He travelled mainly by sea from his home at Samos to parts of modern-day Turkey, Greece, Sicily, Egypt, Iraq, and Iran. Herodotus wrote accounts of his travels that are still read today.

Besides travellers on pilgrimage, other travellers had three main motives, all of them related to wealth-gathering. They were members of armies intent on conquest, or officials checking out options for tax-collecting, or traders looking for a hot bargain in a foreign marketplace. Travel was expensive, because they needed not only equipment and reliable means of transport (small boats with new-fangled sails for waterborne travel and camels for land travel), but also interpreters, guides, and a battalion of guards to ward off those who preyed on tourists. The hospitality venue was usually well fortified and capacious—to provide room to park the many draught animals required by a caravan.

One of the more popular and profitable routes for business travellers was the 'Silk Road' which stretched from the eastern Mediterranean to western China. The accommodation along the way was generally good, in the sense that travellers could find good reliable water and supplies at reasonable cost.

Two thousand years ago, the leading entrepreneurs were often referred to as 'Emperors'.[8] They encouraged 'tourism' by their use of taxation officials and armies who were responsible for seeking new business opportunities and profit. To that end, the emperors improved communications—such as the canals of eastern China (of up to two thousand kilometres in length), and the military roads of the Romans. Officials could stay at imperial posts, and common travellers who used the roads and canals could stay at the small

Figure 1.2 *Two thousand years ago, usually only the very wealthy could afford to travel*

Kevin Baker

inns that sprang up at intervals of one day's journey (about twenty kilometres). These hospitality ventures varied in quality. Many a traveller complained of rapacious innkeepers and bed bugs—both described as 'bloodsuckers'.

The Roman official Sidonius Apollinarius (who lived from 430 CE to 489 CE) was a frequent tourist. He looked forward to some of the holidays (that took up about one half of the Roman year) to get away from the city and travel to his resort at Avitacum, where he could enjoy rural pursuits as well as Alpine walks.

The tenth and eleventh centuries in Europe saw a growth in the popularity of pilgrimages. Groups travelling to local shrines, or as far afield as the eastern Mediterranean, numbered in the hundreds and sometimes in the thousands. Like all tourists, they brought souvenirs back to their homes and told stories that inspired others to travel the same roads.

Within the African continent there is evidence of extensive trade and travel routes. The stone tower and ruins at Great Zimbabwe appear to have been a centre of travel centuries ago.

Activity 1.2 *Trek to Great Zimbabwe*

To consider how time-consuming and expensive travel was before the twentieth century, undertake the following exercise.

You wish to travel to Great Zimbabwe by wagon (assume it is in a time when travel by wagon is possible). Great Zimbabwe is 450 kilometres away and your wagoner estimates that the trip will take thirty days, provided that there are no delays due to floods or other obstacles, but there will be no places en route where stores or quality fodder for the draught animals can be obtained.

The team who will assist you in your travel will be: your wagoner, two guides/interpreters, five armed men for an escort, and your personal servant—a total of ten people, including yourself. You will need a kilogram of food and other supplies per person per day. Fortunately you need not carry water for it is plentiful along the way at this time of year. You will also carry a hundred kilograms of trade goods and gifts to ease your passage through the countryside and to assuage officials at your destination.

Each wagon is drawn by two draught animals that will each need six kilograms of supplementary fodder in addition to what they can pick at along the route on the way. Each wagon needs a wagon driver, who also needs a kilogram of food per day. Each wagon also has to carry twenty kilograms of spare parts for the journey. Each wagon can carry either six people (that is, the driver and five passengers) or 500 kilograms of freight.

You have to pay your people in silver coins. The nine people in your team want two coins per day each. The wagon drivers want one coin per day and one coin to hire their wagon. The cost of fodder is one coin for a hundred kilograms; and the cost of food for your crew is one coin for twenty kilograms.

In your strongbox you have two thousand silver coins.

QUESTIONS

- Can you afford to travel to Great Zimbabwe?
- How much extra should you add in case floods delay your travel by five to ten days?
- Can you afford to pay for the return journey if the above costs are the same for the return?
  (For the solution to this Activity, see page 31.)

A thousand years ago, there was an increase in entrepreneurial tourism. The Vikings from Scandinavia took up travel with enthusiasm, both west to North America and east to Persia, using their highly developed vessels to cross oceans and traverse rivers.

There were also individuals such as Ibn Battuta, a scholar from Tangier who left his home town on 13 June 1325 for twenty-nine years travelling around Africa and Asia, writing travel diaries that were social, political, and economic treatises. Other Muslim travellers, such as Al-Bakri and Al-Masudi, visited different regions of Africa. The practice of the annual pilgrimage to Mecca encouraged many Muslims to travel. There were the Venetian merchants Nicolo and Maffeo Polo (and Nicolo's son Marco) who set off for Peking on business in 1256 and purportedly came back to Europe with a spaghetti/noodle 'franchise', and there was the Chinese sailor Cheng Ho who voyaged around the Indian Ocean and the Cape of Good Hope to East Africa via Java, Sri Lanka, and Vietnam. The fourteenth century saw a decline in travel in Europe and parts of Asia by merchants, pilgrims, and adventurers —caused partly by the Black Death, a plague carried from central Asia and spread by travellers.

From five hundred years ago

From the fifteenth century onwards, with economic recovery and the technological advantage of the sailing ship, Europeans set out to all the corners of the globe—to explore, to trade, and to occupy. They did not always prebook accommodation! Nor did they pay fair rates for the hospitality that they received!

At the same time, there was an increase in travel for health reasons. Spa resorts and 'taking the waters' (bathing in supposedly health-giving spa waters) became more popular with the wealthy. By the eighteenth century, there was a great increase in travel and tourism. In Europe, the 'Grand Tour' of the major centres of the continent became popular with those who could afford it—hence the origin of the word 'tourism'. Gibbon noted in 1785 that no fewer than 40 000 English citizens were travelling on the continent.

Peter the Great of Russia spent a year journeying through the countries of western Europe. Roads were improved—usually by the forced labour of local peasants, which practice was called the 'corvée'. Coaching inns became common, wherever it was necessary to change horses on the coach at the end of a 'stage' (hence the word 'stagecoach'). These small inns were generally little more than private houses or farms that were conveniently situated. The quality of these inns was not always acceptable. There were few regulations, and the hazards included watered-down beer and biting bugs. An Englishwoman who wrote as 'Mrs Cradock' kept and published a journal of her travel around Europe from 1783 to 1786. She stated that the universal problem with all the inns she stayed at was the bed bug. In one hotel, she and her maid killed 464 bugs before 'Mrs Craddock' considered the bed safe to sleep in!

In 1788, European settlement of Australia began. Australia must be the only nation on earth that commenced as an 'accommodation facility'! As such, it was reliant upon the 'services sector' for the first fifty years of its existence under British rule—although the convicts who made up the bulk of the population were 'guests of the Crown', rather than 'tourists'; and clearly the penal colony at Sydney Cove was not a resort!

In the early nineteenth century, networks of coach routes were developed, and these made it possible to travel to a timetable. The central coach depots became important transport hubs. In 1825, an anonymous French writer described the central coach depot of Paris, and made the observation that there were fifty arrivals and departures each day. Assuming a minimum of fifteen passengers per coach and, perhaps, thirty kisses each person (one for the departing person and one for the person seeing them off), the writer calculated 1500 kisses per day. This meant 45 000 a month and 540 000 per year, so that '. . . in less than a hundred years you will have enough salt water [that is, from the tears] to float a large battleship'.[9]

In 1830, Stephenson's 'Rocket' steam engine drew the first train—a mixed load of coal wagons and passenger wagons—at the previously unimagined speed of sixteen miles per hour from Liverpool to Manchester in England. Forty years later, the long-distance trains of the United States were famous, and entrepreneurs such as George Pullman built and operated trains that offered a range of luxurious appointments. Some of the hotels did not match the standard of railway accommodation. A writer named Baedeker recommended that travellers take with them their own pillows, sheets, and insecticides, and be prepared to haggle with the innkeeper on the tariff, always offering 10–20% less than the innkeeper asked for.[10]

Figure 1.3 *Modes of travel are always changing*

Kevin Baker

Improvements in technology have always heralded an expansion of travel and tourism and, in the nineteenth century, the development of railway systems and steamships saw another increase in travel opportunities. Even the less well-off could afford to travel to other regions and countries, and to a newly developed concept—the beachside holiday resort. With the popularisation of travel, hotel chains were established, and the hospitality model as we know it came about.

With the mass appeal of travel to the middle classes in the twentieth century—greatly aided by changes in labour practices, namely the granting of public holidays and extended leave—the hospitality manager became more than a mere innkeeper. Hospitality became more than providing a roof for the night and protection from marauders. It became an integral part of the tourism sector, offering a multifaceted product. A profession had been born.

Activity 1.3   A local history

Using local archives, libraries, and historical societies, explore your immediate area to ascertain the earliest recorded history of hospitality activity. Find the first accommodation service, and the first food & beverage service.

The global hospitality industry

The industry worldwide

The tourism and hospitality sector of the world economy is enormous. It makes up approximately 12% of the world gross domestic product (GDP),[11] employs 8% of all employees, and accounts for approximately 11% of capital investment throughout the world.[12] This makes the global tourism and hospitality industry one of the largest in the world in terms of employment and economic activity. Moreover, as global economic growth continues, this growth overflows into hospitality because business travellers make up one of the most important markets for the accommodation sector.

The industry is labour-intensive (because of its nature as an individually based service industry), and tourism and hospitality enterprises are generally decentralised, because they are spread widely and are often small enterprises such as tourist shops, restaurants, and small accommodation venues (although, of course, there are also some extremely large corporations in the industry). Tourism spending has a substantial 'multiplier effect'—that is, the money spent at a hotel or resort flows through to local suppliers of goods and services and also flows into the local economy through the wages paid to staff.

The industry is of vital importance to many national economies. It is a source of employment and economic growth through consumption and investment in infrastructure (such as hotels and airports), and it also produces foreign exchange (that is, currencies other than the local currency). Foreign exchange brought into a country by the tourism industry is important because it is gained by domestic production and offsets current account deficits that result from an excess of imports over exports. Tourism and hospitality operations are also economically important because of taxes on revenues and profits.

The world's tourism remains skewed towards the wealthier countries. Approximately 60% of the world's tourism industry is in Europe, and 12% is in North America—although other destinations and markets (such as China, Thailand, and Australia) are increasing their market shares. Reflecting this distribution, the people who travel are from the United States, the United Kingdom, Germany, France, and Japan. These five countries account for approximately half of the world's tourism expenditures.

There are several forces driving the growth in world tourism. These include the expansion of the economies of many countries, the spread of technology, and the expansion in international trade relations. Travel is becoming more affordable, thus allowing more people to travel. The World Tourism Organization and the World Travel and Tourism Council have produced optimistic growth forecasts for world tourism—of 4% per year—as development spreads throughout the world, and as new tourist destinations are publicised (for example, in eastern Europe). Improved employment conditions have given many employees more leave and hence more time to travel. Increased life-expectancy (and the consequent 'ageing' of the world's population) also contributes to the growth of tourism and hospitality—because retirees often have the means and the leisure to travel and enjoy the experience. Increased global trade means that there is also more business travel.

Activity 1.4   *Writing about travel*

There have been many authors who have written about the travel experience. They include: Stendhal; Robert Louis Stevenson (*Travels with a Donkey*); Joseph Conrad; Balzac; and Jules Verne (*Around the World in Eighty Days*).

This activity explores modern travel writing and other media presentations of travel.

QUESTIONS

- Using the Internet, create a list of modern-day travel writers (but select those who have written books rather than journal or newspaper articles). List their specialist areas and appraise their writing style.
- List television travel programs available on your local channels. Do they have any regional or travel specialisations (such as focusing on air travel, for example)?

There are some drawbacks in expanding the global tourism and hospitality industry—just as almost every human activity has costs as well as benefits. Some of the drawbacks of expanding tourism and hospitality operations and infrastructure include the following.

- Local services such as roads and airports can become congested.
- Some areas and attractions can become crowded, setting delicate environments and heritage constructions at risk.
- The demand for labour can attract workers from other crucial areas of the local economy, and can drive up wage rates across the board.
- New demands for local products can distort local markets.

There are many issues facing the industry worldwide. Some of these issues include the following questions.

- What is the appropriate role of governments in regulating tourism and hospitality enterprises and to what extent should the industry be deregulated?

- How can the economic expansion of tourism infrastructure be carried out to take account of the environment and ecosystems?
- What is the appropriate role of global organisations and should they have effective control of subsectors (for example, airline operations) within the industry?
- How will technology change the delivery of hospitality services?
- What are appropriate education models for the industry?

The industry in the Asian region

The Asian region experienced an economic and financial crisis in 1997–98. One of the results of this was a fall in inbound tourism arrivals in 1998 but, as the regional economies improved in 1999, so did the tourism industry. Inbound tourism arrivals increased by 4.7% in 1999, and currency devaluations in 2000 benefited tourists from Europe and the United States who chose vacations in countries such as Malaysia and Thailand.[13] Despite the improvement, hotel occupancies remained generally low, and hence profitability was also down. The Arthur Andersen Hotel Industry Benchmark Survey of fifteen capital cities in Asia reported that there was a wide variance in occupancy rates between one capital city and another. In only one city (Seoul) did the average occupancy rates reach 80%. In Jakarta, the average occupancy rate was only 29%.[14]

In 1998, ten Asian countries ranked among the world's top forty destinations in terms of arrivals—including China (6th), Hong Kong (18th), Thailand (21st), Singapore (26th), Malaysia (27th), and Australia (33rd). In terms of receipts, India and the Philippines jumped into the list of the top forty highest receipt-earners, because visitors tend to stay in those countries longer than in some others. For example, the average length of stay in India was 24 days—whereas, in China, it was seven days and, in Hong Kong, four days. There were 76 million visitors to the Asian region in 1998, growing by 7.9% to 2001, and by 6.7% to 2004.[15]

Sectors of the industry

The tourism and hospitality industry has been divided into a number of areas, and the variety of tourism enterprises is almost unlimited, embracing such specialised areas as ecotourism, farm tourism, heritage tourism, pilgrimage tourism, and so on.

Hospitality enterprises are also multifaceted. Under the broad heading of 'tourism and hospitality' there are several service areas that, themselves, are subdivided into components.

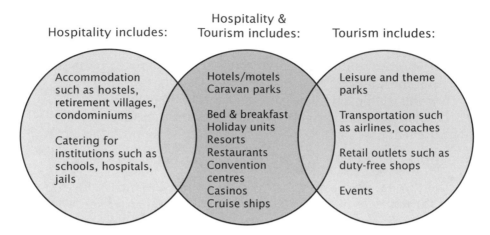

Figure 1.4 *Hospitality and tourism*

Kevin Baker

The lodging services sector

This sector includes short-stay and long-stay accommodation facilities. The sector can be subdivided into hotels, motels, boarding-houses, resorts, convention hotels, caravan parks, and long-stay accommodation institutions (such as retirement units). The standard of facilities extends from five-star hotels to backpacker hostels (so-named because their guests are often young people on holiday with their clothes and belongings in a backpack). Camping grounds can be added to this list—depending upon the level of services.

Food & beverage services

Food & beverage (F&B) services can be subdivided into:

- stand-alone restaurants;
- food & beverage outlets that are integral with other businesses (such as hotels, clubs, banqueting, and function venues); and
- other institutions (including commercial operations and institutional food services).

Food & beverage services can be designed to a theme (or a concept), or be menu-driven. They can range from a top-class restaurant to a roadside van. Fast-food outlets can be included under this category, although there is an argument that this sort of food service better sits under the definition of a 'retailer' because the customers are more likely to be locals than visitors.

Specialised wine merchants and bottle shops (that is, off-licence liquor outlets)[16] are also on the boundaries of the 'F&B' definition, servicing local trade as much as (or more than) hospitality consumers.

Travel and tourism services

This category of services is linked to some of the above lodging and food & beverage enterprises, but this heading also includes tour operators and travel agents—as well as the network of transportation services (sea, air, and land). Transportation services include services such as car rentals.

Activity 1.5	*Tourism and hospitality infrastructure*

Search a library or the Internet for details of an island or oceanside area with pristine beaches and sealife. Consider some issues surrounding the construction of tourism infrastructure in the area. Such infrastructure might be airport or harbour facilities (to enable tourists to arrive for a day visit) or might be accommodation facilities (such as a hotel or a resort to cater for extended stays by visitors). How many issues can you list?

Recreation and entertainment services

This category overlaps with some of the above, but also includes functions and events. One of the largest activities within this sector is the gaming industry, which includes casinos and gambling facilities within clubs and hotels. In Australia, the gambling sector of the hospitality industry includes not only casinos but also TAB (Totalisator Agency Board) outlets, Keno gaming, and other gaming activities—such as poker machines. Recreation services also include facilities such as golf courses and theme parks.

Tourism-related services

This heading includes some retail outlets (such as duty-free shops and souvenir shops) that rely on tourists and visitors for the majority of their custom. It also includes tourism attractions such as natural attractions (for example, cave formations as at Jenolan, New South Wales, or thermal areas as at Rotorua, New Zealand) and built attractions (for example, underground houses at Lightning Ridge).

Space Tourism?

One of the (possibly) more far-fetched proposals for tourism encompasses space tourism. The company putting forward the proposal is Space Adventures, which plans to offer suborbital space flights. Each six-day flight will cost travellers US$90 000. Another firm, architects Wimberly, Allison, Tong and Goo, has prepared preliminary plans for an orbiting 100-room hotel. The hotel will require artificial gravity—otherwise guests will have to be stuck to the walls with Velcro![17]

Figure 1.5 *Space tourism*

Kevin Baker

Apart from subdividing hospitality enterprises by the *type of services offered*, enterprises can also be subdivided on the basis of the *groups who make use of the service*. For a hotel or a resort, and its associated restaurant facilities, the demand for services comes from three main groups:

- business travellers;
- conference travellers; and
- recreation or holiday travellers (generically referred to as FITs—free independent travellers).

These groups can be subdivided further—for example, business travellers can be subdivided into private-sector and public-sector travellers; or holiday travellers can be subdivided into travellers on a tourism package and backpackers. Other subdivisions are also possible.

Apart from the main three groups (business, conference, FIT), there are also other groups—such as sporting groups and other special interest groups.

The product of the hospitality industry

The nature of an accommodation service

The basic hospitality product in the first category described above (the lodging services sector, page 16) is *accommodation*. This is offered in the form of the hotel room or, more properly, the *licence to use* the hotel room for a period of time. This period of time is usually defined as 'a night'—although it is really for 24 hours. Hence, hotel or motel services are usually quantified as a room for a night, or as a 'room–night'. Most of the world's supply of hotel rooms is in Europe (45% of world supply) and North America (30%). The Asia–Pacific region accounts for 13% of the world's supply, and Africa and Latin America contribute the remaining 12%.

The product offered to consumers by the hospitality industry has an unusual feature compared with, say, manufactured products. The hospitality product cannot, in effect, be 'touched'—it is *intangible*. It cannot be picked up and taken away for use by the consumer. Moreover, if the service is not used immediately when it becomes available, it becomes instantly *perishable*. That is, once the night has passed, the hotel cannot sell that particular accommodation to a guest; the product has 'perished'. Nor for that matter can a restaurant provide extra meals next day for the seats that were empty the night before. The airline industry is comparable, in that once the aircraft takes off, no more seats on the flight can be sold.

This *perishability* means that correct pricing and a knowledge of the market—local, regional, and international—are very important. Hotel operators discount their rates heavily if this means that they can increase the number of guests occupying rooms (the occupancy rate). In theory, operators can make a profit out of a very low room rate (the price charged to guests for occupying the room) because otherwise the room could be empty and producing no revenue at all. However, the problem then is that all their other guests expect to pay the same amount, and overall revenue can fall. The characteristics of the hospitality product will be revisited in the chapter on marketing (page 186) when, in addition to *intangibility* and *perishability* (as noted above), the *inseparability* and *variability* of the product will also be outlined.

A pioneer of tourism and hospitality— Isabella Bird

Isabella Bird was born in 1831 and died in 1904. During her life, she travelled and wrote about many countries and cultures—living with the local peoples, describing their customs, and photographing ordinary people and places. She travelled widely throughout Korea, Japan, Tibet, and China, as well as the Middle East. The Royal Geographic Society of England admitted her as its first woman member.

Hospitality and tourism agents and systems

Most bookings for hotel/motel rooms, resorts, and travel are made through agents who acts as brokers between hospitality providers and visitors/travellers. These agents usually operate out of suburban shopfronts or commercial offices. Travel agents can:

- sell travel in general; or
- be specialised wholesalers (who reserve bulk reservations with airlines and hotels); or
- be corporate travel agents.

Most countries and states operate their own tourism offices to encourage visitors to travel to their regions. Private operators who specialise in a like fashion are referred to as 'destination-management companies'.

Tourism agents use computerised booking systems—some on a global scale called 'global distribution systems'. Because of the size of the system required, and the number of agencies to make them effective, most computerised booking systems were established by large corporations, especially airlines (which had a higher number of reservations than any hotel chain due to the number of flights involved). Examples of some computerised reservation systems are Sabre (which is overseen by American Airlines and has 100 000 outlets), Apollo, Galileo, and Worldspan.

Hotel guests

Who are the people who stay at hotels? The Worldwide Hotel Industry Study indicated in 1998 that 52.6% of hotel room–nights were sourced from foreign travellers, whereas 47.4% were domestic.[18] Leisure travellers made up 34.1% of the market, business travellers 28.5%, tour groups 17.7%, and conference participants 10.1%. These are worldwide averages, and individual countries showed large variations from these norms.

Within Australia, most domestic travel is by leisure travellers. The motives for their travel are as varied as the people themselves. Business travellers include both private-sector and public-sector travellers, and this business sector tends to be the most attractive to hospitality operators—not only because of the frequency of their travel and the repeat business, but also because they are not as price-conscious (because their travel expenses are usually met by their businesses or their employers).

Activity 1.6   *Ethical consideration*

You are a member of the bell staff at a four-star hotel. It is late on your shift. A VDG ('very demanding guest') has just rung down and demanded copies of the first edition of the finance journal due out that day. This particular VDG has rapidly gained a reputation for being rude to staff who try to assist. And he never tips.

You check the clock. You have only ten minutes before you go home and you are tired after a very busy shift during which a pop group booked into your hotel, accompanied by television crews and groups of fans at every door of the hotel.

Would you be justified in 'losing' the service request for ten minutes? After all, when the demanding guest rings again in ten minutes (as he surely will do!), the task can be carried out by your colleagues on the bell staff who are due on duty shortly. What are your ethical responsibilities here—with respect to the demanding guest, to your colleagues, and to the hotel?

The hospitality industry in Australia

Overview

The tourism and hospitality industry is important for Australia. The industry directly employs approximately 700 000 people, and indirectly employs another 350 000—approximately one-eighth of the Australian labour force. According to the *Tourism Satellite Account* released in 2000—the first official study of how the tourism industry relates to Australia's national accounts—the industry makes up approximately 4.5% of gross domestic product (GDP), with a financial impact of AUS$58 billion. International tourists made up 21% of the industry's contribution to GDP in 1997/98, and the balance (79%) was generated by domestic tourism.

The history of the industry in Australia has been patchy. In the 1980s there was a boom period for hoteliers with a large increase in inbound tourism. Worldwide economic activity reached a peak and financial deregulation resulted in a ready supply of finance from institutions. Hotels raised room rates, and there was an unprecedented number of new hotels built. At the start of the 1990s, economic activity dived—resulting in a recession. Due to this recession and room oversupply, there was a drop in sales and profitability for many hospitality operations. There was also an extensive airline pilots' strike in Australia in 1989 which delivered a sharp blow to demand for hotel accommodation. Overall, during the first years of the 1990s, the hotel industry experienced losses, staff cuts, and declining service. Many tourists sought lower room rates, and four-star and five-star hotels particularly suffered.[19]

In the Australian hospitality market as a whole, the average occupancy in the year to June 1999 was 72%, and the average rate was AUS$141. The largest player in the Australian hotel market is the Sydney area—where there is a strong demand, due especially to the convention sector. However, the impact of hotel construction to cope with the influx of visitors for the 2000 Olympic Games has resulted in an oversupply of rooms. In terms of room numbers, the supply of accommodation in Melbourne rates behind Sydney. However, in the year ending June 1999 the occupancy rate in Melbourne was 79%, the highest in Australia for a capital city, just shading Sydney's 78%. The Gold Coast and North Queensland continue to benefit from mainly Asian visitors. Adelaide had a 3% growth in yield (a function of occupancy and rooms rate) to June 1999—the highest capital result for the country. Perth has shown some effects of oversupply, although the situation is improving.[20]

The types of hotels in Australia

There are many different types and concepts of accommodation available for visitors and travellers in Australia—including hotels, motels, caravan parks, cabins, and boarding houses. Hotels and motels are the most numerous type

How Phileas Fogg travelled 'Around the World in Eighty Days'

Phileas Fogg was a fictional character in a novel by Jules Verne. The plot of the novel revolved around a bet—whether Phileas Fogg could circle the globe within the (then) unheard-of time of eighty days.

His itinerary was: London to Suez by train and steamship (7 days); Suez to Bombay by ocean liner (13 days); Bombay to Calcutta by train (3 days); Calcutta to Hong Kong by ocean liner (13 days); Hong Kong to Yokohama, Japan, by ocean liner (6 days); Yokohama to San Francisco by ocean liner (22 days); San Francisco to New York by train (7 days); and New York to London by ocean liner and train (9 days).

The same trip by airliner today would take 24–48 hours!

of lodging property in Australia—comprising approximately one-third of the accommodation market (in terms of number of establishments and number of rooms). Broadly, hotels can be divided into:

- full-service hotels;
- budget hotels; and
- self-catering hotels.

Full-service hotels, as the name implies, provide a wide range of services for guests—including food & beverage, personal services (such as valet and laundry), and the provision of facilities for business.

Budget hotels provide basic rooms for guests, with limited food & beverage. Consequently, they are cheaper than full-service hotels. In the suburbs and small towns and crossroads of Australia, there are numerous such hotels, many dating back to the early days of European settlement. These are commonly referred to as 'pubs'. They are typically small, run by owners, and rely on bar trade. The names date from the nineteenth century, and it seems that almost every small town has a 'Royal Hotel', or a 'Commercial Hotel', or an 'Imperial Hotel'.

Included under the heading of 'budget hotels' are small hotels that are often referred to as 'bed and breakfast' (B&B) enterprises. These can be found in suburban settings in larger popular resorts, but can also be rural-based. Usually a B&B is run by a family–owner, as an extension of a private home, and can have as few as two or three rooms available for guests.[21]

Self-catering hotels are different again. These are more like conventional hotels, but provide rooms only, and often those rooms are shared. Guests fend for themselves with regard to food, laundry, and cleaning, although some such hotels supply limited cleaning services.

These three broad categories (full-service, budget, self-catering) can be extended into a larger number of distinctions—such as 'economy', 'mid-range', 'up-scale', 'luxury', 'presidential', and so on. The problem with using extended categories is that the distinctions among categories become blurred, and the categories become unwieldy to use. For example, the term 'luxury' is often used in hotel marketing, and its interpretation can be subjective. It is probably better to use the clearly understood distinction of *full-service*, *budget*, and *self-catering* in describing the range of services offered, and then add the star-rating to indicate the quality of the services.

Other types of classification

There are other types of classification sometimes used for hotels—besides those based on the level of service (as outlined above) or the price.

One such classification is based on location. Hotels can be called 'central hotels', 'suburban hotels', 'airport hotels', 'highway hotels', and so on.

Another classification is based on length of stay. Some hotels are termed 'short-stay', whereas others are called 'extended-stay'.

> ## *The biggest hotel in the world*
>
> The biggest hotel in the world is the MGM Grand Hotel in Las Vegas in the United States. It has more than 5500 rooms. One of the largest hotel chains is Hospitality Franchise Systems which runs more than 4000 properties—including the Ramada hotels and the Super 8 motel chain.

Motels

Motels fill a different category from hotels. In the years when motor vehicles were becoming popular, motels were established as 'motor-hotels'. They were usually close to major highways and offered rooms or units with separate entrances and parking facilities close by. Budget motels offer basic accommodation and might or might not offer some food services (such as breakfast). At the top end of the motel market, four-star and five-star motels differ little from four-star and five-star hotels—other than in size and number of floors.

Ownership

Hotels and motels in Australia are privately owned, with very few exceptions. (Several long-established properties were originally built as tourist accommodation by government—such as Jenolan Caves House in New South Wales, which has since been privatised.)

Hotel ownership can take the form of:

- private ownership of an independent hotel by a partnership, company, or sole trader; or
- group ownership of a number of hotels by an Australian-based company; or
- group ownership as part of an international chain.

Hotels can trade independently, or under the terms of a franchise agreement. A franchise is an arrangement whereby a property pays a franchiser (based on revenue and set fees) to use a brand name. The franchiser markets the brand and arranges reservations. The franchisee benefits from the marketing and also through the bulk purchase of goods (such as advertising and other goods).

A concept that is similar to franchising is a partnership of property owners with a marketing company that owns a well-known brand.

The expansion of franchising is an issue in the hospitality industry, as noted below (page 28).

Another form of partnership ownership comes about when a group of investors purchases a hospitality enterprise and operates it through a manager or a management company. In the hospitality industry, this form of partnership is referred to as a 'syndicate'.

The standards and rating of accommodation in Australia

The need for standards and hotel ratings grew out of the need to meet minimum service requirements, and to ensure quality control and consumer protection when mass tourism expanded in the 1960s. Classification is a category rating which ranks a property according to its type, facilities, and amenities. Grading is used to reflect quality assessment. Hotels and motels, a range of accommodation properties, and restaurants can all use ratings as part of their marketing.

The rating of accommodation in Australia arose from assessments of various hotels and motels compiled by motoring associations for their members' reference in the 1950s.[22] These assessments were supported by the Australian Hotels Association. The earliest ratings systems ranked hotels by stars, allocating four stars to the highest, three to the next, then two, and one star for the lowest rating. As the hotels were inspected, they were given points for the level of facilities offered and the standard of the furnishings. It was soon discovered that the ratings were too broad, especially between two and three stars, and so half a star was allocated where it was considered appropriate. The star-rating reflects such aspects as location of the property and details of room amenities. The star-rating of a hotel (or motel, or whatever) is, of course, reflected in the room rate.

In 1990, the system was reviewed by Standards Australia with input from Tourism Training Australia, and hospitality standards were brought into line with comparable international ratings schemes. The standard is entitled AS/NZS 3905.3:1994. Standards Australia holds a register of hospitality properties that meet the quality assurance standards that are recognised globally. This register of standards is distinct from the ratings scheme.

The Australian Automobile Association (AAA) has nearly 16 000 properties on its rating system, under five categories:[23]

- hotels/motels;
- camping and caravan parks;
- onsite park accommodation;
- holiday units and cabins; and
- B&Bs and guest houses.

The following are only two examples of accommodation ratings for hotels, and the standard of facilities and services required for the award of the rating:[24]

- *two-star:* well-maintained establishments with good furnishings, bedding, floor coverings, lighting, heating, and/or cooling facilities; all bedrooms have handbasins with hot and cold water;

- *four-star:* exceptionally well-appointed establishments with high-quality furnishings and offering a degree of comfort; quality lighting including bedlamps for each sleeping position; fully airconditioned with individual control; full diningroom/restaurant service and attractive quality furnished lounge or reception area; room service meals/liquor at least 6 p.m. to 11 p.m.; some rooms with queen-size beds and two armchairs.

Some properties attempt, with greater or lesser success, to claim a rating outside these officially recognised categories. For example, the Arab Tower Hotel in Abu Dhabi in the United Arab Emirates claims seven-star status—but its suites include gold-plated taps for the handbasins and similar fittings, so it seems there might be some justification for such claims!

Activity 1.7   *On the trail of Phileas Fogg*

Follow Phileas Fogg's itinerary (page 22) and see if you could replicate it exactly. If so, answer the following.

QUESTIONS

- How long would it take you?
- How many days would be spent delayed in cities?
- Would you encounter any difficulties that Fogg would not have encountered?
- What would the total cost be? (Assume that you use three-star accommodation for the days of waiting, add $70 per day for food and incidentals, and use economy standard transportation.)

Selected issues of the hospitality industry

Information technology and other new technologies

Developments in information technology (IT) have had profound effects on hospitality and tourism, just as they have had on all areas of commerce. If it were not for the fact that IT changes have permeated all areas of hospitality operations, the topic would merit a separate chapter. However, because IT can not (and should not) be divorced from all aspects of hospitality management, specific IT issues will emerge in the course of later chapters and be considered as they arise. IT changes are flagged here to put the issue in context, and to provide a general description of some important areas.

Developments in IT comprise the most important issue facing hotel managers. IT is all about information, and information provides knowledge for decision-making. As one writer has stated:[25]

Knowledge, knowledge, knowledge is what it's all about as the hotel industry frantically tries to reinvent itself for the 21st century.

The same article also claims that hospitality management has not been as quick or as ready as airlines and credit-card companies to utilise new information technology.

Recent technological advances have changed the way in which hotels operate, in addition to changing the way they are promoted and marketed over the expanding Internet. Figures from the Australian Bureau of Statistics, for the period February 1999–February 2000, indicate that 43% of all adults in Australia have access to the Internet. Of those who purchased goods and services over the Net, the top spending category was tourism and hospitality products—comprising 12% of all online purchases. The Australian government has established a National Online Tourism Strategy to take account of the growing importance of the Net to the industry.[26]

Because so many intending travellers use the Net and online information when planning their travel, virtually every hospitality enterprise that wishes to compete effectively in the marketplace now needs its own website (ideally with a strong keyword function to allow speedy access), and its own e-commerce strategy. Some hotels not only offer information on prices and facilities, but also include pictures of their rooms and panoramic scans of views from the property. Best Western Australia is only one example of a hotel chain that has developed an e-commerce strategy, with 85% of its properties adopting the strategy.[27]

As well as researching accommodation and other hospitality options, the prospective tourist should also be able to check visa and currency information, as well as physical aspects of the destination such as the weather and local attractions.

After intending travellers have researched their destinations and itinerary, they can then check availability, make bookings by email, and arrange deposits electronically (although care must always be taken when transmitting details of credit cards). If they so choose, intending travellers can also use online travel agents. Online agents in Australia usually have an Australian licence, and consumers thus have a degree of protection because such licensed agents support a Travel Compensation Fund.

Apart from the convenience of being able to access excellent information from home or office, the Internet also provides access to special deals. Some organisations even offer 'web-only' deals.

Other technological changes have also had an impact upon the hospitality product. Rapid changes in telecommunications technology mean that connections for television, computers, and business telecommunications might be desirable in guest rooms. Smart-card access systems can enhance and monitor guest security, and can monitor the movement of staff. Computerised reservations and check-in/check-out functions can change the way in which front offices are designed and operated.

IT can also improve the hotel's marketing function, using database management and warehousing to tailor approaches to prospective guests, and then being able to customise their stay, and subsequently offer them loyalty benefits.

Expanding reservations systems

Global Distribution Systems, or linked reservation systems, were originally developed by airlines. They have become indispensable for large hotel operators, although only about 7% of all reservations worldwide are handled by the systems,[28] and this proportion is being eclipsed by the Internet.[29] There is a tendency for large hotels to set up marketing consortia to handle advertising and marketing to global customers through their linked systems, and the expanded capabilities of these systems means that such factors as rates and rate displays can be updated frequently.

Although large hotels might thus appear to have a market edge, developments in IT can 'level the playing field', so to speak. Smaller operators can compete by repositioning their hospitality property to appeal to niche markets, with more specialised products, and can utilise Internet opportunities by developing websites that attract consumers in a cost-effective way and compete with the larger systems.

One sector of the industry in which small operators can compete effectively with larger properties is the backpacker sector. Backpackers, generally young and well-educated, are frequent users of the Internet for communications and information. Hospitality operators in this sector can thus market their products among prospective clients at least as efficiently as can large properties.

The expansion of franchising

Franchising is a concept that covers tourism and hospitality operations of many types, including restaurants (for example, Pizza Hut, McDonald's), motels (for example, Holiday Inn, Best Western), and theme parks. Typically, franchisers have established a quality product, marketed the product so that it is widely known, and then demonstrated their expertise in the field by a lengthy period of profitable operation. The franchisers are then able to market their format, their brand name, and their skilled support through a franchise package. Those who purchase the franchise, the franchisees, are able to enter the marketplace with a reasonable hope of success, being backed by specific expertise and market exposure. Franchising is especially attractive to small investors, because they have tailored support. This support often makes it easier for the investor to obtain finance, because banks and finance institutions usually take account of the strength of the franchiser in assessing the franchisee's application for finance. An example of franchising in Australia is that of Flag motels, which began as an owner-run consortium, but which has reorganised into a franchised product.

Themed hospitality

There are always new fashions in hotel design and development. One of the continuing trends is a 'boom in small, offbeat hotels where the interior design is cutting-edge or richly opulent . . .'.[30] These are also termed 'boutique' hotels and cater for a particular market segment, usually people who have the wealth and inclination to seek something different and exclusive. Another fashion is the trend towards privacy. In earlier times, there was a certain imperative to 'see and be seen', but now this is less important, although it still exists in parts of Asia and the Middle East.[31]

Food & beverage outlets are also being 'themed', and can be contracted out in 'innovative, symbiotic relationships in hotel dining that help build incremental revenue and foster brand identity'.[32] Brand restaurants, in particular, are creating new demands for hotel services, often from the general public as well as from guests.

Touring old battlefields

There are numerous tour opportunities to former battlefields and sites of military interest. An example of one such opportunity is a tour of former battle and prisoner-of-war sites in Singapore. Small groups of tourists— some consisting of former servicemen and servicewomen, and/or their relatives—can join local groups of schoolchildren who visit sites such as Changi Prison, with its associated museum. More than 130 000 British imperial troops were imprisoned at Changi. The story of these people is told, and afterwards there are simple ceremonies under the flags of Singapore, Malaysia, India, the UK, and Australia to commemorate the 24 000 Allied soldiers killed in the Pacific War.[33]

Focus on business travellers

Business travellers make up one of the largest segments of the hospitality market. They have particular needs including telecommunications (for example, video-conferencing) and support services (such as small meeting rooms for client appointments, and secretarial support).

The guest room for business travellers often becomes a 'business room' with in-room fax, on-call printer, access to the Internet, and two or more telephone lines. Studies have indicated that video-conferencing and telebeaming facilities are becoming increasingly attractive to business travellers.[34] These facilities can include news services and various e-commerce applications. To support these services, high-speed broadband Internet access is essential.

The Bass hotel chain (which includes InterContinental Hotels and Resorts, Crowne Plaza, Holiday Inn, and Staybridge Suites) negotiated a deal for in-room Internet technology to cover 120 000 rooms outside the United States. The cost to a typical Australian user is approximately US$20 per day.[35]

Chapter review questions

1   What were some of the 'ancient values' of hospitality?
2   Are hotels really hospitable?
3   Has the concept of 'hospitality' changed much over time?
4   What is the relationship between the hotel industry and the tourism industry?
5   What are some necessary factors for the development of tourism?
6   Which is the major partner—the hotel industry or the tourism industry?
7   What is the importance of quality assurance in lodging properties?
8   Describe some ways of managing hotels, and the advantages of the different setups.
9   What factors must be taken into account when deciding the market mix (the various types of potential customers) for a given hotel?
10 What are some of the benefits of information technology in tourism and hospitality?

Solution to Activity 1.2

THE GREAT ZIMBABWE TOUR

(See page 9 for details of this activity.)

Each wagon needs 12 kg per day of fodder for the animals, and 1 kg food for the wagon driver. Therefore, over thirty days, 390 kg of fodder and food is required for each wagon, as well as 20 kg of spares, giving a total of 410 kg.

Each wagon has a load capacity is 500 kg. Therefore, taking away this total of 410 kg (for fodder, food, and spares for the wagon alone), leaves only a mere 90 kg available for other freight. This was the problem with travel in those times. Travel was very slow and a traveller had to carry food for draught animals in many cases.

The freight that had to be carried was food for the 10-person team of interpreters, guards, and so on. For thirty days, this meant 300 kg, plus 100 kg of gifts. However, do not forget that the two wagons required to carry the team cannot carry their own fodder, so an additional 780 kg (390 × 2) must be carried by other wagons. Hence, the freight that must be carried totals 1180 kg. Dividing by 90 (the weight able to be carried by each wagon over and above fodder, food, and spares) means that at least fourteen wagons are needed for freight, plus two for passengers. This means that your caravan will be 16 wagons long.

Costs will be:

- for the team: 30 days × 9 people × 2 coins a day = 540 coins;
- for the drivers: 30 days × 16 drivers × 1 coin a day = 480 coins;
- for the wagon hire: 30 days x 16 wagons × 1 coin a day = 480 coins;
- cost of fodder: 30 days × 32 animals × 6 kg per day/100 = 58 coins;
- cost of food: 30 days × 26 people × 1 kg/20 = 34 coins

    Total 1592 coins.

    Cost for extra five days = 265 coins.

    Cost for extra ten days = 530 coins.

Therefore, with your 2000 coins, you could travel to Great Zimbabwe with a caravan of twenty-six people, including yourself, and sixteen wagons. You could afford a delay of five days (assuming you can buy fodder and food off another caravan perhaps, or even adding two wagons with extra stores), but you could not afford a delay of ten days. You would not have enough money for a return trip.

Clearly, travel by wagon was only for the very rich!

CASE STUDY

The HB Hotel

Figure 1.6 *The coat of arms of the HB Hotel*
Kevin Baker

The HB Hotel is a boutique four-star hotel of forty rooms with a stand-alone cottage in the grounds. It operates from a heritage-listed building in a coastal resort region called the Blossom Coast.

The hotel is set in two hectares of land on a promontory with sea on three sides. All of the grounds are well-kept gardens with an indoor/outdoor pool, children's play area, and grass tennis court. Next to the tennis court is an aviary, with the hotel's resident mascots—a white cockatoo called 'Turkey' and a bronze-wing turkey called 'Cocky'.

The rooms have been designed so that all face the sea. The rooms breakdown is as follows:

- 1 cottage suite ('Blossom Cottage');
- 1 honeymoon suite;
- 19 twin-bedded rooms (all with ensuite);
- 20 queen-sized rooms (all with ensuite);
- STD and IDD (International Direct Dialling);
- colour television and radio in all rooms; and
- free in-house videos.

The hotel also has a small 50-seat restaurant and bar, and a function room that holds up to 200 people. There is also a shaded parking for a hundred cars.

The owners, Huyton and Baker, are not resident and have recently placed the property in the hands of a manager, who faces a number of challenges. The first challenge is a review of the demand for hotel accommodation in the region. The owners have asked the manager to begin investigations for a profile of visitors to the region and a listing of the competition for hotel accommodation.

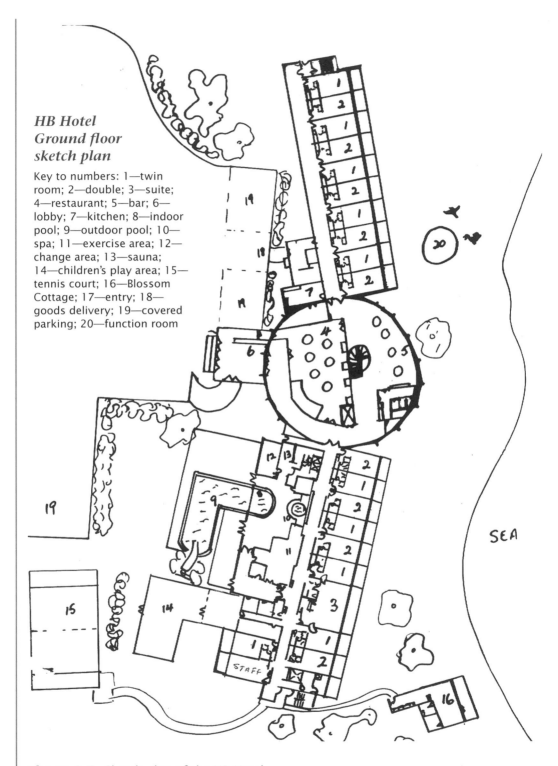

HB Hotel Ground floor sketch plan

Key to numbers: 1—twin room; 2—double; 3—suite; 4—restaurant; 5—bar; 6—lobby; 7—kitchen; 8—indoor pool; 9—outdoor pool; 10—spa; 11—exercise area; 12—change area; 13—sauna; 14—children's play area; 15—tennis court; 16—Blossom Cottage; 17—entry; 18—goods delivery; 19—covered parking; 20—function room

Figure 1.7 *Sketch plan of the HB Hotel*
Kevin Baker

The owners have thus asked the manager to write a brief report outlining:

- what information sources should be examined with a view to compiling a profile of the typical visitor to the Blossom Coast; and
- what information sources should be examined with a view to compiling useful information about competitors.

In the report, the manager is expected to give reasons for choosing the sources suggested.

What are your suggestions for the manager in undertaking the task set by the owners?

[Note: The HB Hotel is a fictional property. It will stand as a setting for consideration of various issues and matters related to hospitality. Each chapter will conclude with reference to the HB Hotel and the case study will be developed from chapter to chapter.]

HB Hotel
First floor
sketch plan

Key to numbers: 1—twin room; 2—double; 3—suite; 4—restaurant; 5—bar; 6—lobby; 7—kitchen; 8—indoor pool; 9—outdoor pool; 10—spa; 11—exercise area; 12—change area; 13—sauna; 14—children's play area; 15—tennis court; 16—Blossom Cottage; 17—entry; 18—goods delivery; 19—covered parking; 20—function room

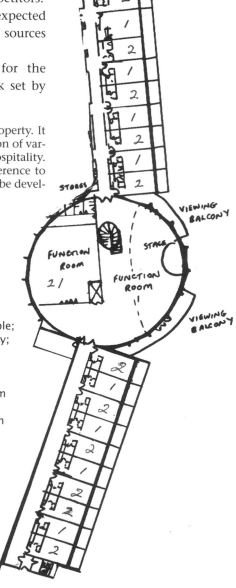

Figure 1.7 *Sketch plan of the HB Hotel (continued)*
Kevin Baker

Chapter 2

The General Manager

The measure of a person's greatness is not the number of servants they have but the number of people they serve.

Anonymous

Synopsis of chapter

This chapter examines the nature of management, with special emphasis on the role of the general manager. The chapter describes career paths in hospitality, and then moves on to a discussion of some issues in the industry. These issues include customer service, and the reasons for hospitality managers' aspiring to excellence in service. The chapter includes discussion on environmental and cultural awareness, and occupational health & safety.

The work—management in hospitality

The general manager is responsible to the owners of the enterprise (perhaps through a board of directors) for the smooth and profitable functioning of the enterprise. This involves dealing with staff and guests, ensuring quality of service, and overseeing the economic success of the operation. In carrying out these functions, the general manager assumes overall responsibility for a variety of departments and functions. This is done through the managers of these department who report to the general manager. Of these managers, those who have direct responsibility for the supervision of staff who provide services to guests and customers are commonly referred to as 'line' managers. Managers of sections that do not deal directly with the product or service, but fill a support function (such as accounting or marketing), are commonly referred to as 'staff' functions. General managers, in their decision-making, combine both line and staff functions.

Later chapters will consider the various areas of line and staff management in detail. For the present, we will consider the organisational structure within which line and staff managers work under the authority and direction of the general manager.

Hotel organisational structures

As an example of a hospitality enterprise, consider a large four-star hotel. A hotel has a complex structure that has been designed and refined to meet the guests' requirements and to provide the level of service desired. There are many different departments—including large operational areas (such as the rooms division, and the food & beverage operation) and support divisions (such as finance, maintenance, and marketing).

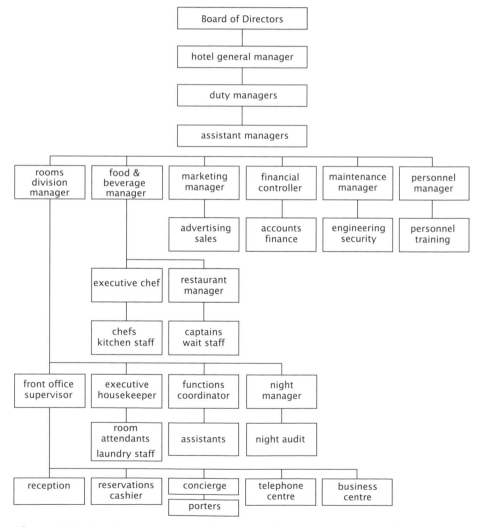

Figure 2.1 *Hotel organisation chart for a four-star or five-star hotel*

Kevin Baker

The various functions of staff reflect the organisational structure. These include:

- front office;
- housekeeping;
- sales and marketing;
- food & beverage;
- kitchen;
- accounting & finance; and
- maintenance (including engineering and security).

General managers should have an understanding of all these roles. They will have usually progressed through supervisory and management positions in one or more of these departments.

The people

The role of the general manager

In considering the role of the general manager, it is useful to consider what management is all about. There are many views and descriptions of what makes 'management' and 'managers'. Management can be broken up into several constituent elements, and these can be summarised as follows:

- planning;
- organisation;
- coordination;
- direction;
- control and evaluation;
- motivation; and
- other roles.

Some thoughts on each of these are presented below.

Planning

Planning involves the broad lines for carrying out the operations of the enterprise—the policy, the general program, the overall plan, the costs, and the organisation structure. Preparing the appropriate methods for effective action means acquiring and effectively implementing the equipment, tools, material supplies, working instructions, and techniques for given procedures. Planning also involves setting targets of expected performance and outcome (such as guest traffic and occupancy levels). Planning means setting marketing targets for product line divisions—including rooms, food & beverage outlets, business centres, functions centre, and so on.

Organisation

The organisation of a hospitality enterprise involves departmentalisation— the setting-up of the departments to meet all the functional requirements.

This requires the organisation of management teams within the departments, and then the recruiting and training of staff to carry out the duties of each area.

Coordination

Coordinating activities means that management has to balance competing interests and keep the various operating activities together. It also means ensuring that functions, be they ongoing functions or new projects, are performed in harmony. The guests take away their impression of a whole experience—if one service area within a hotel does not meet service expectations, the total experience is flawed.

Direction

Managers are required to direct staff in day-to-day activities, communicating the objectives of each day, inspiring those who are responsible to them, coaching or mentoring those who are having problems, and working towards the objectives with a style that is accepted and respected by employees. Managers, through their direction of all those responsible to them, build a *corporate culture*.

Control and evaluation

Controlling an organisation includes developing and maintaining quality standards. This involves checking current performance against objectives and targets in terms of predetermined standards contained within the plans, and evaluating whether adequate progress and satisfactory performance has been achieved. If performance standards have not been achieved, the hotel manager might have to review all aspects of operations—from room rates to staffing levels. Evaluation also involves making decisions to continue or change the plans. This involves assessing the experience gained from the working of these plans—as a guide to future operations. Controlling and evaluation also means reviewing operational data on a daily, weekly, and monthly basis.

Motivation

Motivation demands, first, that a manager be skilled at getting the members of the team to give their loyalty to the group. The aim is to encourage staff members to 'pull their weight' effectively in their individual tasks—to carry out properly the activities allocated, and to play an effective part in the over-all task that the organisation has to undertake. This process is commonly called 'leadership'. It might involve the manager in representing the property to owners on the one hand, and to staff members on the other. It might also be a very public role in which the manager is called upon to represent the property to the guests and public. In other words, the general manager is the public face of the enterprise.

Other roles

The various elements of management outlined above can be applied to any large or small hospitality enterprise—be it a restaurant, hotel, institution, or airline. The work of the hotel general manager encompasses all of these attributes of management—plus many more. For example, the hotel general manager is also an ambassador for the property. He or she is the principal greeter for very important persons (VIPs), and thus has to have an understanding of the appropriate protocol. As Guerrier and Lockwood (1989) observed:[1]

> The traditions of hotel management emphasise the hotel manager as the person who is always around to greet guests as they arrive. The Victorian hotelier was almost like a host welcoming a guest into his own home.

The general manager might also have to be the arbiter of disputes between the hotel and guests, or between staff members. He or she will have to be an effective chair of committee meetings. Most importantly of all, the general manager must be a *leader*, with a sense of the 'big picture', while maintaining a sense of the details that matter.

Each hotel general manager has a style of management—be it an autocratic style (that is, a style in which orders are given in the expectation that they will be promptly carried out) or a cooperative style (that is, a style involving delegation, listening to opinions, and leaving subordinates to fulfil their responsibilities without close supervision). Whatever the style, every manager needs a range of skills to carry out the leadership role. A later section in this chapter (page 41) considers some of the more important management abilities that have to be exercised in the unique role of the hospitality general manager. These include knowledge and skills in the following areas:

- service quality, and how it can be achieved;
- negotiation and conflict resolution;
- communication;
- health & safety; and
- cultural awareness.

Challenges to general managers

General managers face challenges resulting from change across the range of management roles.

First, effective general managers need to examine the labour situation constantly. They will be on the alert to maximise the efficiency and effectiveness of the labour force, and to reduce (where possible) labour overheads. In a small organisation, this could mean, for example, examining the effectiveness and the appropriateness of rosters and changing them as frequently as is needed.

Secondly, the equipment situation should be examined by analysing new equipment and new technology. Cost-analysis exercises should be conducted on costs of overheads and ongoing maintenance costs as opposed to costs of capital replacement. In particular, managers should be looking at the potential application of technical improvements and information technology. They should be actively involved in purchase and supply decisions regarding such equipment.

Thirdly, general managers should be continually searching for alternative options for controlling and monitoring the operational situation. They should be constantly alert for economies—including financial economies, economies of effort, and economies of scale. Managers will always be evaluating all aspects of operations by conducting audits—for example, the energy utilisation of various departments.

Career paths to general management

There are many career opportunities and entry-level positions in such a large industry. Even if the area of discussion is narrowed down to the front office of a hotel operation (a common entry point for aspiring general managers), there are numerous branching career paths. In the front office of a typical hotel, duties include:

- check-in/check-out;
- room allocation;
- accepting payment of accounts;
- handling of luggage and personal effects;
- security services;
- provision of advice on hotel services, business support, local tourist attractions, and so on;
- handling guest communications; and
- booking ongoing accommodation.

Base-level staff positions in the front office include:

- front-desk clerk;
- telephonist;
- concierge;
- reservations clerk;
- records clerk;
- accounts clerk; and
- night auditor.

Any of these positions can lead to more responsibility, including:

- cashier;
- concierge; and
- supervisor.

Management positions that are opened up through experience in front office include:

- head receptionist;
- front-office manager;
- night manager; and
- sales and marketing manager.

The career path to executive management for a trainee manager in a large chain-operated hotel has been summarised as follows:[2]

Table 2.1 *Career path to executive management*

General manager	after 10 years
Deputy manager	after 8 years
Front-office manager	after 4 years
Assistant front-office manager	after 2 years
Front-desk shift leader	after 1 year

One should note, however, that not all large hotels have five levels of management as per the organisational structure shown in Figure 2.1 (page 36). Many hotels have implemented a concept sometimes referred to a 'flatter structure'—with as few as three levels of management. This provides a more efficient decision-making environment, but it also has the effect of reducing career-path opportunities.

Skills and knowledge required of the general manager

Appreciation of customer service

The essence of the hospitality contract is the service relationship. The level of service is the central quality that makes a hospitality enterprise successful or mediocre, and the responsibility for achieving high service levels lies squarely on the shoulders of the general manager. Competition among hotels (or among competitors in other sorts of hospitality enterprises) comes down to a competition to provide the best service. The 'service encounter' is all-important in the services sector.[3]

The present authors define customer service in the following terms.

> Customer service is the provision of the necessities and preferences of the customer to the complete satisfaction of that customer.

The beauty of this definition lies in its simplicity, but the simplicity of this definition obscures some problems. A service provider has to *judge* the preferences of the customer and then meet those preferences. But the preferences of

Top management requires excellent communication and presentation skills
Courtesy Hotel Kurrajong, Canberra

individuals differ widely. A service that is good overall is not enough—very often, it is the details and the atmosphere that will make the difference between good service and excellent service.

If a hospitality manager is to seek and achieve excellence in service, he or she must develop certain qualities. Among those qualities are:

- an expectation of excellence;
- an understanding of what customers want;
- an appreciation of high levels of skill in service;
- the ability to lead and inspire others with the vision of excellence; and
- personal integrity of character.

The expectation of excellence is a quality that all managers must develop within themselves. It is a self-motivating factor, built on enthusiasm and, indeed, on a love of their business. They want to be the best in what they do; they want to strive for excellence. All managers, whether or not they have a share in the ownership of the business, should have a deep desire to make the business grow and succeed. If these desires are absent, they should look for a new job! From the expectation of excellence flows an energy that carries managers through the day, so much so that they can start their duties at the beginning of the day, and be surprised, later, to find that eight hours have passed. Expectation of excellence must be 'in the blood', and pumped to every part of the body with every heartbeat. If the manager is enthusiastic about service, it shows. It shows in a smile.

High levels of skill grow from a technical proficiency in all aspects of hospitality service, and are developed from a day-to-day involvement in all aspects of hospitality operations—that is, from an involvement in all the 'nuts-and-bolts' details of service provision. To take a practical example, it is not enough to have skills in finance and accounting; rather, to provide top service, the manager should also know where the accounting receipt books are kept! A manager must know details, even if he or she is also responsible for the 'big picture'. Even the most experienced of managers can learn something new each day. As an old aphorism goes: 'A day without something learnt is a day wasted'.

Because managers cannot do everything themselves, they need the assistance of staff, and they therefore must have the ability to lead and inspire others with their vision of excellence. A manager must not only have high standards, but must also teach those standards through word and example.

Integrity of character is an essential of service. From integrity flows trust, and trust is especially important in a service organisation. A hotel provides a service like few others. Because guests are in a strange environment, and because they are especially vulnerable while they are sleeping, they entrust themselves to the enterprise. Customers thus have a special need to trust the service provider, and they rely on the integrity of the hospitality manager. The manager must therefore possess integrity of character, strong moral principles, and a willingness to put these into practice.

Bonnie Knutson, who writes on issues of customer satisfaction, proposes ten principles of customer service. They are:[4]

 1　recognise your guest;
 2　make a positive first impression;
 3　fulfil your guest's expectations;
 4　reduce the effort required of your customer;
 5　facilitate customer decision-making;
 6　focus on the customer's perception;
 7　avoid violating the customer's unspoken time limits;
 8　create memories the customer will want to recapture;
 9　expect your customer to remember bad experiences; and
10　put the customer in your debt.

These ten principles can be summed up in different ways and, indeed, other writers come up with different lists. However, most writers are conveying the same basic tenets of customer service.

These ten principles can be restated in a few words.

First, *value* your customers. They are the reason you are in business. If they were not there, you would not have a business. Value them by recognising them and creating a positive initial impression.

Secondly, give customers what *they want*. By knowing their expectations, you can help customers make decisions by offering them clear and distinct options. You should offer them what they need, not what you want to give them. Customer surveys are one means of establishing this, but surveys must always be treated with caution—because the opinions that come out of them can reflect the quality of the survey, and the ideas of the person who designed the survey, rather than what the customers really think.

Thirdly, related to the second point above, see the service from *the customer's point of view*. Managers should focus on the customer's perceptions and understand why they will recall poor service. Customers are entitled to privacy, respect, and empathy.

The Ritz-Carlton's three steps of service

The Ritz-Carlton Hotel Company has three steps of service that employees must follow. They are:
- a warm and sincere greeting; use the guest name, if and when possible;
- anticipation and compliance with guest needs;
- fond farewell; give them a warm goodbye and use their names, if and when possible.

In addition, each employee is trained in twenty basic service standards.[5]

A strategy to achieve excellence in service

A strategy for achieving excellence in service should include three interrelated elements:

- trustworthy service;
- service recovery (that is, response to problems); and
- service fairness.

Each of these will be considered below.

1. Trustworthy service

An important tenet of customer service is that the customer should be able to trust the service provider to provide a quality service. It is a fact of life that there can be problems with service, and that errors will be made in attending to a customer's expectations and needs. Indeed, a positive response to problems can lead to increased customer satisfaction, not less. But if there are too many problems, especially if a pattern of errors develops, a customer can no longer trust in the reliability of the service and it becomes very difficult to re-establish a reputation for delivering a quality product. (For more on this, see 'Service recovery', below.)

There are some aids to improving service reliability (such as automating some procedures), but the key is in establishing appropriate management and employee attitudes. People must *want* to be trustworthy. With such an attitude, the inevitable mistakes that are made can become worthwhile learning experiences.

2. Service recovery

Service recovery is an essential aspect of service strategy because even the most carefully planned service delivery can contain glitches. As noted above, one mistake, promptly and courteously corrected, can improve a customer's assessment of a service. But an ineffective response, or a pattern of several small mistakes, can make the situation irrecoverable. Generally, in response to a mistake in service delivery, customers expect four things:

- a prompt response that demonstrates management's concern regarding problems;
- an apology that is sincere and personal (that is, not mere 'empty' words, delivered impersonally);
- an alternative that rectifies the problem; and
- recompense for any inconvenience caused.

Some organisations do not encourage complaints because they can be troublesome, and because other customers might hear about the problem and make a similar complaint. However, in cost/benefit terms, this strategy can be counterproductive. If customers do not have an avenue of complaint within the organisation, they might take their complaint outside the organisation— a much worse prospect in terms of adverse publicity and reputation.

A good service-recovery strategy is based on a good attitude to customer service. Management and staff must have a vision of service excellence, and must recognise that learning from mistakes can improve service. An error is not a problem if it is an opportunity to learn. Errors should be logged and reviewed with a view to changing procedures and practices.

TARP, a United States government agency that studies service, has found that if customers have their complaints handled effectively, efficiently, and with sincere regrets for the inconvenience caused, 90% of these customers will remain as loyal users of the company's services. Upsets or inconveniences to customers, if handled properly, are thus an excellent means of reinforcing sales, and can be used to build loyalty.

3. Service fairness

Customers expect to be treated fairly and with integrity. Customers understandably feel that they are not being treated fairly if they are subject to doubtful practices—such as misleading advertising, or service conditions being written in the smallest of print. Customers will trust a service provider if the customers feel that the provider has integrity, credibility, and competence. Fairness is developed by having fair procedures, and by ensuring that these procedures are actually followed by management and staff.

If an organisation is perceived to be unfair in its services to customers, that attitude can flow through the organisation. Staff will not take pride in their work—or worse, might be tempted to cheat and pilfer. In contrast, an organisation with a reputation for fairness will have a loyal clientele, and a loyal staff.

In addition to the three essential aspects of a service strategy outlined above, a good manager should consider aiming a little higher than guests expect. Leonard Berry states that customers generally expect a reliability of service, but companies 'that surprise customers with unusual caring, commitment, or resourcefulness during the service process receive the extra credit . . . they 'wow' their customers and build deeply felt loyalties'.[6]

It requires only a little extra effort to plan a 'surprise' aspect of service. The surprise should not, of course, result from mistakes and disappointments, but should result from planning to exceed customer expectations of service. The strategy means that management seeks some additional service or benefit that the customer does not expect, and has not experienced from competitors. The 'surprise' can be one thing or a series of things that are more than the customer expected. Very often, it is the small details of service that the customer notices—for example, a complimentary cold bottle of mineral water in the refrigerator instead of a warm chocolate on the pillow. Personalised welcome cards might also be preferable to a posey of flowers. The imaginative manager will think of these sorts of things, and others besides.

A pioneer of hospitality—Conrad Hilton

Conrad Hilton died in 1979 aged 91. He had become a famous figure in the hospitality industry, not only for the size and extent of his hotel chain (from the Waldorf Astoria in New York, extending to Hilton hotels in many major cities of the world), but also for his innovations and his readiness to embrace new ideas. He was among the first to develop management contracts, and was instrumental in establishing Carte Blanche, one of the first credit card companies.

Although he was a courageous innovator, Conrad Hilton knew the value of tradition and atmosphere in a hotel, and he sought to make each of his hotels individual, rather than giving them all a mass-produced atmosphere.

Conrad Hilton started with just one small hotel, the Mobley Hotel of Cisco, Texas, with a mere forty rooms. He purchased the hotel in 1919.

The ability to negotiate and resolve conflict

In addition to an appreciation of customer service (page 41) and the development of a strategy to ensure delivery of that service (page 44), a good manager must possess knowledge and skills in conflict resolution.

In the authors' opinion, managers spend 20–25% of their time in resolving conflict. The conflict might involve a fundamental policy disagreement (over what is to be done and how it is to be done), or it might involve a conflict of personalities. The latter is the more difficult to resolve—often involving high emotions, anger, mistrust, and resentment.

Conflict can come about through a lack of communication, or through differing expectations, or through a work crisis, or through some combination of factors or events.

Conflict can arise at different levels. The conflict can be between different organisations, between different groups within a given organisation, or between individuals. A conflict between two employees of approximately equal status (be they two staff members or two managers) is often called a horizontal conflict. A conflict between two people of unequal status (between a staff member and a guest, or between a manager and a staff member) is often called a vertical conflict. A conflict can even exist within the mind of a single individual—in being undecided about a course of action to follow.

Some conflicts can be productive if they are kept at the level of a controlled rivalry to produce the best service. However, many conflicts are destructive, and the ability to handle the conflict revolves around recognising what the conflict is all about, what stage it has reached, and what is to be done to negotiate a resolution.

A conflict can be viewed as involving five stages:

1 existence of the underlying conditions that create the conflict;
2 participants in the conflict feeling sufficiently aggrieved to take some action with regard to the differences;
3 open expression of the conflict;
4 action being taken to suppress or resolve the conflict (either by the parties themselves or by an outside party); and
5 the conflict having created some change in personal relationships, or in the organisation itself.

A manager requires multifaceted skills in negotiating the resolution of conflicts. It is best, if possible, to resolve conflicts at the first stage, when the conditions for differences exist. To do this, a manager needs insight and awareness of potential areas of conflict. A manager needs to be sensitive, empathic, and creative if he or she is to be aware of potential conflict before it actually arises. Recognition of the needs of others is important here, alongside an ability to imagine potential problems before they actually arise. Communication skills are also important in this regard—to have established a management style in which staff members have sufficient confidence in the manager to mention their concerns about a situation, or their concerns about other people. Communication skills are also important in helping the manager to recognise hints and suggestions that might not be fully articulated.

If the conflict has advanced to the second or third stages—where participants have taken some action to express their differences, or if the conflict has blown up into an open dispute—the manager can take one of a number of courses.

1 The manager can make a decision that imposes a resolution on the conflict—for example, by directing staff members to take some action or other. If the conflict involves a guest, the manager might be able to resolve the guest's problem or offer compensation for the matter (as in the strategy of service recovery noted above).

2 The manager can make a compromise decision after consultation with the parties on the possibilities of 'trade-offs'. This might take more time than the first course, but is usually preferable.

3 The manager can defer a decision for a set time period to allow participants to 'cool off', and then address the matter in private in a neutral venue at a future time.

4 The manager can refer the matter to a higher authority for resolution. For example, if the conflict is about working conditions, the manager might feel that the board or the owners are the more appropriate authority to resolve the conflict. If the matter is serious, there might also be value in referring it to a professional mediator.

5 The manager can leave the matter unresolved, but separate or quarantine the conflict by separating the parties. For example, if there is a personality clash between two people, it might be best to transfer one or both of them.

The skilled and experienced manager might even be able to use conflicts to strengthen staff relationships, especially through the design and use of conflict-resolution procedures that are publicised among staff members at all levels of the organisation. In this way, the manager becomes a respected mediator, and the chances of a 'win-win' resolution to conflict are increased.

Communication skills for general managers

The hospitality industry is labour-intensive, and the quality of services depends upon how well people work together. To work together with efficiency and effectiveness, and without conflict, requires cooperation. The maintenance of such effective cooperation is another responsibility of general managers.

Cooperation requires communication one with another—by voice, gesture, writing, or other means. Because hospitality is based upon encounter and interaction, the ability to communicate well and effectively is an important skill in a hospitality manager.

A day in the life of a hotel manager [7]

6.00 a.m.	Alarm clock!
6.15 a.m.	Swim ten laps of the hotel pool
7.15 a.m.	Shower, suit up, and leave for the office via the lift
7.30 a.m.	Breakfast with a senior European travel journalist in one of the hotel's restaurants
8.30 a.m.	Meet with your secretary to discuss day's appointments
8.45 a.m.	Weekly management meeting with all department heads
9.45 a.m.	Scrutinise reports on sales & marketing, finance, and occupancy
10.30 a.m.	Meet with marketing manager and an incentive company regarding an integrated customer loyalty campaign
11.15 a.m.	Meet, greet, and charm a famous visiting celebrity
12.00 p.m.	Interview a prospective food & beverage manager
12.30 p.m.	Attend a charity luncheon in the hotel ballroom
1.45 p.m.	Return a call to the local paper with a prepared statement on the shortage of good chefs in the industry
2.00 p.m.	Meet with the hotel's occupational health & safety officer for an update on the increasing number of claims for workers' compensation
2.30 p.m.	Approve next year's marketing plan
3.00 p.m.	Dismiss a senior member of staff and arrange immediate pay-out
3.30 p.m.	Hold meeting with other senior staff to discuss the dismissal
4.00 p.m.	Meet with a group of ten of the hotel's top producing inbound travel agents and host an afternoon tea
4.45 p.m.	Attend tourism industry meeting (of which the manager is a board member)
5.50 p.m.	Meet with an irate (and important) guest
6.15 p.m.	Attend 'Staff Member of the Month' function at the hotel; announce and congratulate the winner
6.30 p.m.	Attend monthly meeting with the hotel's owner
7.00 p.m.	Dinner with the hotel's owner and parent company representatives
9.30 p.m.	Read through mail and make action notes for secretary
10.30 p.m.	Take the lift home—tired, fulfilled, a little richer, and a little wiser

1. The communication model

There is a common model of the communication process involving the communicator (sender) and the audience (receiver). Faults in the communication can be due to the sender or to the receiver, or could be produced by an external factor. Such an external factor is termed 'noise'—which means any factor that impedes the reception of the message. In the case of a verbal message, this might be literally true—when loud conversation or loud music makes reception of the message difficult.

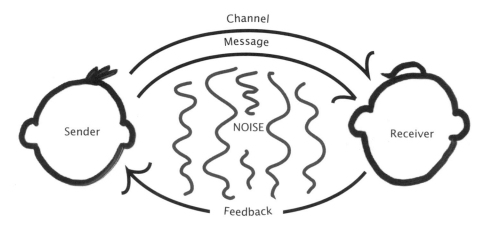

Figure 2.2 *The communication process*

Kevin Baker

To avoid problems in this communication process, skills are required at various steps in the model.

Skills are necessary at the first stage in the process, when the information is encoded. If one person of a certain background attempts to communicate with a person of a different background, the sender might use a word that has a different meaning for the receiver. For example, for an English person, the word 'duchess' means a titled lady; but for an Australian from Queensland, it means a dressing table. As another example, the word *susu* in Indonesian means 'milk', in Turkish it means 'be quiet', and in Mandarin it means 'uncle'. Thus, encoding skills are important, and the communicator must recognise that different words can have different meanings to different people.

Skills at choosing the right channel, then forming an adequate message for that channel, are also of importance.

Finally, there are skills in selecting the right message that will show that communication is achieved.

CASE STUDY

In the hotel kitchen

The Fictional Hotel kitchen is extremely busy at 11.45 a.m.. There is a high guest occupancy in the hotel, a fully catered conference is running in the function room, and several coach groups have been booked in for lunch (with some of the coaches having arrived early).

The new kitchenhand comes up to the chef and says: 'You know when I filled in my form for the superannuation fund when I started last week, what did question 4 mean when it referred to a section of the superannuation rules, and said that I had to have preserved portions of my fund when I retired?'.

- What is the chef's likely reaction?
- Did the kitchenhand choose the best medium for conveying his message?
- What medium should he have used?

2. Communication 'rules'

(a) Keep the message simple

With clear purposes and a clear message, the likelihood of imparting the desired information (and of obtaining the desired reaction) is much improved. It is best to use words that are as direct as possible. When extra words are used, there is a risk that there might be inconsistency between one statement and another.

Activity 2.1 '*Chinese whispers*'

'Chinese whispers' is a very old parlour game, but it is a game that is, perhaps, even more relevant today than it was hundreds of years ago.

- Stand or sit a group of people in a circle.
- The nominated first person thinks of a sentence.
- Whisper that sentence to the neighbouring person.
- That person passes on what he or she heard to the next person.
- Continue passing the message in whispers until it goes around the circle to the person who started it.
- Match the original message with the one received at the end.

(b) Choose the right channel or medium

The communication channel must be chosen with care. The communicator must choose a medium that will do the job. Moreover, it must be a medium that can be handled competently.

	For staff	For guests	For the public
face-to-face	X	X	X
group meetings	X		
telephone	X	X	
email	X		
letter		X	X
notice	X		X
TV ad			X

Figure 2.3 *The communication matrix*

Kevin Baker

Circumstances can affect the choice of medium. For example, urgency can affect the choice of medium. If it is necessary urgently to advise a small group of people of a set of circumstances, a spoken message (related personally or passed on by word of mouth) is probably the most appropriate medium (as opposed to a written memo). In other cases, a disability might render certain forms of communication inappropriate or inadequate.

Hospitality managers might therefore employ several communication channels for the same message—such as audio-recordings, in addition to printed notices, voice-mail, and email.

Activity 2.2 Communication consideration

A guest who has an intellectual disability asks a staff member the way to the hotel restaurant. The reply is: 'Two floors down, then across the lobby and through the double glass doors, then first turn right, down a corridor, and next turn left, and you'll find it adjacent to the bistro.'

The guest does not find the restaurant.

You are a member of the front-office team.

What is the correct way to handle this request?

(c) Avoid barriers to communication

One of the less obvious problems that arise in the communication process is that caused by preconceptions—ideas already held about the communication before it actually occurs. Each of us, according to the ancient Greeks, stands upon a pillar, and that pillar is made up of the background and experiences that have formed our ideals, judgments, and values. Everyone has a different background, and these different backgrounds can make for difficulties when one person standing upon a certain pillar has to make contact with another person standing upon a totally different pillar.

Prejudice towards a particular group of people is the most obvious form of preconception, but there are many other preconceptions that are not so obvious. Every person has an image of himself or herself in the world, and a mental image of other people or groups. These images make it easy and almost 'natural' to categorise receivers in the communication process. This is particularly so in business situations where the sender might not know the receiving person or group very well. Thus the sender must consciously determine to whom the communication is relevant when dealing with people in a group. The sender must consciously communicate with each person individually—and not with some preconceived idea of the group, or the person perceived to be in charge of the group.

Figure 2.4 *Different people stand on different pedestals*

Kevin Baker

The sender's 'body language' or 'paralanguage', can also be a barrier (or an aid) to communication. A sender of information conveying the same message to different people will use different body language, depending on the circumstances. Vertical communication (to a supervisor) will be different from horizontal communication (to a member of a peer group). The body language differs, according to perceived roles and expectations.

Activity 2.3   *Ethical considerations and context of communication*

You are a duty manager of a hotel, working in your office. Down the corridor, you can hear the sound of laughter and singing coming from a family celebration in one of the function rooms. It is clear that it is a very joyous occasion for all those involved.

Then you receive a phone call. One of the guests, en route to the family function, has been in a motor vehicle accident and is in hospital seriously injured. You are asked to inform the family of the tragic event.

QUESTIONS
- How do you communicate this message?
- Should you wait a while until the celebration is close to concluding—rather than halt the festivities with your bad news? Or should people be informed immediately?
- If you decide to inform the people immediately, what is the most appropriate way to do this?

Another barrier to communication can arise from using the wrong context. The point of a message can be lost if it is communicated in the wrong context. The context should facilitate the passage of information, not impede it. For example, if a message likely to cause tension has to be communicated, a stressful environment will not facilitate acceptance of the desired information. If a manager has to reprimand a subordinate, this should be done in private, in a measured fashion. To choose the wrong context for a reprimand means that the essential message can become lost in the clutter of the surroundings.

'Context' is here taken to mean the many factors in the environment that surround the message in the communication channel. In the case of written messages, factors such as courtesy titles and phrases, spelling, punctuation, and ambiguities are all factors of the context that could distract from the essential information. Verbal messages could be disrupted by contextual factors such as other activity or sounds.

Activity 2.4 | *The importance of communication*

A large metropolitan hotel has a busy period in which it is nearly fully booked, and has a number of conferences in the building. Some of the guests and conference delegates are:
- a Japanese tour (of whom only the guide speaks English);
- a national conference for people with hearing impairment (who are using signers at all their sessions);
- a visiting soccer team and its supporters; and
- three different teams for the local meeting of the paralympics selections.

QUESTIONS

- As the general manager, how would you stress the importance of all the guests and clients to your staff (individually, at a meeting, by memo, or by some other means)?
- However you decide to communicate with staff members, what advice do you wish to give staff members? That is, what do you want to say in *general* about the situation?
- What *specific* advice would you give staff members regarding such matters as procedures for a possible emergency evacuation—taking into account the characteristics of people in the various groups, and their abilities to understand and respond to such an emergency situation?

Cultural awareness in general managers

Cultural values

The term 'culture' refers to the sets of characteristics, values, mores, attitudes, customary behaviours, lifestyles, and traditions of groups of people. The Oxford English Dictionary defines culture as: 'the customs, civilization, and achievements of a particular time and people'.

Different groups of people obviously have different cultural habits and values. Differences exist among different races of people, and even within particular races. Indeed, it is sometimes possible to note certain cultural differences between people of the same nationality and race if those people come from different cities or regions. It is also possible to note that the cultural values of one particular group of people change over time.

Cultural differences among different groups of people, and within a single group of people over time, are thus complex and important. Each of us has grown up in a certain cultural environment, and each of us has developed an understanding of the world and humanity as a result of these cultural experiences. In this sense, it is 'natural' for each of us to view other cultures from the perspective of our own culture. This is known as an 'ethnocentric' view of the world and is, to a certain degree, understandable and unavoidable. However, if carried to an extreme, such an ethnocentric view of the world can lead to some people judging all other cultures to be inferior to their own.

In Australia, it is illegal to discriminate against people on the grounds of racial and cultural differences, and there is a general policy of 'multiculturalism'—that is, a policy that attempts to recognise and respect cultural differences.

Cultural awareness and hospitality

For the hospitality industry, a policy of multiculturalism makes sense—not only legally and morally, but also commercially. Hospitality is all about 'the friendly and generous reception and entertainment of guests or strangers' (see page 3). To do this successfully, hospitality managers and staff members need to be aware of the background, preferences, and expectations of their guests.

The need for management to embrace multiculturalism has become more important because of the growing trend to globalisation of corporate operations. Few large companies operate entirely within the borders of a single country any more. Similarly, guests travel larger distances than used to be the case. The combination of multinational corporations and transnational travel makes cultural awareness and sensitivity more important than it has ever been.

Hospitality managers must be sensitively aware of cultural differences and preferences if they are to implement culturally appropriate policies and practices—for both guests and employees. It must be remembered that, in Australia, the workforce is more multicultural than those of many other countries. Hospitality managers must therefore recognise that they have an increasingly multicultural staff providing service to an increasingly multicultural clientele.

Cultural awareness and sensitivity in the hospitality industry means more than simply learning a few words and phrases in other languages. It involves being aware of habits, manners, and gestures that are appropriate in other cultures. For example, if you get into an elevator, how close would you stand to another person? Personal space is a major indicator of culture, for our notion of personal space helps to define ourselves and our worldview. In some cultures, personal interaction is more intimate, even crowded, and the personal space a person expects might be approximately 150 mm (six inches). They would not be uncomfortable even feeling the warmth of another person's breath. Yet in other cultures, an arm's length marks a comfortable personal space. A porter showing a guest to a suite might make the guest feel very uncomfortable by standing too close in an elevator and not allowing the guest the personal space that person expects. The discomfort of the guest will mean that the first important impressions of the hotel will not have been pleasant ones.

Consideration—personal space

'Personal space' refers to the area around a person—a type of 'zone of safety'. When other people enter that area, we are put on our guard—we feel uncomfortable if others stand too close.

The people of Hong Kong are used to a small personal space, whereas Australians expect a greater space. Australians generally like to keep people at a distance of approximately 600 mm in front of them (about 'arm's length'). If someone approaches an Australian more closely without invitation, this can be perceived as being an 'invasion' of personal space and can make an Australian feel uncomfortable. To come even closer and engage in the aggressive style of contact sometimes referred to as 'in-your-face' or 'eyeballing' will be perceived as being openly hostile and offensive by most Australians.

Other forms of personal interaction can also be perceived negatively in various cultures. For example, in many Asian cultures, direct eye contact for an extended period can be perceived as very offensive and personally intrusive.

Another area of cultural divergence is the area of communication—both verbal and non-verbal. Most cultures mix verbal and non-verbal communication (such as gestures and body language), but to different degrees, and using different gestures. A person from a culture where communication is mostly verbal might not be looking for gestures, or might misunderstand gestures. Moreover, cultures that use mainly verbal communication expect language to be detailed and specific, and might not understand the imprecision and the symbolism that is more common in cultures where verbal and non-verbal communication are given equal value. This division is sometimes referred to as the 'high-context/low-context' aspect of language and communication. In a high-context culture, as the term implies, the context of the words might convey just as much as do the words themselves. For example, Japanese people seldom use the word 'no'—because its use seems impolite to them; however, they might convey disagreement by gestures or associated expressions.

It is important for hospitality general managers to be aware of cultural values and cultural differences so that they can understand the people with whom they are interacting, and so that they can clearly fashion and communicate responses. This cultural awareness is vital both at the stage of developing strategies and at the stage of taking concrete actions. There is a need to consider perceptions of time and space, power relationships, attitudes to materialism, communications expectations, and ethical considerations.

The need to understand cross-cultural communication does not apply only *within* a hospitality operation. Hospitality corporations and chains exist within a network of business contacts, and this is especially so in the Asia–Pacific region, where suppliers of hospitality services frequently operate within a set of Western cultural norms, whereas the tour wholesalers have a background in Asian norms and values.

Historical background, ideologies, values, norms, and language also have impacts upon employer–employee issues—including matters such as job tasks and duties, education, rewards, motivation, and communication. Japanese, Australian, and Filipino managers, for example, are mostly likely to support the right to strike, whereas the least likely managers to approve of a strike by employees are Singaporeans, Thais, and Taiwanese.

Some cultures value the work ethic more highly than others. In the West, there is a strong emphasis upon individual achievement and often people are valued by their status in the workplace. In other societies, in which there is more emphasis on family, clan, and tribal values, there is less emphasis upon work and more emphasis upon the overall wellbeing of the group. This difference between cultures can make a difference to motivation strategies. Promises of bonuses or promotion might not be effective if employees place less emphasis on improved status and reward as an individual.

Even the development of a hotel project should take into account cultural beliefs and practices where appropriate. For example, in parts of Asia, or indeed in other countries where hotels cater for a large number of Asian guests, it would be appropriate to take into account the principles of *Feng Shui* when designing the layout of the hotel and the layout of the individual guest suites. To do this, the development team could employ a *Feng Shui* master.

Culture and authority

Cultural differences also exist in the relationship between authority and the individual. As described by Hofstede,[8] different cultures place different emphasis on such matters as individualism, hierarchy, and power–distance relationships.

In some cultures, authority is commonly exercised through a strict hierarchy, whereas in others (an example being Australia) there is less emphasis upon hierarchical management and more emphasis on an egalitarian relationship between the leaders and those whom they lead. These different perceptions of power–distance relationships means that, in Asian cultures, business contacts are often made through intermediaries rather than through direct approaches and face-to-face negotiation. Australians have a tendency to be blunt, and to seek prompt decisions on business propositions, whereas Asians tend to take more time to consider an issue and to seek consensus among the parties involved.

Cultural values must also be taken into account when management interacts with employees from a different cultural background. For example, in some cultures, there might not be the same urgency with regard to time as in Western culture.

Building a multicultural environment

Building a multicultural environment within a hotel operation means that the management can provide a better level of service to guests from a different cultural background. It also means that the hotel can build upon the strengths offered by the different cultures of staff members, and the unique culture of their environment. All in all, a multicultural environment means making a strength out of what might have been a weakness.

Concerns that individual cultural values must be protected have resulted in the development of guidelines for equal employment opportunity. These guidelines are frequently enacted in legislation that establishes the legal right of all individuals to be treated fairly in terms of employment opportunities, workplace conditions, and promotion opportunities. Such legislation differs from jurisdiction to jurisdiction in Australia, but generally means that employers are required to make reasonable allowance for employees of different cultural backgrounds—for example in the wearing of traditional head-coverings, such as turbans in the case of people of Sikh background.

Preconceptions and negative opinions about people from different ethnic groups are referred to as 'prejudices'. Prejudice can result in inappropriate behaviour towards those who are perceived as being different. This behaviour can include making offensive or unfair comments, making ethnic jokes, or discriminating in various ways. Such behaviour is commonly called 'harassment'. Prejudice can impede a manager's ability to see the benefits of ethnic diversity in the workplace.

The key to making due allowance for other cultures is in making an effort to understand those cultures, and the reasons for certain cultural practices. This can be achieved through spending time with those of other cultures, bringing an open mind to discussions, and being prepared to respect different insights into the world and the ways of doing things.

CASE STUDY

Joe's Stone Crabs Restaurant [9]

Joe's Stone Crabs Restaurant is a large restaurant in Miami, USA. In 1997 the restaurant was found to be a discriminatory employer—even though none of its employees ever complained about discrimination. The discrimination was unintentional, but a complaint was made by the Equal Employment Opportunity Commission and a court found it came about because the restaurant usually hired staff who had already worked there, or who attended an interview and were evaluated on appearance, attitude, articulation, and experience. The court stated that this policy amounted to a form of cultural discrimination for it had an impact upon disadvantaged groups. The court held that the restaurant should have taken steps to ensure that its employment policies did not 'unintentionally' discriminate.

Culture-specific operations

A well-developed multicultural awareness can also assist in developing a hospitality operation using local cultures as a theme for the development. Stanley Selengut, owner of resorts in the Virgin Islands and Florida expresses it simply: 'Bringing guests into a sense of place is essential'.[10] By doing so, visitors to an area experience the whole range of factors that make the place unique.

Activity 2.5   *Ethical consideration*

You are a senior manager of a hotel, but it is your first month in the job and you are subject to confirmation in the position.

An extremely wealthy guest arrives and insists that his servant must sleep at the door of the presidential suite all night. If you protest that this is against hotel policy, it is likely that the wealthy guest will leave and make a complaint about you. It is possible that the complaint will be that you are 'culturally insensitive'. This sort of complaint might mean that you will find it very difficult to get employment elsewhere in the industry.

QUESTIONS

- Do you take a firm line with the guest and insist that hotel policy overrides his cultural sensitivities? Or do you accede to his request?
- Give reasons for your answer.

Occupational health & safety in hospitality enterprises

Hotel general managers must be well aware of safe and unsafe working conditions, and have a legal and moral obligation to minimise risks to their staff as well as to their guests.

Definition of occupational health & safety

In 1950, the World Health Organization (WHO) and the International Labour Organization (ILO), through their joint Committee on Occupational Health, produced a definition of the objective of 'occupational health':

> . . . the promotion and maintenance of the highest degree of physical, mental and social well-being of workers in all occupations; the prevention among workers of departures from health caused by their working conditions; the protection of workers in their employment from risks resulting from factors adverse to health; the placing of and maintenance of the worker in an occupational environment adapted to his physiological and psychological equipment and, to summarise, the adaptation of work to man and of each man to his job.

This definition includes not only the minimising of the risk of accident, but also the provision of good, healthy working conditions.

Every employee has a right to a safe working environment, and every guest has a right to enjoy safe surroundings. This chapter, in its discussion of elements of health and safety, also includes the health and safety of guests within the provisions of the above definition, for the hospitality industry is special in that its class of customers (that is, guests) remain on the premises receiving services for a substantial period of time, and are therefore commonly exposed to the same hazards as employees. Therefore managers need a proper understanding of occupational health & safety principles, for they are responsible not only for their employees, but also for their guests. If the working environment in a hospitality operation is hazardous for the people who work there, guests will also be put at risk.

Costs of occupational health & safety

Injuries to employees or guests in a hospitality operation are costly, and it is commonsense for hospitality managers to provide safe conditions that prevent accidents—rather than react when accidents have already occurred. Preventative measures are more economical than reactive practices.

All employers in Australia and New Zealand are required to have insurance for injuries to employees. Such insurance covers costs such as medical fees, rehabilitation, compensation for wages lost during time off work, and compensation for employees who are unable to resume work. In addition, employers should insure against claims for injury to members of the public, and for damage to property caused by accidents such as fires or natural disasters.

The importance of preventing problems—rather than merely reacting to them—is emphasised when it is realised that insurance premiums will rise if there is an increasing number of accidents (and hence an increasing number of claims) in an unsafe workplace. An employer will also incur costs that insurance might not cover. These include:

- wage costs for employees who are idle during an accident;
- wage costs for employees (or outsider contractors) who have to clean up after an occurrence;
- the costs of 'down time' when the facility might have to be closed;
- decreased custom due to bad publicity; and
- reduced productivity among employees due to impaired morale.

Occupational health & safety also implies other costs that cannot be avoided—even with proper preventative measures. There are costs in providing and maintaining materials and personnel in first-aid rooms.

The costs of unsafe working conditions can be very high for any organisation, but can be especially damaging for a hospitality operation—because it is dependent upon its staff for the quality of service, and dependent upon its special relationship of trust with its guests.

Teamwork and safe working conditions

Teamwork is the key to the creation and maintenance of safe working conditions. Unsafe working conditions can be reduced (or even eliminated) only if everyone in the workplace pitches in together to work as a team. A cooperative, consultative, considerate workplace also decreases stress—which is, itself, a factor in occupational health & safety.

> ## Three 'Cs' for teamwork
>
> - Cooperation
> - Consultation
> - Consideration

Teamwork leads to good 'housekeeping' by which everyone shares responsibility for safety and tidiness. This includes such matters as putting power leads back where they belong after use, keeping aisles clear of obstructions, and ensuring that doors are closed.

Managers have an important role in establishing this sense of teamwork for safety. The owners, as employers, bear the overall legal responsibility for ensuring safe working conditions, but this responsibility is exercised on the employers' behalf by the manager. Good managers should:

- inspire employees towards safe working practices by example—that is, by obvious personal commitment to high standards on the part of the manager;
- conduct regular inspections themselves to ensure that working conditions are monitored and maintained;
- ensure that sufficient resources are budgeted for safety checks, training, and the rectification of problems; and
- provide channels for feedback from employees.

Note that the provision of safe working conditions implies more than minimising the risk of accidents from physical objects in the environment. It also includes minimising the potential for injuries from improper work postures and positions—based on the science called 'ergonomics' (which deals with movement of the human frame in workplaces and work situations). For example, a kitchenhand should not have to hunch over a bench while preparing vegetables, but should have a good posture with work materials available at the correct height.

Employees also have a role to play in teamwork for safe working conditions. Frontline employees have opportunities to notice problems and unsafe areas—such as wet floors or damaged electrical equipment. They should be encouraged to communicate concerns, and be aware of formal channels to pass on information concerning hazards.

The occupational health & safety team in the hospitality enterprise should formulate its strategies through a representative committee that has members from all sections of the organisation. Such a committee should consult widely, and meet regularly, and should have resources to publicise its decisions and policies. The committee should record and monitor safety information in the wider industry, and should be a source of reference. For example, there should be a ready source of reference on chemicals used throughout the hospitality operation, with full advice on procedures to be followed in case of poisoning or chemical fire. The occupational health & safety team might also include outside consultants from time to time—such as government officials from health & safety authorities, or experienced professionals from specialised private agencies.

Steps to workplace safety

Step 1 Recognise and remove the causes of accidents and health hazards.

Step 2 Use safe work practices and safety gear at all times.

Step 3 Know what to do in an emergency through attending safety education and promotion programs.

Accident-prevention practice

A workplace accident is an incident arising out of the circumstances of employment that results, or could result, in personal injury or damage to property. Every employer, through management, must seek to reduce the number of accidents and to minimise the injuries caused by accidents.

The first step in reducing accidents and minimising injury through accident-prevention practices (assuming the health & safety team is already established) is to conduct a survey of risk identification and risk assessment. The survey should consider the property as it is now, and the past history of the property with regard to accidents. The survey should be completed by experienced personnel—either from in-house or from an external organisation.

Some questions must be asked.

- Are the job specifications and job designs adequate?
- Do the working conditions comply with legal requirements?
- Do the fire safety procedures and equipment comply with legal requirements?
- Are the storage and disposal of waste (such as chemicals and fats) safe and adequate?

- Is there an emergency plan?
- Are there particular problems in this specific property (for example, with hot cooking liquids in the kitchen, or with water safety requirements in the pool area)?

Signs are an important part of ensuring safe procedures in the workplace. Signs can be advisory in nature ('what to do if an emergency should occur'), or they can be more direct warnings ('beware of this wet floor now').

Example—hotel fire emergency notice

If you see a fire and there is no alarm sounding, you must:
- Immediately dial reception and state: (i) your name; (ii) floor where you are; (iii) location of fire; (iv) what is burning.
- Notify anyone else in the area.
- If practicable, operate the appropriate fire extinguisher.
- If the fire is too severe, leave the area immediately, closing doors behind you.
- Leave the building (do not use lifts).
- Gather in the Evacuation Assembly Area to be counted.
- Do not re-enter the building until instructed to.

Hospitality managers should ensure that there is documentation and advice available to staff on occupational health & safety issues, and they must ensure that staff members know that they can access such information.

Health & safety information can be incorporated into other advice to employees. An example might be advice on clothing—advice that can be incorporated into the establishment's grooming requirements. Such advice might be worded as follows.

Clothing tips for hospitality workers to prevent accidents:
- clothes must be neat and clean;
- roll sleeves down to protect against heat and spills;
- wear non-slip shoes;
- wear shoes sturdy enough to protect against hot spills;
- aprons should reach below the knees;
- gloves should be worn where necessary;
- long hair must be tied up or covered;
- jewellery can catch on things, retain heat, and contaminate food—all jewellery should be removed (with the exception of wedding rings if desired).

Activity 2.6   *Safe working conditions*

An employee is responsible for photocopying and reproducing documents. He works alone in the photocopy room which has been set up in the basement of the building. He is responsible for three photocopiers of various sizes.

The room is ventilated, and its walls are all painted grey—even the three photocopiers are grey and the shelves holding paper are grey. There is a plastic grey chair for the man to sit on when there is no work. The documents requiring photocopying come down vacuum tubes. He photocopies them and sends them back up the vacuum tubes. He sees no one else all day—other than when he signs on and off at the staff entrance. He eats his lunch alone in the room.

QUESTIONS

- List some of the occupational health risks that the man might face (referring back to the WHO/ILO definition of the aim of occupational health on page 60).
- List some of the steps that you would take to minimise any health hazards.

The accident-prevention program must be based upon an appropriate strategy.

1 There should be a health & safety policy document that is authorised by top management. The policy should mandate initial safety training and on-the-job safety training for all employees. Management and supervisors should have advanced training. The policy must reflect certain legislative requirements (such as the requirement to wear safety apparel in some circumstances).

2 There should be safety rules that are backed up by sanctions. Incorrect use of equipment or actions that are hazardous to others should invoke punishment.

3 There should be regular safety checks and inspections—not just of the hospitality premises, but of the jobs themselves.

4 There should be procedures for the reporting and investigation of accidents, including the reporting and investigation of 'near-miss' situations. This should be followed by communication of events to all staff members as part of a safety-promotion program.

5 There must be provision of adequate first-aid facilities and treatment stations.

6 There must be an active program to identify remove work hazards, such as replacing harmful chemicals with less-hazardous ones.
7 There should be preparation for disaster and catastrophes. Because a large facility such as hotel can be a focal point for local community relief in the case of an emergency, such preparation should include surrounding areas, and not just areas within the property itself.
8 There should be worker involvement in the safety programs, with provision for feedback to senior management.
9 There should be a positive attitude towards rehabilitation, with programs in place to assist injured employees back to work when they able.

The health & safety audit of risks within the property, should not neglect a review of any vehicles. Motor vehicle accidents are a common cause of workers' compensation claims. The review of vehicles should ensure that there are adequate policies for vehicle use, and that drivers are licensed and trained. The vehicles must be properly maintained, and accurate records should be kept of the maintenance status of each one.

Example—notice concerning preventative measures against fire hazard

- Be careful with naked flames.
- Avoid loose clothing near flames.
- Isolate flammable materials.
- Keep filters and drainage channels clear.
- Prevention of injury is a first priority; protection of property is a second priority.
- Inform a supervisor of fire.
- If a fire cannot be fought, contact the fire brigade, evacuate the area, and warn other people.

Example—notice concerning fighting a fire

- Cut the gas or power supply.
- Use a fire blanket correctly.
- Use the correct fire extinguisher for the type of fire.
- Test the extinguisher before approaching the fire.

Other issues relating to general management

Ethics in hospitality management

Stephen Hall, in *Ethics in Hospitality Management*,[11] has emphasised that ethics are inseparable from quality. A survey of a thousand American Hotel and Motel Association properties (of 300 rooms or more) resulted in a working understanding of ethics as applied in the hospitality industry. According to the survey, ethical behaviour consisted of 'treating others in a fair and equitable manner'.

It is important that hospitality managers work to create an ethical and legal environment in the areas under their responsibility, and by so doing create a milieu in which illegal and immoral activities are clearly seen to be unacceptable. There is a heavy responsibility upon general managers to be honest and ethical, for if management does not set an example of ethical and legal behaviour, it is more difficult to encourage such behaviour in the staff who report to management.

In industry at large, there has been a proliferation of ethical codes in recent years and there have been several academic studies of those codes—see Pitt and Groskaufmanis (1990),[12] and Rogers and Swales (1990).[13] However, Stevens (1996) has found that ethical codes are generally framed from a defensive position designed to protect the organisation, rather than as an educational or inspirational device to encourage and support ethical behaviour.[14]

How ethical are students? Surveys of students in university business courses in Australia have indicated that many students do not have an appreciation of ethical behaviour. A survey at Monash University found that 61% of 380 business students surveyed said that they would engage in insider trading—an unethical and illegal practice.[15] A survey reported in the journal of the Institute of Chartered Accountants found that a large minority of accounting students stated that they would accept bribes of $5000 to $75 000 to keep silent about fraud and theft by company directors. Interestingly, there was a difference between sexes. Of males, 48% of first-year accounting students would accept a bribe of $75 000, but only 25% of female students would take the same bribe.

The present book includes ethical discussions in each chapter to encourage a frank consideration by readers of their own ethical attitudes. Those who aspire to management positions in hospitality operations should be well aware of the importance of their own ethical values.

Risk management in hospitality

From studies of mathematical principles and actuarial theory, the field of risk management has become important as modern management techniques and practices have developed. Every manager who has stewardship of assets is involved in the managing of risk. Risk management now includes review of:

- security against outside theft or destruction of assets;
- internal control;
- health & safety issues;
- disaster plans and relief;
- protecting investments against changing political environments or policy change; and
- assessing the likely return on new projects.

Risk management is especially important for hospitality managers because they bear the responsibility for the welfare of the guests who enter their property, and because the properties themselves are generally high-value assets.

Definition of risk

'Risk' is a word that is commonly used in the English language. Losses can result from the hazards of nature and human activity, or from the consequences of a decision (for example, to invest or not invest in a new project). The Oxford Dictionary definitions sum up the action-focused essence of risks—'to expose to the chance of injury or loss' and 'to venture upon'. The definitions go on to emphasise three basic aspects—'the magnitude of loss, the chance of loss, and the exposure to loss'.[16]

Some experts on the subject state that it is too restricting and impractical to define risk. Jan Doderlein prefers to discuss risk without attempting a definition, which he sees as generally lacking practical usefulness.[17]

A 'risk', as it understood in the field of risk management, encompasses much more than the threat of loss. The context in which 'risk' is used in risk management is comprised of four main factors—threats, resources, modifying factors, and consequences.[18] This view of risk is much more than issues of insurance, or considerations of investing in futures or commodities markets. This broad view of risk includes *all aspects* of managing for the security of assets, including developing new applications of those assets in entrepreneurial projects.[19]

There is risk in all human activity. There is risk in every new venture attempted or modified each day. But risks should not always be classified as threats of loss; some risks can constitute opportunities for gain.[20] Types of risk that face the hospitality manager include:[21]

- natural perils—fire, storms, and so on;
- loss of personnel—through death or injury;
- labour risk—lack of a suitable workforce, or trained workers;
- liability risk—the threat of being sued;
- technical risk—the development of new technology;
- marketing risk—the launch of new products or properties;
- political and social risk—nationalisation, terrorism, hijacking, and so on;
- environmental risk—pollution, and so on.

More general categories include 'risks to property', 'risks to employees', 'interruption risks', and purely financial risks.[22] Possible losses under these heads can be difficult to estimate.

Profiles of risk-takers

All of us take risks. All of us make decisions every day. However, some of us have responsibility for managing large assets and must make decisions with regard to those assets. There have been several studies of business executives who, in their decision-making, are involved in risk management. It is of interest to consider briefly the profiles of those risk-takers because these profiles are pictures writ large of risk-takers generally.

Research has established that a large proportion of executives are noticeably unwilling to accept risk where it involves a substantial (that is, more than 34–40%) risk of loss of personal investments. In terms of corporate investments, only a very small proportion (1%) of executives can be classed as 'significantly' risk-taking.[23] The results show a widespread refusal among executives to accept risk even where there is also the possibility of significant financial gain. The survey does indicate that executives are more willing to accept risk in business rather than in personal dealings.[24] Older managers are markedly more conservative than their younger counterparts.[25] Other factors—such as postgraduate education, higher income, executive position, higher authority, success, and a smaller firm—all increase risk-taking. Some industries, notably banking, are significantly less likely to accept risk in their investments than others.[26]

How should the manager gain the information to manage risk and, by so doing, gain control over the risk factors involved in a situation? Briefly, the four steps are as follows:

- analyse the situation;
- describe the objective of management in controlling the risk;
- list the options available to reduce the risk of loss (and their relative riskiness); and
- weigh up the costs/benefits involved in each option.

Insurance and risk management

Insurance cover is a benefit that must be purchased. The cost of the cover will depend upon the likelihood of the occurrence of the loss—or, in other words, the degree of risk. Insurable losses can incorporate:[27]

- loss of human life;
- reduction in life-expectancy;
- loss of human health;
- material losses;
- environmental damage; and
- societal disturbances.

Risk management takes in many aspects of the wider functions of management. Central to all these is the security of assets and their conservation against loss or destruction outside the ordinary course of business activity.

Environmental practices in general management

The importance of environmental issues and practices to management

The tourism and hospitality industry has not been exempt from the imposition of environmental controls. Environmentalism has become an international issue with international ramifications. There are now international standards for good environmental practice (for example, ISO 14001).

Environmental controls should not be seen as an unnecessary burden upon general managers, or even as a passing fad. Some property owners who have endorsed environmental values have found that they have enhanced the value of their investment. Properties with good environmental programs increase the efficiencies of their operations, and extend the economic lives of their facilities through sustainable operations. They also gain important public relations benefits. There is always potential to promote minimisation and recycling programs, and to develop a marketing edge. A hospitality operation that qualifies for a 'green' label can advertise the fact. An increasing public awareness and support for 'green' products means that consumers' decisions will be affected by a company's environmental posture.

The incentives are many and, in some jurisdictions, even include tax benefits for complying with waste-minimisation targets. Taxation advantages can offset required investment in environmental protection programs, and cost savings over time can make such programs very positive in any cost/benefit analysis.

Some initiatives involve substantial capital outlays that, in time, will be recouped through efficiencies and savings. But it is also possible for properties to implement a range of programs which need little investment—such as colour-coded bins for various recyclable wastes.

Hotels use large quantities of energy and generate large amounts of solid and liquid wastes. The activities of a hotel that contribute to the large amounts of waste materials and energy consumption include the following.

1 Dining facilities providing breakfast, lunch, dinner, and 24-hour services for guests use considerable amounts of water, energy, and cleaning products. These facilities also generate significant solid and liquid wastes in the restaurants, kitchens, and food-preparation areas. The kitchens also use energy in cooking, baking, and refrigeration.
2 Guest-comfort requirements use large amounts of energy—mainly in airconditioning and ventilation.
3 Guest facilities such as showers, baths, spa baths, and swimming pools consume large volumes of water and energy. Water usage, including

What motivates hotel managers to save water?

A survey of fourteen hotels in Rotorua, New Zealand, indicated that most managers in the survey were motivated to conserve water because they could reduce overheads and increase their profit:[28]

- nine hotels conserved water to increase profits;
- two hotels conserved water to develop a better environmental image;
- one hotel conserved water because of corporate policy;
- one hotel conserved water to reduce runoff; and
- one hotel conserved water to reduce strain on the sewerage system.

Conclusion: Conserving water makes financial sense.

that in kitchens, is estimated to be approximately 500 litres per guest per day. To put this another way, a 150-room hotel with 80% occupancy, and double occupancy in half of its occupied rooms, has 180 people staying per day. Those 180 people use 500 litres of water each—which equals 90 000 litres. This means that an Olympic-sized swimming pool of water is consumed every eleven days in a small-to-medium-sized hotel.

4 Laundry and drycleaning facilities (whether onsite or offsite) consume large volumes of water, solvents, chemicals, and detergents, as well as energy. These facilities also generate a large volume of waste water which is usually discharged into the sewerage system.

5 Solid wastes are generated by in-house guests and by guests at other functions such as conferences. One example is the huge number of plastic covers used for drycleaned clothing returned to the hotel.

6 Hotels also generate considerable amounts of paper wastes, particularly in the provision of eating facilities (napkins and table covers) and in marketing their services (brochures and pamphlets).

Hotels make other impacts upon the environment. For example, the ambient air temperature in Frement Street, Las Vegas, is measurably higher than that of Las Vegas as a whole, due to the enormous use of power to illuminate the hotel signs and displays.

Although the overall environmental effects of a single hotel might not be as damaging as a large industrial facility, it is nevertheless true that responsible management demands that these effects be minimised.

Many hotels have been in the forefront of recent campaigns to use energy sensibly, and the lead they have taken can inspire domestic users to conserve energy. After all, the difference between a hotel kitchen and a household kitchen appears to be one of scale, rather than one of function (with apologies to some fine hotel chefs!).

The Christmas Tree at the Melia Bali Villas and Spa Resort

The management of the Melia Bali Villas and Spa Resort at Nusa Dua in Bali, Indonesia, was reluctant to cut down a living tree for the centre-piece of their Christmas decorations. But the alternative was to pur-chase a 'tree' made of synthetic materials. They resolved their problem by constructing a Christmas Tree using dry native grasses called *alang-alang* decorated with fruit.[29]

Stakeholders in environmental programs in hospitality

Management

Through the environmental programs that it develops, management has a valuable opportunity to raise community awareness of environmental issues. Such programs can also act to raise the morale and support of staff, and improved morale flows through into a more efficient and effective operation.

Capital costs are involved in instituting environmental programs, but there are paybacks over time as reductions in energy and waste result in cost-savings and a positive impact on the bottom line.

Management must also be conscious that there is growing community pressure to improve environmental practices. This pressure is exerted through government and public-sector agencies. It is clearly better for man-agement to be seen to be taking the lead, rather than being perceived as being forced by government into taking action. It is also advantageous for management to be seen to be a step ahead of the pack in this regard, rather than being mere followers.

Staff

The Hotel Bel Air in California, USA, instituted a comprehensive environ-mental management program, and one of their employees, a kitchen man-ager, summed up the feelings at the hotel:[30]

> This is a great opportunity that is good for everyone. There are cost savings, the employees feel great, and it is good for the environment.

Involvement in programs that are at the cutting edge of hospitality ser-vices, and programs that are of benefit to the general community, engenders a commensurate improvement in staff morale. Staff members can feel that they are making the world better in a small way through their employment. And there can also be career advantages for staff who take a leading role in developing environmental programs.

Taking part in programs can also contribute to team-building, and to the development of group loyalties within hotel departments. At the Hotel Bel Air, the committee members who brought in recycling programs and reduced energy usage were called the 'Guardians of the Grounds'. At the Hyatt Regency at Scottsdale, Arizona, USA, the committee charged with operating a comprehensive recycling program was comprised of representatives from each department, and was known as 'The Green Team'.[31] Of course, staff members are also members of the community at large, and improvements to the environment will flow to everyone in the community.

Some specific programs that employees could undertake to improve environmental practice include car-pooling to get to and from work.

Guests

Guests can benefit from a more widespread awareness of environmental issues, particularly if programs at one hotel stimulate competitors to improve their operations. If more hotels institute green practices, the demand for environmentally friendly goods will grow, and the greater demand should result in cheaper goods that are readily obtainable.

A hotel that implements environmental improvement programs can improve its corporate business. If such programs are recognised by community awards (and such awards are now not uncommon) there is significant marketing leverage to be obtained.

Environmental programs can assist in establishing rapport between staff and guests. At the Renaissance Cottonwoods at Scottsdale, employees wear buttons with the line: 'Ask me why I'm green'.[32] Environmentalism has become a common topic at the hotel, and most guests are aware of the intent of the programs. The opportunity to discuss with staff what is involved can thus serve as an 'icebreaker' in initiating conversation.

The surrounding community

The wider community is an important stakeholder in environmental programs. It is essential that any hospitality operation takes into account the community within which it operates, and recognises that both the operation and the community benefit if the property enhances natural assets. For this reason, proposed projects require master plans for development. These plans must be shaped according to a full appreciation of the surrounds—which include topography, flora and fauna, geology and water resources, local cultural resources, socioeconomic factors, and local history. In a very real sense, the local community, whether a big city or a rural region, is a 'host' for the hospitality operation.

It is obvious that if a hospitality operation damages the surrounding area, it damages its own attraction to the guests who want to come and stay there. If the environment is not protected, and is made unattractive by waste or overuse, visitors will go elsewhere.

Steps in developing environmental programs

The first step in developing an overall effective environmental program is to ensure the full support of senior management. The role of the general manager is therefore crucial to sound and effective environmental programs. Without support at the top, initial obstacles—such as the provision of funding for investigations, and the allocation of valuable staff time—can prove to be insurmountable. If other senior members of the organisation are expected to provide their support, the top level of management must endorse the initiatives, give direction to the programs, and display their genuine personal commitment. Management's support for environmental initiatives can be effectively communicated through the circulation or display of a concise document, entitled 'Our Company's Environmental Policies', or similar.

Secondly, before moving to detailed programs, a relatively senior staff member should be appointed as coordinator of the effort to achieve 'an environmental culture'. The coordinator should act as a focal point for the programs, and should gather material and information.

Thirdly, under the guidance of senior management, the coordinator should develop targets and timelines with the assistance and input of a working group made up of specialists from various important departments, such as housekeeping, and maintenance. The targets should be short-term and long-term. For example, there could be a target of reducing energy usage by 5% over the first twelve months of the programs, and by a total of 10% over three years. Targets should be practical and achievable.

The fourth step should be to develop staff awareness, and to win the support and commitment of staff members in establishing an 'environmental culture'.

Fifthly, having established targets and general staff support, specific programs should be developed in conjunction with departmental staff. It is crucial to have staff involved in the development of specific programs. Without their input and support 'on the ground'—or even worse, if there is active cynicism about the programs—success is unlikely. Examples of specific programs that could be designed with the cooperation of staff include a review of excessive electricity usage, or a review of waste practices and the possibilities of recycling.

The final step in the process is to establish a mechanism to support staff efforts, and to recognise and reward the achievement of set goals. A poster can be set up in staff areas on noticeboards, with staff achievements being regularly noted, and perhaps a sticker shaped like a green leaf signifying that a staff member or section has reached an important goal.

Recycling of solid waste

There are significant economic and environmental benefits associated with the minimisation and recycling of solid waste. Environmental benefits include more efficient reuse of natural resources through recycling, and a

'Environmental conscience'

Novotel (UK) has developed environmental programs with the aim of applying an 'environmental conscience' to all aspects of its operations. Six words that summarise the concepts within its programs are:

- rethinking
- reducing
- recycling
- reusing
- rationalising
- recovering

decrease in the quantity of waste sent to landfill. The economic benefits include decreased waste-disposal costs and the possible generation of a small income-stream for the hotel.

Larger hotels can establish a recycling operation using, for example, cardboard bailers or aluminium crushers. All hotels generate many newspapers daily, and these are relatively easy to recycle. Glass bottles can be recycled, although some organisations have noted that recycling glass by breaking bottles into 'clear' and 'coloured' glass containers has resulted in hazardous conditions for employees involved, and extra safety procedures might be required.

Community programs

The hotel can share in (and even lead) community projects such as clean-up campaigns, and the development of local parks, beaches, and amenities. The hotel can be a sponsor of local educational programs, or a tree-planting program in the local district. The area selected for regeneration need not be adjacent to the hotel property. For example, the Hotel Continental in Sydney offered to assist in the regeneration of bushland south of Sydney that was devastated by bushfire in 1995. The hotel grew plants from seedlings on their own property and then planted them out in an 'adopted' section of the fire-devastated area.[33]

An incentive award for a good idea

Ma Shan is a stores officer at a large city property. He received the hotel's 'employee of the month' incentive award for his suggestion to use shredded paper from the administration office as packing in boxes of goods, instead of bubble-wrap. Thus, with one idea, he reduced the need to purchase packaging, and encouraged an alternative use for shredded documents.

Hotels in resort areas, or those close to natural features attractive to tourists, can start education programs for guests. The Sheraton Miramar at El Gouna, on the Red Sea in Egypt, has taken responsibility for a mangrove-covered sandbank island which is a native habitat for bird life.[34]

Hotels in nature reserves can take special care that their impact upon flora and fauna is minimised—even to the extent of conducting professional research on the effects of their operations upon the area. For example, a resort development, including a golf course, near Khao Yai National Park in Thailand operated successfully for several years, but the deer in the park were dying. Research discovered that the deer were eating golf balls—which proved fatal. The resort development was halted.[35]

Larger organisations can also reduce the material going into landfills by separating out material and items that could be useful for community groups. These could include computers and office equipment from administration, beverage containers and food leftovers from the kitchen, and even items such as paint from the maintenance department. All of these items might be no longer useful to the hotel, but can still be useful for less sophisticated purposes in the wider community. It is not a question of giving people 'second-rate' goods. Rather, it is a question of making productive use of resources that would otherwise go to waste.

Activity 2.7   *Ethical consideration*

You are duty manager of a resort on a subtropical island. The most popular activity for guests is a seaplane flight from the lagoon in front of the resort out to coral reefs nearby. Six guests are shortly due to board the aircraft which is moored near the beach in only a metre of water.

The resort's director of activities, somewhat disconcerted, comes to see you. A saltwater crocodile has appeared near the seaplane. The crocodile apparently obviously believes that the floats of the seaplane are other crocodiles.[36] It will not go away, and it is becoming aggressive. The director of activities does not want to cancel the seaplane flight, reminding you that some very important guests have come a long way and spent a lot of money to see the beauties of the coral reefs.

It will take weeks before wildlife officials can come from the mainland and make arrangements to capture the crocodile and move it elsewhere. One member of the maintenance crew is an experienced and licensed shooter. He proposes that a shot or two at the crocodile might scare it away. If this does not work, the animal itself can be shot. It could be justified, says the shooter, as removing a hazard to the safety of the guests.

QUESTION
- Would you give instructions for the shooter to go ahead with his plan?

An analogy—hospitality management as the 'art of the bath'

A good manager must determine the exact purpose of the operation, and how that purpose can be achieved efficiently and effectively. Consider an analogy of general management—that management is like immersing oneself in a bath. What is the purpose of taking a bath? The primary purpose is to achieve a state of cleanliness, but taking a bath is more than that. Besides the basic washing, bath-taking is also an experience. It can be a time of relaxation and unwinding.

So also with the hospitality experience. Is hospitality merely the provision of a roof over a guest's head? That is the basic function, but surely it is much more than that? Hospitality involves giving guests an enjoyable experience—making them feel relaxed and comfortable, and helping them to enjoy their stay. That's real hospitality. It involves many aspects and many managerial skills. Hospitality, like bath-taking, can be an art as well as a function.

First, the art of bath-taking requires preparation. What are the basic tools and equipment that the bath-taker requires? It is too late to look for the scrubbing brush when one is neck deep in the water! These things must be prepared beforehand, and the process must be planned. How much water will be needed? Besides quantity, the bath-taker must make judgments on quality (for example, how hot should the water be?).

Figure 2.5 *The art of the bath*

Kevin Baker

The environment should be properly prepared. The bathroom must be designed and built to function well if it is to provide the desired experience. All the elements of the environment should blend together so the operation is a success. A successful bath is judged not by the amount of grime sluiced off, but by the measure of satisfaction of the bath-taker. It is not sufficient merely to fill the bath and leave it at that. The bath-taker must make ongoing judgments about the degree of relaxation in the bath. Have the deeper objectives of the exercise been achieved?

Bath-taking, like the hospitality industry, also has 'added value'. There are little extras that make the experience more memorable—such as bath essence, whirlpool effects, and bath pillows. Hotels too have added extras such as minibars, in-house movies, and health-spa facilities.

Of course, hospitality management involves much more than this simple (rather offbeat!) analogy. But the analogy does serve to make the point that effective hospitality management is definitely an art that requires imagination.

Chapter review questions

1 Why should customer service be the primary focus of every hotel operator?
2 How would the organisational structure of a small hotel differ from a large one?
3 What special services do business travellers require during their stay and how could a hotel provide these?
4 Discuss why the art of communication is paramount to the success of any business operation.
5 Why is listening as important as speaking?
6 What is 'body language'?
7 In considering a model of communication (see page 50), list some of the sources of 'noise' (that is, communication interference) in a busy hotel kitchen.
8 Look up the words *sympathy* and *empathy* in a dictionary and note the differences in the definitions. Explain the difference between *sympathy* and *empathy* in a communicative situation.
9 To what extent are you ethnocentric (see pages 55–6)?
10 Why is it vital for any hospitality industry to fully understand the need for multicultural management?
11 What sort of problems are likely to be encountered by an expatriate manager (that is, a person from another country), and by the manager's family?

CASE STUDY

The HB Hotel

The owners of the HB Hotel are returning from a conference on the Gold Coast and are discussing the details of the presentations at the conference. They are most impressed with the way that customer service can increase business, enhance profit, and empower staff (thus improving staff morale).

The owners decide that, as soon as they return, they are going to implement a management program to improve customer care and service. They telephone ahead to the hotel general manager, and ask the manager to think about ways in which such a program could be implemented.

Accordingly, the manager calls together the head receptionist, the housekeeper, the chef, and the head waiter to obtain their views. The manager gives each of these departmental supervisors the following headings for their service program:

- research of guest likes and dislikes;
- training of the staff;
- monitoring of the success of the program; and
- consideration of what could be done in each area of responsibility to give the customers 'added value' to their experience.

Instructions for student exercise

Make up teams of five, with one person nominated as the manager, and the other four to take the roles of the department heads (head receptionist, housekeeper, chef, and head waiter). Establish a customer-care program using the four headings given above. The general manager must then collate the individual programs to create an overall strategy for the hotel. As a team, the five participants are then required to present the program to the owners.

Chapter 3

The Front Office

Your guest forms an impression of your hotel within a minute of coming in the door.

'Big Tex' Reilly

Synopsis of chapter

This chapter first considers the accommodation product and the guest cycle, and then considers the roles and duties of front-office personnel, along with the personal qualities required of the front-office team. The chapter includes a discussion of interdepartmental liaison, and concludes with sections on multiculturalism, environmentalism, and occupational health & safety issues that affect the front office.

The work of front office—the accommodation product and the guest cycle

The accommodation product in detail

The essential accommodation product is the room. This product varies according to the type of establishment—be it a five-star hotel, a two-star hotel, an hostel, or a residential institution (such as a home for the aged or a hall of residence at a college). The product varies in terms of the number of beds in the room, the types of bed, the other facilities provided, the location of the room, and the view.

Because most guests do not view the room before their stay, they are reliant upon the front-office staff to describe the room and its facilities adequately and accurately. It is therefore of the utmost importance that all members of the front-office staff have a clear knowledge of every room in the property.

Because there are differences in the quality of accommodation offered, there are also obviously differences in the prices charged. The standard rate that is charged for a bedroom is called the 'rack rate'. This name stems from the days when all hotel room details were kept in a rack on the reception desk.

Table 3.1 shows some terms commonly used with respect to room rates.

Table 3.1 *Room rates—commonly used terms*

Rate Name	Description
Rack rate	the standard rate for a room with no meals, discounts or deductions
Corporate rate	the rate charged to business houses which guarantee that they will use the hotel regularly; the greater their use of the hotel, the greater the discount they receive
Airline rate	the rate negotiated between an individual airline and the hotel; the discount being based on the volume of business that the hotel receives from the airline
Conference rate	the rate charged to a conference organiser or company for the use of the hotel's conference facilities as well as the bedrooms and meal outlets; instead of a room rate, the whole package is usually charged at a daily rate for each conference delegate, fully inclusive of meals, room, and conference facilities
Group rate	a specific rate agreed for a group of people who will all be arriving together; this rate is agreed upon in advance of the group's arrival and is based upon the numbers of people staying in the hotel, and whether or not they have meals

As can be seen from Table 3.1, the provision of rooms is not merely based upon someone who wants to spend the night. The following criteria all have a profound effect upon the selection of a hotel property by a potential guest:

- the level of luxury that the client wants;
- the facilities that the client wants in the hotel;
- the location of the hotel;
- whether the room has one bed or more; and
- the reason for the guest's stay.

Activity 3.1   *Types of accommodation*

Explore the various types of accommodation in your area and use the following headings to list what they provide:

- number of rooms;
- type of room (single, double, twin, and so on);
- facilities in the room (ensuite bathroom, television, mini-bar, in-house movies, and so on);
- facilities in the building (pool, gym, bar, restaurant, and so on);
- facilities in the grounds (pool, car park, gardens, and so on); and
- location and views.

The guest cycle

The front office of a hotel works very much on a chronological cycle—that is, the work of the front office is based on the timing of the needs and desires of guests. These include:

- the timing of the decision to stay in the hotel;
- the timing of the arrival;
- the timing of the stay in the hotel; and finally
- the timing of the check-out.

Thus, the whole cycle can be seen as a clock. See Figure 3.1.

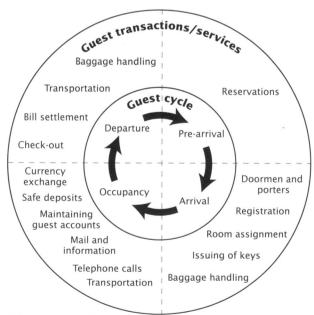

Figure 3.1 *The guest cycle*

Based on Baker & Huyton 1999

During this cycle, the guest has many dealings with the various departments within the front office. Many different groups of people work together to make the guest feel welcome.

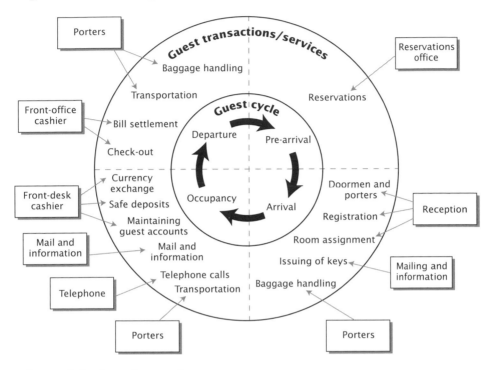

Figure 3.2 *Guest interaction*

Based on Baker & Huyton 1999

In larger properties, information technology (IT) systems are important in recording information on the guest cycle. Computerised systems such as Fidelio and Maxial can be used, in addition to a large number of specialised packages. The use of these systems allows guest information and preferences to be tracked, and all relevant data to be included for billing purposes. In some properties, smart cards have eliminated paper billing of guests and customers. Ideally, a property should operate an integrated system of reservations, property management, and database functions that includes guest, statistical, and financial information.

The people—roles, duties, and attributes

Reservations

The reservations staff includes the reservations supervisor and the reservations clerks.

The reservations supervisor or manager is in charge of the section and ensures that staff members are operating effectively and efficiently. The supervisor also ensures that the hotel operates with the maximum occupancy levels possible while, at the same time, ensuring that rooms are achieving the best possible revenue returns. The supervisor determines the levels of over-booking each night. (Overbooking refers to the practice of taking a larger number of reservations than there are rooms available—as insurance against guests not arriving, or guests leaving earlier than expected.)

In medium-sized hotels the reservations section might not have a separate manager. In these cases, the reservations supervisor reports daily to the front-office manager. In small hotels, the supervision of reservations is often part of the duties of the receptionist or telephone operator.

The reservations staff records the bookings. These can come to the hotel by telephone, fax, mail, email, or even in person. Records are kept of the daily number of bookings taken for each type of room. Additional information is recorded to ensure that the guest gets exactly the accommodation required. In most cases, the reservations clerk asks the potential guest to guarantee the booking with a credit card—and these details are also recorded.

It is becoming more common for the reservations clerk to be seen as a sales agent. In fact, in some hotel companies, the reservations department has been relocated within the marketing department. The sales component of the reservations job requires that staff members try to 'up-sell' the hotel. This means that the staff member will try to get the guest to stay in a more expensively priced room than that first suggested by the guest.

Activity 3.2 Budget and five-star accommodation

Describe the differences between budget and five-star accommodation, and explain the reasons for the different tariffs that apply for each.

Reception

Staff in the reception section of the front office can include:

- the reception manager or front-office manager;
- the reception supervisor; and
- reception clerks and trainee receptionists.

The front-office manager controls the front desk, and it is the manager's duty to work in collaboration with reservations to ensure that occupancy and revenue are maximised. The front-office manager is also responsible for staff rosters, and the effective use of front-office staff. The manager assists in maintaining staff morale and, at the same time, ensuring high levels of customer service and satisfaction.

The front-office supervisor's role is to guarantee the smooth operation of the front desk. The supervisor handles any guest complaints or difficult customers, and is responsible for the notification to all relevant departments of VIP ('very important person') guests. In the absence of a cashier's section, the daily banking reconciliation can also be part of the supervisor's responsibilities. In conjunction with the front-office manager the reception supervisor has responsibility for allocating rooms for group tours before those groups arrive, and for preparing all documentation that will be required upon group's arrival. The supervisor then takes charge of the actual arrival and coordinates the whole process while keeping all other relevant department informed.

The receptionist (or front-desk clerk)

The role of the receptionist in receiving guests includes:

* preparation for the guest's arrival;
* greeting of the guest upon arrival at the front desk;
* obtaining all necessary information from the guest for registration and payment of accounts; and
* checking the guest into a suitable room.
  Other duties of the receptionist include the following:
* keeping details of the hotel rooms status, and creating the daily rooms reports required for senior management;
* liaising with housekeeping on a regular basis regarding cleanliness and readiness of rooms—which rooms are dirty, which are clean and ready for letting, and which are out of order (OOO); and
* giving out room keys, dealing with mail (guest and hotel), and acting as an information desk.

Personal profile—a lodging manager

General Manager Art Sapanli has high praise for one of his managers, Judy Pratt. He considers her one of lodging's best managers, for she will never refuse any request as being outside the scope of her duties. 'Pratt dearly enjoys the creative opportunities her position presents her,' he observes.

Judy Pratt herself says: 'If a group has a beach party theme, it's a challenge for me to come up with something that looks good to them'.

Sapanli also praises Pratt for getting involved in planning employee events, decorating the hotel for Christmas, and coordinating small gifts for elderly people during the holidays.

Pratt states that customer service means, 'to always be a step ahead of the guest's expectations, [to] anticipate and create for them the best possible situation they could have'.[1]

Because the 'mail and information desk' has all but disappeared from hotels (except in the very largest of hotels), the receptionist and the concierge are the main suppliers of information about the hotel, the local area, and the country nationally. Receptionists also often sell stamps and stationery, as well as toiletries (if the hotel does not have its own shop).

The cashier

The specialist cashier has disappeared in most hotels—with a far greater emphasis being placed upon hotel staff being cross-trained in a variety of skills. In most hotels the cashiering function is conducted by the receptionist (or 'front-desk agent' as the receptionist is becoming known).

If there is a designated 'cashier', the role is to keep the guest's account with the hotel fully up to date. The cashier prepares guest accounts and takes payment at the time of check-out. The cashier also looks after the guests' safe-deposit boxes, and conducts any foreign-exchange dealings.

The concierge department

The concierge department consists of:

- the head concierge (or head porter);
- door staff;
- bell staff (porters); and
- car jockeys (in those hotels with parking facilities).

Head concierge

The head concierge is in charge of the bell staff, door staff (if the hotel is large enough), car jockeys and, (in some cases) public area cleaners.

Front office staff must enjoy dealing with people

Courtesy Parkroyal Hotel, Canberra

Les Clefs d'Or

In 1929, a number of hotel concierges formed an association named 'Les Clefs d'Or' (meaning 'Golden Keys'). Admission to the prestigious 'Clefs d'Or' is difficult and demanding—a minimum requirement being that the aspirant be bilingual. Graham, an invited member of the 'Clefs d'Or' at the age of nineteen, was the head concierge at the Lourdes Hotel in London by the age of twenty-four, by which time he was fluent in seven European languages. The association now includes many of the best (and best-known) concierges.

A former president of the 'Golden Keys' defined what makes a good concierge by giving a simple example—whereas a booking agent could get a guest a seat at a Grand Prix, a good concierge ensures the guest gets a seat in the front row in the best stand.

Members wear a crossed-keys emblem on their uniform.

The principal duties of the head concierge include:

- the effective and efficient control of the concierge staff;
- the maintenance of close liaison with all hotel departments (especially the front office);
- acting as a centre for information for internal and external facilities, places of interest, and services;
- the control of accurate message and mail delivery;
- the booking of external tickets for theatres, exhibitions, transport (air, rail, car hire), and so on; and
- security (in those hotels where specific security staff is not employed).

Other concierge staff

The duties of other staff in the concierge department can be summarised as follows:

Table 3.2 *Duties of junior staff in concierge department*

Staff member	Duties
Door staff	initial greeting of all persons entering the hotel; opening of car and taxi doors; organisation of baggage-handling for guests (both arriving and departing); calling of taxis
Bell staff/porters	running of errands and taking messages for both hotel staff and guests; carrying bags to and from rooms; keeping the lobby area clean and tidy
Car jockeys	taking guests to and from external destinations (such as the airport or railway station); parking and collecting guests' cars

Telephone services

The staff in this section includes the switchboard supervisor and the telephonists—for both day and night shifts.

Staff members in this section handle all incoming calls. They also handle some outgoing calls, although most hotels have STD (subscriber trunk dialling) and IDD (international direct dialling) systems. Telephone staff members also look after the in-house paging system for staff and management, and operate the public-address system if the hotel has one.

Switchboard staff members have to be able to handle stressful situations easily and to remain calm under such circumstances (see 'Bomb threats and other extreme threats', page 98). The switchboard is also the 'nerve centre' should the hotel experience an emergency (such as a fire or flood).

Night audit

A separate night team of staff—usually working from approximately 11.00 p.m. until 7.00 a.m.—staffs the front desk overnight. This team could consist of specialist receptionists, cashiers, and a night auditor. However, in most hotels today the roles are combined, and the members of the team work together to cover reception, cashiering, and audit duties.

In the past, most billing and audit systems were manual. However, with the advent of computers, most of the work is completed automatically. Now much of the night auditor's duty is involved with verifying that the computer system is accurately recording, calculating, and reporting the hotel's revenue. The night auditor is usually responsible for closing down the computer (if appropriate), after performing a 'back-up' of the whole system. This 'back-up' involves making copies of all appropriate files in the computer for use in the event of a system crash. The night auditor might also be responsible for printing and duplicating management reports and other documents required for the next day's administration.

Personal qualities of the front-office team

All members of the front-office team must 'look the part', and most hotels provide a uniform for such staff members. If this is not provided, dress must be functional and smart (without being flamboyant). Often, basic black and white is most appropriate. It must be remembered that staff members should dress for the client and for the environment—rather than according to their own personal preferences.

Front-desk staff members have to be aware that they are part of a 'close team'—both in terms of teamwork and in terms of physical proximity to one another. They therefore need to be conscious of personal hygiene and personal grooming in all respects.

Personal profile—a chief commissionaire

Peter was chief commissionaire at the Hotel Australia in Sydney for 44 years. He was a foundation member of the 'Clefs d'Or' (see page 87), and wore the emblem proudly on his blue-and-gold uniform. He had started at the Hotel Australia as a porter and had worked his way up. His daily working hours were 9 a.m. to 8 p.m., with two two-hour breaks.

One coworker commented that Peter ' . . . had information on all aspects of Sydney at his fingertips. Anything you wanted to know he could tell you instantly. His knowledge was outstanding, a perfect commissionaire who knew how to look after guests.'

Another coworker commented that when Peter blew his whistle to summon a taxi, the blast could be heard all the way to Central Station![2]

Because of the style of many modern hotels (with an emphasis on luxury and opulence), front-office staff members are expected to be extensions of this style in the way that they behave. Front-office staff members see many people in circumstances that might be viewed as delicate, inappropriate, or downright 'ugly'. The three wise monkeys were supposed to 'see no evil, hear no evil, and speak no evil'. The professional front-office person operates on a variation of this in their dealings with the indiscretions of the general public. The discreet front office staff member 'sees all, hears all . . . and says nothing'—unless the safety and reputation of the hotel (and its staff and guests) are endangered.

A recipe for a successful front-office manager

Four useful ingredients in a 'recipe' for the production of a successful front-office manager:
- develop an ability to remember names and faces;
- develop good communication skills;
- develop a good knowledge of places and events; and
develop a good measure of patience, tact, and discretion.

Mix together, allow to mature, and the 'end product' will be a successful front-office manager who runs a smooth and efficient front office.

Activity 3.3	*How long is a hotel bed?*

This Activity explores the following sorts of very basic, but very practical questions. How long should a hotel bed be? Perhaps 1.9 metres? 2.0 metres? 2.1 metres? What is the average height of a man? What is the average height of a woman? Are there major differences among ethnic groups?

QUESTIONS

- Find official statistics for these measurements.
- Enquire of the front office of a major hotel and ask the length of their beds.
- How would you accommodate a person who is 2.1 metres tall?

The most important quality in front-office staff members is not that they like to meet people. Nor is it that they are friendly. The most important quality goes beyond meeting people and being friendly. They must want to help people. Those who want to help people automatically have most of the other attributes required.

Skills and knowledge in the front office

Maintaining interdepartmental liaison

The reception department of any hotel plays the principal role in the maintenance of guest records. It is therefore vital that the department maintains very close links with other hotel departments. Most of the guest information

Personal profile—the concierge

Liu Chifu has been the concierge at a five-star hotel in the Pudong development area of Shanghai for two years. He had previously gained experience at the Portman Shangri-la Hotel, learning all aspects of the busy role of a concierge. Chifu takes a special pride in being able to answer any question or meet any unusual needs of the hotel's guests. Late one night, Chifu received a message from one of his porters—a guest simply had to have a pair of ballet slippers! It took Chifu only twenty minutes to arrange the delivery of a pair of white ballet slippers (large size) from a small store in Nanjing Road.

is obtained from the guest registration form and is circulated to all the other departments via a variety of reports.

The most common reports prepared by the reception department are:

- 'in-house' list;
- extra arrivals;
- guest amendments;
- arrivals and departures list;
- checked-out list; and
- VIP list.

These are examples of only some of the lists used. The exact lists prepared and used by any given hotel depends on the size and particular needs of the hotel concerned. Smaller hotels have fewer arrivals and departures on a given day, and might therefore incorporate arrivals, departures, and resident guests in a single list. The levels of service that the hotel provides affects the types of report issued. Top-class hotels provide a wider variety of services, have more guests, tend to attract more VIPs, and generally have need of a greater number of more complicated lists.

Table 3.3 shows some of the departments that exist in a hotel, and the reports that can be issued by the front office to assist in the work of the various departments.

Table 3.3 *Departments and reports*

Department	Type of report	Purpose of report
Restaurants	• arrivals/ departures list	• to inform restaurant staff of the number of people in the hotel at meal times
	• in-house list	• as above
	• VIP list	• to note any VIPs who might choose to dine in the hotel restaurant
Housekeeping	• room-status report	• to inform housekeeping which rooms are dirty, which are clean, and which are vacant
	• arrivals/ departures list	• to advise how many people will be arriving and departing, and how many rooms will be used; this assists in efficient staffing
	• in-house list	• to advise which rooms will be occupied; again for staffing reasons
	• VIP list	• to add extra touches to a room, or to accommodate special requirements and requests
	• tour group list	• to inform the staff of mass arrivals and departures

(continued)

Table 3.3 *Departments and reports (continued)*

Department	Type of report	Purpose of report
Concierge	• arrivals/ departure list • in-house list • VIP list • tour group list	• to help the head concierge roster staff efficiently • to assist the concierge in providing efficient service to in-house guests • to organise staff for any special greetings and services required for these guests • to ensure that there are enough staff members on duty at the times of arrival and departure
Food & beverage	• in-house list • VIP list • tour group list	• to enable F&B staff members to know who is entitled to sign for drinks or meals • to ensure that F&B staff members are aware of possible food and drink requirements of these particular clients (including room service) • to ensure that F&B staff members are aware of the billing arrangements and entitlements of each group
Banquets	• tour group list	• to ensure that function facilities are available and staff rostered for all requirements
Business centre	• in-house list • VIP list • arrival/ departure list	• to ensure that business centre staff members know who is in which room, for billing-verification purposes • to ensure best possible business centre service for these clients • to assist with staffing and billing procedures
Telephonists	• all reports	• the telephonists need to have an 'up-to-the-minute' record of all arrivals, departures, and in-house guests; telephonists must be able to advise callers accurately of the status of all persons; inaccuracies in this sort of information can cause significant inconvenience and disruption
Management	• all reports	• management must be kept informed of all these matters for a variety of reasons—including managers planning their own days, assessment of service provision, staffing requirements, financial assessments, and a range of other matters

The role of the front office is thus vital to the successful running of the whole hotel, and is not restricted to the service of guests in their rooms.

Activity 3.4   *Ethical consideration*

You are the supervisor of the front office. When you start work one afternoon, you discover that a reservations clerk has overbooked the hotel that night. The night was already busy due to an international car-racing event. You interview the clerk to find out how this happened. The clerk informs you that the general manager had instructed her to accept a group of four business travellers—all good clients of the hotel. Apparently the group had contacted the general manager and had asked that they all be accommodated 'as a personal favour'.

It appears that all guests with reservations will turn up and that you will have to deal with some overbooked guests. You make enquiries and discover that none of the other hotels in town has any vacancies.

You discuss the situation with the general manager. She states that you will just have to 'bump' (that is, cancel the prebooked room of) one or more of the prebooked guests. She suggests that you choose from the casual visitors or vacationers who are unlikely to come back to the hotel anyway.

QUESTIONS
- What is your reaction?
- What should you say to the general manager?

Cultural awareness in the front office

Front-office personnel are a focus of interaction with guests, and must therefore be culturally aware and sensitive. Providing culturally appropriate services to individuals requires forethought and planning across a range of issues.

Important among the issues that must be addressed are dietary practices. Thought must be given to what advice front office should give to house-keeping about foods and beverages to place in rooms and minibars, taking account of dietary preferences and cultural prescriptions. What liquors should be supplied—if indeed liquors should be supplied at all? What about social or religious practices related to the time of year or season?

Checklist #1

Which of the following are especially appropriate reactions when dealing with German people?[3]

- Be well dressed and presented when dealing with these guests.
- Do not address them by first names, but do use appropriate titles and surnames (family names).
- Do not apologise for mistakes (because mistakes are a sign of inefficiency), but do ensure that the guest is aware of your sincere desire to fix any problems efficiently.
- Be precise when describing places and times of events.
- Put them at ease by making jokes whenever possible.

But cultural sensitivity means more than merely paying attention to food and other 'obvious' needs. There are more subtle considerations that require real sensitivity. The key to providing hospitality services in an appropriate fashion to take account of different cultural values is to treat each person (both the employee providing the service, and the guest who receives it) as an individual. If hospitality managers recognise that every guest or employee is an individual (with personal requirements for information, services, support, and expectations), managers can modify universal services as necessary to meet these individual needs. Mistakes will still be made in dealing with persons from a different culture. However, if managers are honest and sincere in recognising and learning from such mistakes, all parties are likely to respect the outcome.

What is most important?

Draw up a list of what you consider are the most important aspects of the guest's experience in staying at a hotel. Consider such issues as security, cleanliness, facilities, free giveaways, service, and so on. This can be done as a group project, or under advice from an instructor.

Then go to a local hotel, or some other venue such as an international college, and interview people from as many nationalities as you can. To get a reasonable sample, interview at least three people from each different nation or from each different culture. Ask these people what *they* think are important aspects of staying in a hotel.

Then compare your own likes (and dislikes) to those of your respondents. Do people from different cultural backgrounds have different priorities?

The rule of giving *personal* respect applies even when individual guests are part of tour groups. Guests must always be treated as individuals. But in doing so, staff members should be aware that different cultures put different value on who may speak on behalf of the group, and who may be addressed directly by staff members. Different cultural perceptions of the respect and deference due to age can mean that staff should address queries and comments through older members of the group. It might also be appropriate to serve older guests first. The mode of address can also be important, and the form of words used should be carefully assessed. In some cases, it might also be inappropriate for staff to address women directly.

Activity 3.7   *Checklist #2*

Which of the following are appropriate when dealing with Japanese people?[3]
- Be formal in speech and behaviour rather then seeking to be casual and informal.
- Do not try to address them by name because their names are unpronounceable by non-Japanese people.
- Make a sincere apology if there has been a mistake made.
- Do not look Japanese women straight in the eye, but avert your eyes a little when addressing them.
- Put them at ease by making jokes whenever possible.

A multicultural environment can be developed by encouraging language proficiency among staff—especially staff who have dealings with guests. Speaking the language can obviously assist in appreciating the exact needs and desires of guests. It is also important in that it can build a deeper understanding of the history and development of another culture. (See Appendix 1, page 276 for more on this aspect of service.)

Training in cultural sensitivity is important in building multicultural awareness. Such training can include training in the art of communication, and in the importance of appreciating how various cultures can have different perceptions of a given communication. For example, in their dealings with Asian people, European managers and staff might not appreciate the importance of maintaining respect and not putting an Asian person in a situation in which that person could suffer a 'loss of face'. The concept of 'loss of face' (roughly equivalent to a Westerner being publicly embarrassed or humiliated) is very important in some Asian cultures. It carries greater significance in such cultures than it does in many Western cultures, and incidents that might be of temporary embarrassment to a Westerner can be a matter of severe and lasting humiliation for some Asian people. It might therefore be appropriate to communicate through mediators, or in some other oblique (non-direct) fashion—to avoid placing an Asian colleague or guest in a situation where that person might 'lose face' and feel humiliated.

Training in cultural sensitivity in relation to Arab cultures should highlight how business and social relationships are intermingled, and how a person seeking to do business in an Arab culture must take time to develop personal relationships with their business partners.

Activity 3.8   *Checklist #3*

Which of the following are the appropriate reactions when dealing with American people?[3]

- Be direct in speech and recognise that your slang words might not be understood by them.
- Be relaxed and laid back and do not take them seriously if they have complaints.
- Do not use polite words such as 'please' and 'thank you' because Americans prefer informality.
- Americans like to hear frank opinions (even if critical) about their military activities around the world.
- Ensure that you provide a frank and detailed response to a detailed request.

Occupational health & safety

Late hours

Front-office staff commonly work until late in the evening, and night-audit staff members in particular have abnormal hours of work. Night staff should be included within the protection ambit of security patrols. There are some safety tips related to personal security that apply to all hospitality staff who work late hours or night shifts.

These include:

- leave the property with another person if possible;
- try to walk only in well-lit areas, and always park vehicles close to main roads where there is other traffic or where there is good street lighting;
- do not drive if tired;
- try to get adequate sleep before reporting for the next shift; and
- do not compensate for tiredness by using drugs or stimulants.

Working conditions

Clerical workers in the front office can be at risk if working in areas that are not adequately lit. They can also face health risks through incorrect posture, and from staying too long in one position. If sitting for long periods, clerical workers should ensure:

- that their backs are supported and upright;
- that any documents they are examining are at a comfortable eye level;
- that their shoulders are relaxed (to minimise muscle tension) and that their arms, forearms, and wrists are straight; and
- that their feet are either flat on the floor or on a footrest, with minimum pressure on the back of their thighs to ensure that circulation is not restricted to the lower legs.

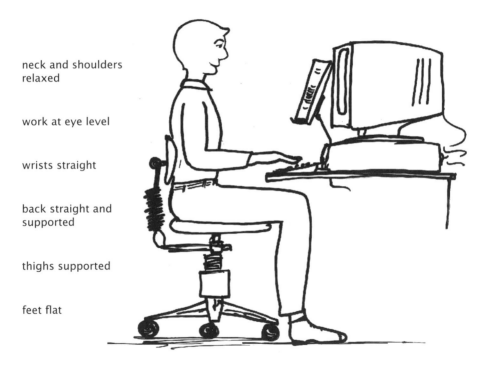

neck and shoulders relaxed

work at eye level

wrists straight

back straight and supported

thighs supported

feet flat

Figure 3.3 *A safe sitting posture*

Kevin Baker

A number of practices can reduce the discomforts of sitting too long during such prolonged tasks as data-inputting. These practices can include alternating between standing and sitting activities, taking frequent short breaks (not working more than one hour continuously), and building up to a steady, comfortable keystroke rate.

Activity 3.9	*The danger of sitting down*

The design of chairs and tables at a work station should be done according to the rules of ergonomics—that is, the study of the human shape and movement.

As a group, check out the physical design of a work station—for example, the workplace of administrative staff, or the study areas of students. One member of the group should sit at a computer and perform a short piece of work, while the other members of the group observe and make notes. Are the arms horizontal? Is the neck straight? Where are the eyes focused? Where does the light fall?

Repeat the exercise at other work stations.

QUESTION

- Write a comprehensive analysis and comparison of several work stations, and note any remedial action that you consider to be required.

Bomb threats and other extreme threats

Although bomb threats and other extreme threats are rare, they do occur. In fact, one of the authors of this book had the unpleasant experience of being present during the handling of such a threat. The incident turned out to be an excellent example of how such matters should be handled.

A telephone call regarding the bomb threat was made to the hotel. The telephonist who took the call remained calm. Indeed, she was so alert that she not only heard the caller's words and responded to them, but she also listened to the background noise of the call. She kept the caller talking, noted the tone of voice and the accent, and noted the background noise. The telephonist recorded excellent detail about all these matters—a female caller with a northern English accent, the fact that the caller appeared to have a detailed knowledge of the hotel (especially housekeeping), and the fact that the caller appeared to be ringing from a particular environment (the background noise). The telephonist's notes enabled the police to make an immediate arrest. The bomb hoaxer was a disgruntled ex-member of the staff who had been dismissed.

As noted above, this proved to be an excellent example of how such matters should be handled. The main point is to remain calm, and to ask questions about where the bomb is, when it will explode, and what it looks like. Authorities then recommend that the telephonist should keep the caller talking so that the telephonist can note anything else (such as background noises). Authorities also suggest that the caller be asked for their personal details, such as their name and address—although it is unlikely that these will be given. However, the caller might make a response that gives some hint to his or her identity.

The next step, after getting details of the bomb or other threat, is to alert other staff members who can contact the police and search for the bomb while the telephonist keeps the caller talking. But, under no circumstances, should staff members attempt to touch or remove a suspicious item themselves. The procedure must be to leave the item alone, withdraw people to a safe distance (as suggested by authorities), and leave the specialists to deal with the device.

The risk of violence

Front-office staff have security concerns not usually encountered by other staff members. For example, front-office and reception staff are usually more at risk of violence from guests or the public. Some measures for the personal safety of front-office staff include:

- the provision of intercom communication;
- the provision of 'panic' buttons or pressure pads for the use of staff who feel threatened;
- obvious video surveillance of the area; and
- the rostering of experienced staff with inexperienced staff.

Front-office staff members should also have some training in the handling of violent confrontations. This training could include such strategies as:

- avoiding eye contact with a threatening person;
- not antagonising or abusing a guest;
- keeping a safe distance, or an item of furniture, between the threatened staff member and an angry person; and
- trying to stay calm under provocation.

All aggressive incidents should be recorded and reported to management.

Front-office workers are also at risk of the trauma of violent theft—especially if they are in a cash-handling role. The risk can be minimised by adequate security measures, and especially by ensuring that clerical staff in such roles are never left alone, and never have responsibility for looking after or transporting large quantities of cash by themselves.

Administration staff other than front-office workers are sometimes responsible for cash-handling and security. Like front-office staff, administration staff in high-risk areas should have the protection of alert devices ('panic' buttons and pressure pads) to summon assistance if required.

Environmental awareness in the front office

Front-office staff members should play their parts in the overall 'green strategy' of the hotel (see pages 70–6). In addition, there are specific environmental issues relating to the front office.

The proper use of paper is the most significant environmental issue affecting front-office work. Most types of clean paper can be recycled through contractors, and there are many opportunities to separate and recycle considerable amounts of paper associated with office work and general pack-aging. In addition, there are opportunities to minimise the generation of paper and cardboard waste through the reuse of office paper, double-sided copying, and a reduction in the amount of packaging provided in guest rooms.

Activity 3.10 *Options for the environment*

As a group, list the ways in which hotels in your area help the environ-ment. Also note those that do nothing.

Having made your own assessment, contact your local environment protection agency and seek further information and guidance from experts.

Create a booklet or pamphlet for hoteliers and tourism operators in your area. In this booklet, list all the ways in which they can protect the environment and estimate how much revenue could be saved or generated by these measures.

Chapter review questions

1 Consider the variety of jobs and roles that occur in the front office of a hotel, and prepare brief notes on each role, making out a case for the necessity and importance of each one.
2 Now think laterally, and consider whether it would be possible to combine some of these roles and skills efficiently. Prepare notes on such a 'rationalisation' of roles.
3 What is interdepartmental communication and why is it important?
4 What is the difference between 'front-of-house' roles and 'back-of-house' roles?
5 What is meant by the 'chronology' of the front-office operation, and how does it work?
6 You hear someone say: 'I don't care about the environment because in fifty years I'll be dead'. What would you say to that person in an attempt to convince him/her of the duty of every person to be responsible in the personal use of resources?

CASE STUDY

The HB Hotel

The manager of the HB Hotel is considering a fully automated check-in process, whereby the arriving guests need only swipe their credit cards and they will automatically be allocated their rooms. Their credit cards will be debited with the accommodation charge. The same process will generate a coded card that will allow access to the room.

The manager can see cost/benefits in using the system—such as the elimination of wages for check-in staff. However, the manager is concerned that guests might prefer the 'personal touch' on arrival at the HB Hotel. Even though the coded access card is in a 'friendly' shade of blue (and printed with flowers and smiling faces), it just does not seem the same.

What are some of the issues involved with automatic electronic check-in?

Chapter 4

Housekeeping, Laundry, and Maintenance

> The princess awoke bruised from head to foot because of the pea beneath the mattress.
>
> From a children's tale

Synopsis of chapter

This chapter first considers the role of housekeeping in hospitality operations, followed by a consideration of the organisation of the housekeeping department. The chapter then discusses cleaning practices and laundry operations, followed by environmental issues, and concludes with a section on occupational health & safety issues.

The work—the role of housekeeping in hospitality operations

The housekeeping function in a hotel or motel is important. The cleanliness and maintenance of a hotel, and the state of the rooms, are major determinants in a guest's opinion of the property. Guests expect a clean, safe living environment, and many expect a personalised service to their rooms (such as valet and room-butler service).

For many years, the role of the housekeeper was seen as being menial 'woman's work'. Now it is recognised as a job for the most discriminating and smart people. A housekeeping manager:

- must be up to date with the products;
- must be a counsellor for the staff (housekeeping invariably having the largest number of staff members of any hotel department);

- must be 'systems-literate' in new technology;
- must be a project planner for refurbishment and deep-cleaning requirements;
- must have accountancy skills (the housekeeping budget being very large); and
- must be a diplomat (because housekeeping staff members see the guest in the privacy of the bedroom, and often much more is revealed than is anticipated).

Because of these varied skills, the role of executive housekeeper has evolved from that of a 'flush-and-brush' person, to that of a senior member of the hotel management team.

Housekeeping executives are becoming more technology-orientated. Inventory control and stock records are becoming dependent upon bar-coding. These bar-codes indicate stock levels, make stocktaking quicker and easier, and can automatically re-order materials and products by email when critical levels are reached. Bar-coding can also be used to monitor servicing of designated areas, and staff can assess the work required and the cleaning program for the day by swiping a hand-held computer over the area's bar-code. Supervisory staff can maintain central records and can, at any time, check the status of a given area. When problems are encountered—such as blown fluorescent tubes, or damaged furniture—housekeeping staff members can log the problem on their hand-held computer and a work order can be generated.

Maintenance and cleaning reports—including records of labour hours, costs, and the cleaning and maintenance status of particular hotel units—can be generated periodically.

Mobile telephones are another item of technology that can make house-keepers more efficient. These can be used as pagers when there are urgent messages or tasks, and can also be used to download work schedules.

The people—organisation of the housekeeping department

The housekeeping department is a 'back-of-house' function and is usually included in the rooms division of a hotel—along with departments such as reservations and telephone. Housekeeping generally has responsibility for cleaning public areas (such as corridors and the lobby), as well as responsibility for cleaning guest rooms. The department has a close relationship with the front office which produces the occupancy reports that are reflected in the housekeeper's room-status report—that is, the report on the inventory of rooms in the hotel. Because the inventory of rooms is at the heart of the hospitality operation, the work of housekeeping is crucial to the successful operation of a hotel or motel.

Some terms that relate to room status include:

- *Occupied*—a guest has registered the right to occupy the room;
- *Due Out*—the guest is expected to leave the room at check-out time;
- *Early makeup*—the room is required as soon as possible;
- *Stayover*—the guest will not be checking out that day;
- *On-change*—the guest has left but the room has not yet been serviced and made ready for a new guest;
- *Deep cleaning*—the room is being given extra cleaning attention (a planned, regular occurrence for all rooms in turn);
- *Out-of-order*—the room cannot be registered for a new guest for some reason (possibly because it needs more extensive cleaning, or because furniture is broken.

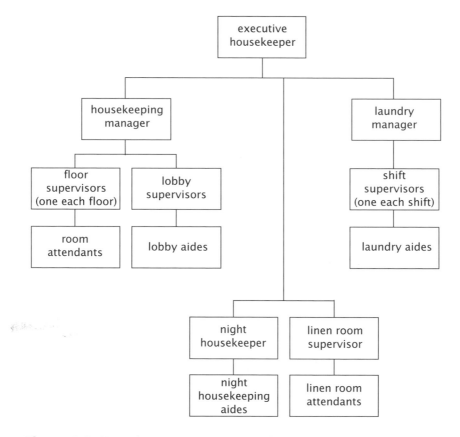

Figure 4.1 *Housekeeping organisation chart*

Kevin Baker, based on Baker & Huyton 1999

To meet their responsibilities, the duties of the department must be specified and allocated to employees through job descriptions. Various housekeeping jobs have descriptions that are self-explanatory of their job duties. These include: linen distributor, lobby attendant, linen clerk, and night cleaner.

Sample job descriptions

Room attendant/housekeeping aide

Basic function: servicing and cleaning of guest rooms under supervision of floor supervisor

Hours of duty: 8.30 a.m.–4.00 p.m. five days a week as rostered

Duties:

- make the bed(s) according to daily assignment; change linen;
- vacuum floor;
- dust surface;
- arrange items in room tidily;
- clean and restock bathroom

Reports to: floor supervisor

Housekeeping supervisor

Basic function: ensuring that all guest rooms, public areas, and working areas are maintained in a clean, safe, and tidy fashion; ensuring that housekeeping and laundry departments operate effectively

Hours of duty: 7.30 a.m.–4.00 p.m. weekdays

Duties:

- select and train housekeeping staff according to hotel guidelines;
- check work of floor supervisors and other cleaning staff;
- coordinate special cleaning projects;
- maintain housekeeping inventories;
- other duties as directed by the duty manager

Reports to: rooms division manager

The organisation of the housekeeping department is determined by the size of the property and the occupancy rate. The various sections are organised according to control and supervision requirements. The department can be subdivided into sections of approximately 13–15 rooms under a section housekeeper, or it can be organised into house divisions that incorporate a whole floor.[1]

Skills and knowledge

Cleaning practices

The work of the housekeeping department requires:

- inventories of the areas to be cleaned;
- schedules for cleaning (that is, which areas will be cleaned daily, weekly, or monthly); and
- required standards of cleanliness.

Each of these will be considered below.

Inventories of the areas to be cleaned

Stocktaking of cleaning materials and guest consumables should be carried out regularly. This includes the checking, counting, and labelling of all materials. By this means, the housekeeping supervisor keeps control over the usage and costs of cleaning materials, and guards against pilfering or outright theft of guest consumables.

Stock can be organised into separate categories of materials:

- housekeeping equipment (such as vacuum cleaners);
- items held for guest use (such as irons);
- linen (a large category); and
- guest supplies (such as soaps and shampoos).

Because stocktakes are conducted regularly they can be incorporated into other staff functions—such as purchasing and stores—so that as levels of stock items fall to a minimum carrying level, they are automatically replenished by stores orders.

A pioneer of housekeeping equipment— William Hoover

William Hoover did not invent the electric vacuum cleaner that bears his name, but he was instrumental in marketing it.

Hoover owned a business specialising in saddles and leather goods. In 1908, the business was declining as horse-drawn carriages were replaced by cars. Fortunately, Hoover came across a new device—an upright sweeper made of wood and tin, with a filter and rotating brushes, and a vacuum supplied by a small electric motor. Other vacuum-cleaning machines were powered either by petrol engines (and were so big and noisy that they had to be left outdoors) or by hand-turning a lever. Hoover saw the potential of the new electric device and started manufacturing the invention. When World War I reduced the number of servants available to the wealthy, the new machine came into its own and sales 'took off'. Hoover set up the Hoover Company in 1922 and never looked back. He died a multimillionaire.

The original inventor of the vacuum device, a man named James Spangler, had devised the machine because he had asthma and needed to sweep his home every day. Unfortunately, Spangler was a department store cleaner and did not have the means to market his invention himself. He therefore sold the idea to Hoover. If Spangler had not sold the invention, people in those parts of the world where the term 'hoovering' has become part of the language might have spoken of 'spanglering' a room—which sounds very odd!

Schedules for cleaning

A schedule is a detailed document that describes what work is to be done, where and when it is to be done, and who will do it. The housekeeping schedule commonly divides the property up into work areas. These can include:

- rooms department (guest rooms, room corridors, lifts and landings, stairwells, and work rooms);
- public areas (lobby, front-desk area, public accessways and amenities);
- restaurants and bars;
- kitchens;
- conference rooms;
- recreation and entertainment areas (games rooms, spas and sauna, gymnasium);
- offices;
- employees' amenities areas (locker rooms, cafeteria, and staff rooms);
- engineering areas; and
- outdoor areas.

These work areas are defined and delineated into areas of responsibility by a 'house breakout chart'. This chart is a floor plan of the whole hotel and includes details of every section of the hotel. Areas of responsibility can be defined by colouring—as a key to which personnel are responsible for that area.

Housekeeping staff members must ensure the highest standards of cleanliness and tidiness in their work

Courtesy Parkroyal Hotel, Canberra

Activity 4.1   *Timing the cleaning process*

The following activity might appear to be a tedious activity, but it can provide an aspiring supervisor or manager with important insights. Vacuum a carpeted area equivalent to the area of a typical hotel room.

- Time yourself—starting the timing from when you go to the storage area to find the required equipment until when you replace the equipment after completing the task.
- Check your work by striking the vacuumed carpet hard with the flat of your hand to see if any dust arises. It is best to do this in a shaft of sunlight if possible. Make an honest assessment of whether a supervisor would be happy with the quality of your work.
- This exercise gives you a better understanding of the daily task expected of cleaning staff—in terms of time and quality.

Each area of the property should have its own schedule of cleaning. Particular areas (for example, guest rooms, bathrooms) and particular items (for example, light fittings) should be given separate schedules to ensure that all requirements are met over a full cleaning cycle. The schedule should have a logical basis to make it easier for housekeeping staff to make sure that everything is done—for example, the schedule for bathroom cleaning could state that work starts at a designated point in the room, and that work progresses around the room until the worker is back at the starting point.

Some areas might need specialist care—such as the external parts of the property and landscaping, or the kitchen area with such fittings as range hoods and grease traps. They should all be included in the schedule to ensure that no part of the property is missed.

The cleaning schedules could include provision for recording any maintenance requirements (for example, painting) that might be noted during routine cleaning. This ensures that maintenance is coordinated with more routine cleaning tasks.

Schedules can be further divided into sections that are a team responsibility. For example, a particular team might be given responsibility for a particular floor, or for a major public space such as the lobby.

Schedules can be further subdivided—down to the level of the individual team member. Particular team members can be given responsibility for particular tasks. When the schedule for the team is matched with the schedules for the individuals, the responsibility of each member of the housekeeping team is clear, and each person will know exactly how far he or she must go with their work.

Personal profile—the executive housekeeper

Jenny Bullman is executive housekeeper at a tourist resort near the Victoria Falls in Zimbabwe. She is never flustered—despite what her staff might find in rooms and units after guests have departed.

Jenny has worked at the resort for eight years. She started as a house-keeping assistant and was promoted to supervisor after two years, before being further promoted to executive housekeeper after completing a certificate of management by correspondence.

Jenny says that her biggest challenge is to keep her staff motivated to achieve high standards of service, and she accomplishes this by encouraging a team spirit among her staff.

Such division of schedules also means that the supervisor is clear about who is responsible for any given area. This allows for easy checking of completed work, and rectification of any problems that remain. The supervisor should be an 'itinerant'—that is, a frequent visitor to, and inspector of, all the various areas of the property. The exact timing of a visit should be a surprise, but the fact there will be a visit at some time should not be unexpected. In other words, staff members should be aware that their work will be reviewed on an irregular and unannounced basis.

Another way of dividing the schedules is by shift. The routine work of day staff could form one part of the cleaning schedule, and the work of night staff could form another section.

Activity 4.2   *Costs of cleaning*

Given the floor layout of the HB Hotel (Figure 1.7, pages 33, 34), work out how many cleaning staff members would be needed, and what their duties would be, for a Wednesday. This will require decisions on how many rooms it is fair for a room attendant to be expected to clean, how much public space a cleaner should keep clean, and what tasks are associated with these roles.

Ask a local hotel for staffing wage rates, and then work out how much it costs on a daily basis for room cleaning.[2]

(Note: Room occupancy rates can be found in the case study at the end of this chapter, page 130.)

Required standards of cleanliness

Housekeeping performance standards, and the routine cycles expected, should be documented in detail and incorporated into the schedules. The standards will direct the cleaning methods and materials to be used. Certain tasks require special treatments—for example, the cleaning of wooden parquetry floors.

When defining the performance standards, and when dividing up the schedules, housekeeping management must take care that workloads are not unfairly distributed. Staff schedules, detailing the hours and days of work of all housekeeping staff, should be drawn up in conjunction with the work schedules. Managing the housekeeping function with teams can simplify the business of compiling rosters, For example, if teams of four to five employees are identified, and perhaps named with such titles as 'red shift' or 'blue shift', whole blocks of the roster can fall into place. The staff schedules must have some flexibility to cope with increased occupancy, and the demands of seasonal fluctuation or special functions.

It is a good housekeeping practice to utilise brief room inspection reports which:

- catalogue the status of the rooms;
- ensure that all the cleaning schedules have been kept;
- note any maintenance that is required; and
- record any unusual occurrences or items that should be logged as a matter of security.

Control of guest supplies

As part of their service, hotels maintain a quantity of items for guest use. Long-staying guests might, for example, find ironing boards or sewing kits

The importance of buckets and carts

'Rolls-Royce' is the name of a prestigious car, but 'Royce Rolls' is the name of a company that conceived numerous products that make the lives of housekeepers easier. For example, in 1925, Maria Royce was in hospital and commented to her husband about how much noise the housekeepers made working with buckets in the halls. She wondered whether it would be better to have buckets on wheels. On her discharge, Maria Royce and her husband began to make such buckets in their basement, and the business took off. The company also designed cleaning carts to make the work of housekeepers more efficient by saving countless trips back to storage cupboards.[3]

useful. Guests with mobility problems might require a wheelchair or crutches. For transient or short-stay guests, housekeeping might provide shampoo, hair conditioner, pens, and paper. Some provide toothbrushes, combs, and razors. The array of guest supplies usually increases with the star rating of the hotel.

The housekeeping supervisor should keep an inventory of these items and use a register to control their issue to guests.

Activity 4.3   *What's needed?*

Make a list of supplies that you expect to find in a bedroom of a three-star hotel. Do the same exercise for a bedroom of a five-star hotel.

QUESTIONS

- Compare your list with the actual guest supplies provided by a real three-star hotel and a real five-star hotel.
- Explain any difference between your expectations and the real lists.

Housekeeping security issues

Because it has primary responsibility for guest rooms and public areas, the housekeeping department has special responsibilities with regard to the security of guests and visitors. Special care has to be taken with respect to keys and access to guest rooms. The housekeeper must keep a register of all keys to rooms, and must take special care of master keys—particularly keys that are in the form of computerised card systems that can be copied or damaged.

Some other areas of security concern are:

- noting unrecognised people on the floor (especially those who behave strangely);
- checking that doors are locked;
- noting hotel employees who are outside their normal workplace;
- noting suspicious or unauthorised items in the hotel (such as firearms, large amounts of cash, animals in guest rooms, and so on).

Not all security issues relate to unlawful activity. Housekeeping supervisors must be alert to guests who might be ill or injured in their rooms. The housekeeping division must have a procedure to be followed in the event of a death in a room.

Housekeepers must also be alert to signs of danger—such as a fire, or conditions that increase the risk of a fire occurring. They must ensure that all staff members are knowledgeable about evacuation and emergency procedures—both for themselves and for guests.

For these reasons, it is important that housekeeping be kept informed of any SPAs ('special attentions'; that is, guests with special requirements). For instance, in the event of a fire alarm going off, housekeeping or security should know if there are any guests with hearing impairment who might not hear the alarm. Similarly, guests who require wheelchairs for mobility, or guests with other disabilities, might require particular assistance in the event of evacuation.

Emergency exits and equipment must be clearly marked. For these and other amenities it is a good practice to use illustrative signs—that is, signs and notices that use pictures rather than words. Such pictures can be understood by anyone, whatever their language.

Figure 4.2 *Illustrative sign*
Guest advice card, Maritim Hotel, Köln

Activity 4.4   *What does it mean?*

Examine the example of an illustrative sign in Figure 4.2.

QUESTIONS

- Describe the general intention of the sign.
- Do you think this is effective in its intention?
  (Answer is on page 128.)

Another aspect of housekeeping duties under the broad heading of 'security' is responsibility for lost and found items. Anecdotal evidence of what is left behind in hotel rooms borders on the bizarre. For example, a Great Dane dog was left behind in one hotel room. In another room, a set of musical instruments was found. One of the authors discovered that an unknown guest had left behind a mink coat valued at tens of thousands of dollars. Several previous occupants of the room were contacted, but none claimed any knowledge of the coat!

The housekeeper must have a system for logging the discovery of these items, and for keeping records of any goods that are claimed. A system is required for ensuring the safety of such goods until they are claimed or until the hotel relinquishes control over them in some agreed way.

Housekeeping equipment, furniture, and fittings

The housekeeping division also has responsibility for the care of fixed assets in the rooms and associated areas. The condition of these assets should be carefully monitored, and replacement organised as appropriate. Items such as mattresses and beds should normally be replaced within a seven-year period, and housekeeping should therefore provide senior management with a replacement schedule that allows for the purchase of new furniture for one-seventh of the rooms annually. Other items such as drapes and curtains last approximately five years. Blankets should be replaced every two years.

Laundry operations

Many hospitality operations contract out the laundry function, but there are advantages in conducting a laundry on the premises—notably to ensure quality control and to ensure that an adequate supply of linen is always on hand.

Robotic vacuums

There have been some notable failures among robotic cleaning devices. In the 1950s and 1960s, a 'brave new world' was envisaged in which robots would do all the cleaning and more difficult housekeeping work. Visionaries provided images of human-like machines happily scrubbing and sweeping. The reality was that no robot could match the efficiency of the human eye and hand, and many machines came unstuck when they encountered a step or corner. However, in the mid to late 1990s, several more sophisticated devices were developed that can carry out straightforward tasks.

A manufacturer in Virginia, USA, developed small robots that can sweep and scrub hallways—using a type of sonar to navigate and check the areas to be cleaned. A Swedish design developed in 1994 can clean carpets in a random pattern starting from the perimeter of a room. But, when its steam runs out, so does the robot! Another carpet cleaner first sold in 1999 can cruise a room sucking-up dust, returning to its charging station periodically to empty the dust and recharge its batteries. The more successful robots are patrolling security machines that can sense fire, smoke, or unexplained movement.

The scope of laundry operations

Laundry operations for a small motel can take up 70 square metres of floor space. For a medium-sized operation this could extend to 180–200 square metres of floor space.

A 'rule of thumb' is:[4]

- allow 4 square feet per guest room for laundry space; *and*
- another 4 square feet of space per guest room for the handling and storage of linen (this might be spread throughout the hotel or motel).

The amount of linen to be processed depends upon the nature of the hospitality property. For example, the amount of linen will be increased if the hotel offers a full valet service to guests. It will also be increased if there is a food & beverage service associated with the property (because of the need to launder tablecloths, napkins, and so on). Large hospitality operations (for example, a 400-bed hotel of four-star or five-star quality) will offer a range of service to guests, and the laundry requirements will be substantial.

The quantity of linen to be processed is directly linked to room occupancy. A typical laundry estimate is that 4 kilograms of linen will need to be laundered per occupied bed–day—allowing for all bed linen, towels, and other cloth material in the hotel that requires cleaning. This 4 kilograms is dry weight—obviously the wet linen will weigh much more (which is, itself, an indicator of the hard work required in handling wet laundry). This estimate of the amount of material that has to be processed—each day, seven days a week, fifty-two weeks a year—indicates that the laundry operation must be well planned with respect to layout and equipment, and that the staff must be adequately trained for the job.

How much linen should the property maintain in total? The 'rule of thumb' is that for every item of linen on beds or in bathrooms or restaurants, there should be another item on hand ready to replace it, and a third item in the process of being laundered. In addition, there should be a quantity of new linen available as replacements.

Laundry operations flowchart

The laundry process involves the collection of soiled laundry items and the transport of these to the laundry—where they must be sorted into categories (that is, coloureds separated from whites, and wools from cottons) ready for washing. The laundry is placed into washing machines that are correctly set for the load. After extraction, the items are dried, spread, ironed, and folded. The items are then transported back to linen rooms or service carts.

Laundry operations must meet performance standards. This relies upon having the right flow of work through the process area—as well as the right equipment and staffing (as noted below, pages 115–16).

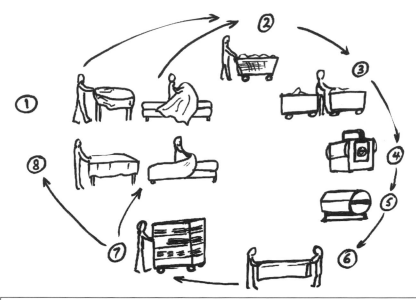

Key: 1—Collect soiled laundry; 2—Transport soiled laundry; 3—Sort laundry into whites and coloureds; 4—Washing; 5—Drying; 6—Folding; 7—Transport clean laundry; 8—Issue clean laundry

Figure 4.3 *Laundry flowchart*

Kevin Baker

Laundry equipment

Hospitality operators must take care in selecting the laundry equipment that is necessary for the job, training staff in its use, and ensuring that the equipment is maintained. Besides high-capacity washer/extractors, a laundry requires dryers, ironers, and folders, and larger properties might require steam tunnels and cabinets. If a valet service is part of the laundry operation, there will be ironers and finishers for shirts and trousers. (The trouser finishing unit has parts known as a 'topper' and a 'legger'; finishing units for general use might have 'single puff' or 'triple puff' irons. Every area of skill has interesting jargon!)

These items of equipment must be properly installed. The equipment must be installed with care to ensure that work surfaces and chutes are at the right height, and that there are no sharp corners or edges to cause injury. Ancillary equipment (such as sinks and drains) are also required, and vapour absorbers and airconditioning are needed to make the work area tolerable for staff.

The selection of equipment will be determined by applying the estimate of 4 kilograms of washing per occupied bed–day (see page 114). Therefore, if the property is a medium-sized operation of 200 rooms, with a calculated occupancy of 190 beds per day, the laundry will require a capacity of 760 kilograms of laundry each day (that is, 190 × 4). This might require one washer extractor of 160–200-kilograms capacity (a fairly large item), with another small unit of 10–15-kilograms capacity for small jobs, and probably two tumblers, each of 50-kilograms capacity. A matching spreader/ironer and folder will also be required.

Once installed, it is vital to carry out a daily routine of cleaning and maintaining the machines. This includes checking for correct temperatures and pressures, and removing lint or other foreign matter.

Additional equipment includes items such as tables (for folding), hampers (separate hampers for soiled, washed-wet, and washed-dry linen), and mobile linen carts.

Laundry staffing

Laundries must be adequately staffed. There must be sufficient staff members to cope with a varying laundry load (which will fluctuate on a daily and seasonal basis). Laundry rosters must be prepared in anticipation of the projected occupancy statistics—which determine laundry requirements.

Staff must also be adequately trained. Laundry work has its own skills, and is often undervalued when hotel operations are considered. There is a range of materials used in hotel linen (including polyester, cotton, wool, and acrylics), and these different fabrics require different laundering techniques. These different fabrics must be processed to a high standard of appearance and odour, and the laundering must also ensure that the materials are sanitised. All this must be done in a fashion that does not shorten the life of the items through overly harsh treatment—for example fading the colour or abrading the material as sometimes happens with granular detergent and minerals in the water (not an uncommon problem in some regions of Australia). Problems such as linting, staining, yellowing, 'pilling',[5] wrinkling, and shrinking must be addressed, and staff must also be able to attend to small repair and sewing tasks.

Laundry staff must be trained in proper handling techniques, and this training must include methods of handling heavy loads, as well as safety in using chemicals and equipment. Laundry staff must be especially trained in handling possible health hazards—such as encountering syringes and needles in linen.

Energy and water usage should also be monitored by laundry staff, and laundry personnel can take a lead in 'green' hotel initiatives. For example, the temperature of the wash and the chemicals used can be investigated for the optimum mix. This area of operations will be considered in greater detail below (see 'Environmental awareness in housekeeping and maintenance', page 124).

Occupational health & safety

Chemicals and related hazards

There are particular threats to health and safety in the housekeeping division. One special area of risk is from the use of chemicals such as detergents and stain-removing agents. To reduce this area of risk, staff must be aware of, and be trained in, rules relating to chemical usage.

Some special rules for housekeeping staff and others using chemicals

Remember:
- cleaning-up can be dangerous because of tiredness;
- always dilute detergents according to manufacturers' instructions and know first-aid for every chemical you use;
- any spillages or breakages of chemical containers should be cleaned-up immediately and completely, even if this means disposing of a large volume of material;
- avoid fumes of cleaners;
- never mix chemicals;
- store chemical cleaners properly and prevent contamination with other materials;
- when cleaning overhead, use safety glasses or goggles to avoid eye splashes; and
- do not use any material unless you are certain that you know exactly what you are doing and know exactly how that material should be handled.

In the laundry, housekeepers should be aware of the hazards in handling soiled laundry and room rubbish, and they should wear protective garb such as gloves and aprons. Clean laundry should be kept well clear of soiled laundry. Laundry equipment should always be operated within the limits recommended by its manufacturers, and laundry workers must be trained in the methods of operating the equipment.

Whether working in the laundry or in rooms and public areas, housekeepers should always take care to wash their hands frequently, with personal antiseptic cleaning agents. They should be aware of the risk of skin disease through exposure to chemicals and organic agents.

Activity 4.5   Chemicals

Examine as many work areas of a large hotel property as you can and list all the chemicals used in each area. Note how many of the chemicals are toxic or dangerous if not used in the approved fashion. Take special note of any protective wear or equipment required to be used while handling the chemicals. Also note the emergency procedures appropriate to each class of chemical (for example, CO_2 fire extinguishers required with certain fires).

Electrical threats

Rules for using electrical equipment apply to all hotel staff, but housekeeping staff members should be especially careful. They should be especially aware of the following:
- do not allow power leads near water or wet areas;
- do not allow power points to be overloaded;
- ensure that electrical equipment is kept clean and checked frequently;
- be alert for evidence of any damage to equipment (such as cracked powerpoints or plugs, frayed power leads, and so on); and
- ensure that electrical repairs are carried out only by qualified and licensed persons.

A commonsense rule that can save lives

The following rule might seem so simple that it is hardly worth stating (or remembering!). But sometimes the best advice is good plain commonsense. Therefore, always remember:

Have a close look at any electrical equipment before touching it.
Following this simple advice might save your life!

If a person has received a shock from an electrical fault, do not touch the person. Rather, look for and turn off the power point. If this cannot be done, use something that does not conduct electricity (such as a plastic rod) to push the lead or wire or equipment away from the person. Then immediately call for help and apply first-aid.

Other housekeeping tips

Housekeeping staff face particular risks in working alone in guest rooms. To minimise the risk of incidents involving guests, always ensure that the door is left open when cleaning a room. If there is no one else in the room while

Safety blunder

'To check whether curtains in a hotel ballroom were flame-resistant, a Vienna fire-prevention officer held a lighter to them. He thought he had safely extinguished the fire that resulted but, minutes after he had left, the room was ablaze, ruining the stage, valuable paintings and part of the roof—and no doubt the fire officer's reputation.' [6]

the housekeeper is servicing it, the housekeeping trolley could be placed in the doorway to stop other people entering the room without warning. If people do return to the room while it is being serviced, the housekeeper should observe them to make sure that they are the guests who should be occupying the room.

One more tip for housekeepers—always work with a straight back. Even when bending down to clean bedheads and cupboards, bend at the knees and keep the back as straight as nature intended.

Activity 4.6   *Safety procedures*

The general manager of the Yass River Hotel recently tripped over the electric cable of a vacuum cleaner being used by a porter. He badly sprained his ankle and had to rest in bed. During this rest, he got to thinking about the occupational health & safety procedures in the hotel. On his return to the hotel, he found out that there were no written procedures. He contacted the housekeeper to ask for his help in preparing suitable written instructions. In turn, the executive housekeeper enlisted the help of his team to complete the task.

The executive housekeeper, allocated various aspects of the task to his team members. He asked them to prepare written procedures on the following:

- bomb alert;
- fire;
- serious injury;
- death in a hotel room.

QUESTIONS

- Divide into groups of three or four persons, and allocate one of the above tasks to each group. Each group is to prepare written guidelines on appropriate health & safety procedures for the subject allocated to it. These guidelines should consider (a) prevention (if appropriate); (b) what to do if an incident occurs; and (c) appropriate training for staff.
- Once these tasks have been completed, each small group is required to present its report to the full group for discussion.

Particular risks for maintenance and engineering

Like staff from the food & beverage department, and staff from the house-keeping department, maintenance staff members are at risk of injury from lifting heavy weights in cramped spaces, and from using chemicals and electrical equipment. In addition to these shared risks, maintenance staff also commonly use heavy equipment such as welders and the like. No person should use an item of machinery for which they are not trained and with which they do not feel competent. Boilers are a very specialised item of equipment that require special training, and no one without the prescribed current boiler attendants' certificate should attempt to control a boiler.

An area of risk for maintenance and engineering personnel is working in confined spaces with inadequate ventilation. Clearly the prudent measure here is to ensure that all vents are operating to allow adequate airflow. Another area of hazard is working at height—and thus being exposed to the risk of a serious fall. Maintenance people should work in pairs in hazardous situations wherever possible. They must also wear protective clothing and equipment—such as safety helmets and safety boots.

Maintenance staff members are not without their own personal security risks, for they are often required to work at odd times and places in a large property. To reduce personal security risks, they should ensure that vegetation is trimmed, and that containers are not allowed to pile up, because these things can provide cover for malefactors to enter a property undetected, or to hide from observation.

Activity 4.7   *Ethical consideration*

You are the executive housekeeper in a very busy hotel. There is a convention event being planned for the functions room of your hotel. Extra electrical connections are needed because of special lighting required in the front stage area. Consequently, electrical cords are run across the room to service the equipment. The cords can be covered with carpet and connections made under tables where they will not be noticed. You have a feeling that the connections might be in breach of electrical wiring regulations, but you are not absolutely certain. You are comfortable that it all seems safe enough, and anyway the cords will be hidden by the carpets. There is no time to bring in a qualified engineer or electrician to check out the installation.

QUESTION

- Should you allow the situation to remain, or should you insist that the function must be cancelled or transferred to an appropriate venue?

Occupational hearing loss, or 'industrial deafness', is a serious problem in the workplace. It is not as prevalent in the hospitality industry as it is in some manufacturing establishments, but there are some areas of operations where managers should be conscious of this hazard. For example, noise exposure can be a problem for wait staff who work for long periods in a beverage outlet with extremely loud music, or for maintenance workers who work for periods near equipment such as blower fans. The safety inspection of any hospitality property should identify problem areas where noise levels are unacceptable and unsafe. The noise problem should be eliminated if possible, but if it cannot be entirely eliminated, workers should be issued with ear protection, and be rotated through noisy areas.

Activity 4.8   *Animals in hotels?*

Discuss whether a hotel should provide accommodation for a dog.

Your immediate reaction might be negative, but what about 'seeing-eye' guide dogs for visually impaired persons? Should a hotel provide accommodation for a dog which is especially trained to assist physically disabled persons?[7] If such an animal is accommodated, what special arrangements should be made? Should the accompanying guest be charged. If so, how much?

What about cats? The Royal Society for the Protection of Animals (RSPCA) in Australia, and some bookshops and veterinarians, can supply a directory of hospitality properties around Australia that are 'cat-friendly'. The directory contains approximately 300 entries.[8]

What about a pelican? Should a hotel accommodate a pelican?[9] What about a crocodile?[10]

Issues in housekeeping

Contracting housekeeping services

The practice of contracting (or 'outsourcing') various functions and services has become a significant issue in hospitality enterprises. The question is whether specialist outside firms can do the job more cheaply and more efficiently than can the employees of a hospitality enterprise working under direct supervision. This question is of great importance in these times of pressure to contain costs. Every possibility of greater economy and better service must be considered. Almost all of the services offered by a hospitality enterprise can, in theory, be contracted.

A loose (but serviceable) definition of a contract for outsourcing is:[11]

> . . . a contract for the supply of services (as distinct from goods) on an ongoing basis between an institution as one principal and a supplier of services as the other principal.

The argument for contracting housekeeping services (such as cleaning, garbage removal, laundry operations, and so on) is that the enterprise benefits from having a specialist supplier who supplies services more efficiently and more economically than services managed directly by the hotel administration. Much, of course, depends upon the quality of the contracted services and the experience of the supplier of those services. In a competitive market for the supply of each service, the hotel, as a shrewd purchaser, should benefit by obtaining the best service at the best price. For small-to-medium-sized purchasers, an additional benefit (apart from price) is that the contractor will probably have a depth of resources and experience that ensures continuous high-quality service. The general philosophy underlying the supply of services on contract is that the specialist firm can concentrate its staff and resources in one area. The contractor should therefore be up to date in its speciality, and under market pressure to find greater efficiencies by ongoing review of its contractual performance. In theory, the end result should be the best product at the best price.

Activity 4.9   *House rules*

The following is an excerpt from the 'Terms and Conditions of Lodging' in the West End Hotel, Mumbai, India:

> 7. Visitors' Servants—Servants are not allowed to sleep anywhere on the hotel premises . . . Servants may not wash guests' clothes on the premises . . .
> 10. Games—Card-playing and other games are not allowed . . .
> 13. No outside food or beverages to be brought into the hotel . . .

QUESTIONS

- Discuss these house rules, listing the reasons behind them.
- What provisions (if any) should housekeeping make to accommodate the servants of guests?
- What forms of games are included in the prohibition on 'card-playing and other games', and what might be the legal issues involved in this rule?
- How could housekeeping enforce the card-playing rule?
- What should a housekeeper do if the housekeeper becomes aware that guests have brought outside food or beverages into the hotel?

Specialist contractors can usually offer economy of scale and specialist expertise in a range of services. Thus a hospitality institution that once operated its own small cleaning department can utilise a contractor who employs ten times the number of people—but with a spread of overheads on staff and equipment costs. Enterprises in outlying areas can be serviced by a larger depot. Purchasing and supply can be organised on a larger scale.

However, there are disadvantages. The management of the hospitality enterprise relinquishes effective day-to-day control of the service. Although there can be some consultative controls written into the contract, ultimate control remains with the contractor. The ultimate effective control retained by the hospitality enterprise is the threat to terminate the contract. This threat is a significant overall sanction, and should encourage the contractor to fulfil all contractual consultative standards.

There are two basic types of contract:

- the guaranteed-cost contract; and
- the management-fee contract.

The details of contracts vary from firm to firm, but the essentials of each type of contract are:

- under a *guaranteed-cost contract*, the contractor guarantees all labour and supply costs; whereas
- under a *management-fee contract*, the contractor guarantees costs of management and supervision, but the hospitality enterprise is still responsible for labour and supply costs.

Personal profile—the maintenance and security officer

As maintenance chief at the Residence Inn, 'Swanie' Swanberg has studied equipment repair on his own time to save the hotel money. He can fix heating sequencers himself in ten minutes, using a $7 part—a feat that has saved the Residence Inn $5000 in sequencers alone. Because of the property's small size, Swanberg pitches in elsewhere, too, serving coffee at breakfast, helping out in housekeeping, setting-up a meeting room, or running guests to the airport.

'I do whatever. I'm a jack-of-all-trades,' he says, claiming that the flexibility to do so many things is his favourite part of the job.

To Swanberg, service means 'doing whatever it takes'. This includes making a point of calling repeat guests by name. When he recognises a guest he checks the register to ensure that he has all the relevant details. Then he calls the guest's room to make sure that everything is in order.[12]

A *guaranteed-cost contract* operates as follows. The hospitality enterprise operator provides the contractor with the number of bed–days for an agreed period. The contractor offers a guaranteed cost per bed–day. The number of bed–days multiplied by the guaranteed cost per bed–day gives the total cost to be paid by the hospitality operator to the contractor for its services. The advantage of a guaranteed-cost contract is that the hospitality operator knows in advance what the housekeeping department will cost for a given level of activity. The contractor bears responsibility if the guaranteed cost is exceeded.

A *management-fee contract* operates as follows. The contractor charges a management fee that covers the management and supervision provided, start-up costs, and the cost of supporting management services. The cost of supplies, and the wages and associated costs of housekeeping department employees, are paid by the hotel and kept within a budget approved each year by the hospitality management. The management fee is thus paid primarily for the supervision and expertise of the contractors—who are acting as consultants and experienced line managers.

Environmental awareness in housekeeping and maintenance

In addition to the more general environmental concerns affecting hospitality operations, there are concerns specific to housekeeping and maintenance. These include the following.

Chemical usage in cleaning and maintenance

Most hotels and restaurants use cleaning and disinfecting chemicals. They also occasionally use pesticides, insecticides, and fertilisers—in both the garden and the house. Through the proper selection and use of these chemicals, and especially through the proper dilution of the products, there is an opportunity to minimise the environmental effects of such chemicals, as well as minimising the overall volumes used. It is often possible to use dispensers to mete out controlled quantities of these chemicals. It is also possible to purchase these chemicals in more concentrated form—thus using less chemical to do the job. In turn, this reduces consumption and waste.

Where possible, a property should use biodegradable and low-phosphorous detergents and cleansing products. These are more benign in their effects on the environment, and have the added benefit of being less threatening to the health of employees. Properties should also use 'soft' (desalinated) water for dish and glass washers—to ensure that there is no build-up of scale requiring strong chemicals to remove. Properties should use electronic forms of pest control—to reduce the need to use poisons for pest reduction in food-preparation areas.

Activity 4.10 *Ethical consideration*

You are the executive housekeeper of a large three-star property. A member of your staff calls you upstairs urgently because there is a lot of noise, including shouting, coming from a suite.

Consider two alternative scenarios.

▪ You knock on the door of the suite and, after a long delay, the door is opened by a man. Behind him, a woman is sitting on the bed, crying and holding her head. Her face is red and swollen. It seems to be obvious that the man has been beating the woman. He angrily tells you to mind your own business. The woman looks at you and says nothing. What would you do?

▪ You knock on the door of the suite and, after a long delay, the door is opened by a woman. Behind her, a man is sitting on the bed, crying and holding his head. His face is red and swollen. It seems to be obvious that the woman has been beating the man. She angrily tells you to mind your own business. The man looks at you and says nothing.

What would you do?

Water usage

In guest rooms and bathrooms, water usage can be minimised through the installation of:

- low-flow shower heads;
- plugs that fit tightly in sinks;
- dual-flush toilets;
- aerated taps with touch-flow devices that stop the flow when not needed; and
- proper plumbing maintenance (especially to reduce the dripping of taps).

In maintaining outdoor areas such as lawns and gardens, hotels can install time-controlled water-sprinkler systems, and can utilise roof storm-water. The reuse and recycling of water is particularly useful in drier areas, such as regions of Australia that have low rainfall.

Noise pollution

Noise pollution is often overlooked as a form of environmental degradation—but must be addressed. A noisy background can be health-threatening. It can also be a distraction or a downright nuisance. Not only does noise reduce concentration and enjoyment, but it also adds to stress for staff and guests. Staff members have a right to an appropriate working environment, and guests have a right to a quiet, peaceful room where they can rest or work. Hotel owners could even be liable for legal damages if guests or staff members were to sue for injury suffered from the consequences of noise.

Sources of noise can be equipment, human noise, or noise from the surrounding environment (such as traffic). Noise of machinery can be reduced by insulating equipment such as rubber, or even by the simple step of correct maintenance and servicing of equipment. Outside noise can be reduced by double-glazing of windows, or by the use of muting material in walls and ceilings. Human noise can be reduced by sensible house rules—which should be enforced. Some irritating noises within hotels—such as staff work—can be reduced by rescheduling.

Activity 4.11 *Combating noise pollution*

QUESTIONS
- In groups, list the various aspects of hotel life that add to noise pollution—for example, vacuum cleaners used at night; incessant piped music in the elevators; kitchen noise; drunks. Can you think of others?
- How would you combat each of these problems?

Controlled dispensing

Reductions in product use and waste generation can be achieved with careful thought regarding the use of such common materials as towels and soaps.

The use of roll-towels (instead of folded towels) can reduce waste because rolls provide more hand-dries than do folded towels—presumably because people tend to pick up a whole towel or a handful of folded towels if available, rather than the smaller quantity chosen from a roll dispenser.

Within the shower recess or bath, the provision of soap and shampoo in a refillable dispenser (rather than in individual plastic bottles) is also helpful in reducing usage and waste.

Solid waste and recycling

Packaging accounts for one-half of all commercial waste in the United States.[13] Hotels generate considerable amounts of packaging waste that can be effectively eliminated or reduced. Such packaging waste in hotels usually takes the form of personal-care products such as:

- gifts provided to guests (including sewing kits, sweets, and toiletries);
- shampoo containers; and
- soap wrappings.

These items are usually part of marketing the hotel, but they represent very inefficient and sometimes unnecessary packaging that could be reduced by alternative presentation. Opportunities exist to eliminate the items altogether by purchasing in bulk containers, or at least by packaging them more efficiently.

There are other items used in housekeeping that offer opportunities for recycling. For example, liners in garbage tins need not be replaced every day if the garbage is dry and not putrescent (rotting). Waste housekeeping items that can be recycled include a range of materials including bubblewrap and linen. Worn linen can be a major item at larger lodging properties. Instead of simply being disposed of as refuse, worn linen can be converted into aprons or cleaning rags. Failing that, unwanted linen can donated to any number of charities that recycle the material for industrial uses.

Activity 4.12 *The hotel energy audit*

Energy consumption at the Yass Ocean Hotel has been investigated by conducting an energy audit. The results of the audit indicated the following breakdown of energy usage.

Heating, ventilation, and airconditioning	40%
Lighting	22%
Kitchen	20%
Refrigeration	11%
Miscellaneous	7%
Total	**100%**

QUESTION

- List some possible initiatives that could reduce the overall energy usage at the Yass Ocean Hotel.

Chapter review questions

1 Explain how the role of the housekeeper has changed over the last fifty years.
2 Why is the role of the housekeeper now seen as acceptable for men as well as for women?
3 In a standard bedroom of a four-star hotel, how many different items of furniture and equipment does the room attendant have to care for?
4 For most hoteliers, emergencies are very rare. Explain why it is vital to understand and practise what to do should such an emergency occur.
5 What sections of a hotel workforce are most prone to injury?
6 What procedures should housekeeping staff follow in the following circumstances?
   • the discovery of lost property;
   • a guest who is sick and wants a doctor;
   • a guest who has died;
   • guests who have not packed their belongings as expected when the room is needed by reception.

Answer to Activity 4.4

WHAT DOES IT MEAN?

(See page 112 for details of this activity.)

The sign is intended for guests to note any repairs or maintenance required in the room that they are occupying. The guests should tick an attached box depending upon whether there is a problem with the water, the toilet, the lighting, or the television.

CASE STUDY

The HB Hotel

The HB Hotel has prided itself on the fairness of its treatment of staff. Unfortunately, in recent times, the housekeeping staff has become more and more disgruntled. Staff members have been having problems getting any of their scheduled breaks, and they never seem to be informed of their rostered hours of duty until just a few days before the roster takes effect. Much of this is due to the fact that the executive housekeeper has been away sick, and his role is being carried out by the deputy. Figure 4.4 is an example of a typical two-week housekeeping roster.

Shift	M	T	W	T	F	S	S	M	T	W	T	F	S	S
1. Rooms														
10 a.m. to 3 p.m.	X	X	X	X	–	X	X	X	X	X	X	–	X	–
2. Rooms														
10 a.m. to 3 p.m.	X	X	–	X	X	–	–	X	X	–	X	X	–	–
3. Public areas														
7 a.m. to 12 p.m.	–	–	X	–	X	–	–	–	–	X	–	X	–	–
4. Function/relief														
	–	X	–	–	X	X	–	–	X	X	–	X	X	–
5. Laundry														
	X	X	–	–	–	X	X	X	X	–	–	–	X	X

Figure 4.4 *Housekeeping roster*

Kevin Baker

As the rooms-division manager, examine the roster and list the problems with it. Then draw up an alternative roster. This roster is to be a perpetual roster—that is, one that can be repeated one period after the next. It must be effective for the hotel and equitable for the staff. The rooms occupancy and statistics are as shown in Figure 4.5 (page 130). Assume that this is a typical day.

HB Hotel
Room Occupancy/Status Report for Housekeeping

Date: *29 June*

Vacant/Clean

HS	TB 291	TB 104	TB 105	TB 211	QS 323
QS 325	QS 439				

On-change

TB 214	TB 220	QS 440			

Occupied/Stayover

CS	TB 106	TB 107	TB 108	TB 213	TB 215
TB 216	TB 217	QS 326	QS 329	QS 330	QS 431
QS 432	QS 433	QS 434	QS 435	QS 436	QS 437
QS 438					

Blocked

TB 212	TB 218	QS 327	QS 328		

Due Out

TB 103	TB 109	TB 110	QS 322	QS 324	

Out-of-order

QS 321

Function Room

Available

CS = Cottage suite
HS = Honeymoon suite
TB = Twin-bedded room
QS = Queen-sized room

Figure 4.5 *Rooms occupancy and statistics*

Kevin Baker

Chapter 5

Food & Beverage Services

Here with a Loaf of Bread beneath the bough,
A Flask of Wine, a Book of Verse—and Thou

The Rubáiyát of Omar Khayyám (1859), 1:11

Synopsis of chapter

Aspects of food & beverage services could fill a book—and often do. This chapter concentrates on those factors that especially concern managers of hospitality operations. The starting point is the role of food-service managers, food & beverage people, and kitchens. Then the chapter looks at issues related to menus and menu-planning, catering, and buffets. The chapter then discusses purchasing practices and the place of contracting in hospitality food services. The last section of the chapter considers food practices and hygiene.

The work—food services

The structure of the food-service operation

Food services can be divided into the following elements:
- food-service management—preparation, distribution, and quality control of food;
- technical food & beverage function—the application and interpretation of the scientific principles of nutrition and food preparation;
- hotel management—overall organisation structure, communication, budget, personnel, and disciplinary matters; and
- administration—recording and clerical requirements (including provisions and purchases).

Food & beverage service requires a good memory, attention to detail, and the ability not to become flustered

Courtesy Casino Canberra

Types of food services

Food services are divided up as follows:

- hotel food services;
- club food services;
- full-menu restaurants;
- limited-menu restaurants (including take-aways);
- public cafeterias;
- catering services;
- other institutional food services (such as hospitals and schools); and
- transportation food services (such as airlines and trains).

These food services range from small family-owned restaurants or take-away outlets to large food-service operations (such as an airline's inflight catering services). Hotel food services are not insignificant within hospitality operations. Typically, hotel food services (such as in-house restaurants, bistros, coffee shops, and so on) contribute approximately a quarter of the total revenue of a property.[1]

Hospitality food & beverage services are operated by owners, by hotel employees, or by specialist food-service contractors. Anyone involved in hospitality operations should have a grasp of some basic concepts and practices of food services.

Styles of food service

There are many different styles of food service—ranging from full table service (which is, of course, expensive) to self-service options such as buffet and self-service catering.

Full table service is defined as a food service where food and beverages are brought to the guests while they are seated. It can take the form of:

- French-style, where some food items are partially prepared and brought on a cart, or guéridon, to the table for final cooking and serving;
- English-style, where food is brought to the tables in bowls or on platters and either passed around the guests, or served to individual guests to their liking by the server; or
- American-style, where individual orders are given and brought to the diners.

Clearly, these styles of service require high labour inputs and costs, and thus are more expensive than other styles.

Some establishments are catering services. This means that the food is being prepared for a venue other than an attached diningroom. A kitchen that provides a catering service must include in its design means to transport food and keep it hot (or at least capable of being reheated), and the menu must also reflect the special nature of this sort of operation. An example of a very large catering service operation is an airline caterer, in which the kitchen is set up to prepare a large number of meals for airline passengers and crew, and to provide for the meals to be served at a later time in the constricted environment of an airliner.

Hospitals, like airlines, usually serve meals by tray service, in which the entire meal is brought on one tray and placed before a guest. This can be efficient in serving a large number of guests or consumers very quickly, but it has its disadvantages, mainly in keeping the food warm and appetising.

Buffet service, or smorgasbord, consists of food being arranged on large platters from which guests serve themselves.

Cafeteria service involves guests moving down lines of prepared foods, perhaps with the more complex dishes being cooked for them on the spot. Counter services are also common in Australia, in which guests at a hotel place orders at the bar, or counter, and are served their meals within a short period.

In 'fast-food' service, orders are supplied to customers from food that has already been prepared on a production line. The food is provided in take-away bags for consumption on the premises or elsewhere.

Vending machines represent another form of food service. Because of the difficulty of keeping foods fresh, the range of foods that can be offered is limited. In most cases the foods on offer are cold, such as sandwiches or salads. However, hot food can be achieved by selling cold food items (such as meat pies or casseroles) which can then be heated by the purchaser in a microwave oven next to the vending machine.

Catering for banquets or functions can take any of the above forms—depending upon the wishes and budget of the customer. Set menus, with selection from a limited number of choices, supplied to tables, has become a common form of catering at banquets.

Activity 5.1 *Futuristic vending machines*

A number of futuristic science-fiction works feature machines that produce a desired meal on demand. The space hero on board the spaceship simply makes a meal selection, pushes a button, and removes the meal from a slot in the machine. For example, on the mining spaceship *Red Dwarf*, crew member Dave Lister orders a bacon sandwich with French mustard and a black coffee from the food-vending machine.[2] But how could the machine produce hot and cold items together?

On the starship *Enterprise*, orphaned children are beamed up by Captain Kirk and are able to order various flavours of ice-cream in unlimited quantities from the ship's food-vending machines.[3]

But how could a machine supply a large range of products to a large number of outlets almost instantaneously? And how can the machine be kept hygienic if sloppy products such as ice-cream are supplied? Are the products already prepared? If so, how could they be stored and kept fresh? Or are they prepared on order? If so, how could this be done instantaneously?

QUESTION

- Discuss whether spaceship food-vending machines are feasible. List practical problems of food quality and hygiene that would have to be overcome.

The workplace—the kitchen

Design

The design of the kitchen space—including preparation areas, equipment, and stores and receiving areas—is important. The kitchen layout will obviously be primarily influenced by the type of food service—whether that be fast food, full-service, buffet, or cafeteria style. Factors such as the flow of food and beverage products through the system, and the movement of people around the kitchen, must be carefully considered at the time of design. The efficiency of the kitchen, and hence the profitability of the food service, will be enhanced by a layout that allows efficient and easy movement and good supervision. A poor layout can require increased staff numbers if the arrangement is to work effectively, with associated increased labour costs.

The design of a kitchen layout, and the installation of new equipment, must also take into account employee safety factors—such as safe levels of noise and fatigue, maintenance of adequate lighting, and safety in dealing with heated areas and equipment. The design must also take into account maintenance and cleanliness. An open, laid-out plan can mean reduced staff time and costs in maintaining proper standards of cleanliness. Any plan must also meet government regulatory requirements.

Activity 5.2   *Design a kitchen*

Imagine a restaurant of a certain type, and design a kitchen that you think is adequate for the restaurant of your choice.

In drawing up your design you will need to consider the style of the operation and how large it will be (that is, the number of 'covers', or person–meals, that would be prepared at each meal, and over a day).

You will also need to consider the type of menu, and number of menu items you would offer.

Kitchen equipment

The selection and installation of kitchen equipment is a specialised skill that should be undertaken by qualified people to ensure that the equipment is appropriate to requirements, and that it functions in accordance with manufacturers' specifications. Management must be aware that much kitchen equipment is high-tech and requires proper maintenance to keep it safe and efficient. Once the equipment is chosen and installed, untrained staff members must never be put in charge of equipment with which they are unfamiliar.

There is a wide range of automated equipment available for use in kitchens. Many items can be labour-saving, and greatly enhance the efficiency of the kitchen. For example, roll-in/roll-out coolers or food warmers can be a great advantage in kitchens where space is restricted. Budgetary considerations influence the extent to which this sort of equipment can be utilised, and budgetary considerations also influence the choice between stock equipment and custom-made equipment. There are usually cost advantages in purchasing standard stock items, but custom-made equipment can be more cost-efficient in the longer term.

All equipment should be assessed with respect to sanitation and ease of cleaning. Equipment that has wooden parts, such as shelving, is generally hardest to keep sanitised. Metal with a shiny finish is easiest to clean, but is more expensive than plastic equipment.

The food-service product—menus

Types of menus

The kitchen and the diningroom operate on the basis of the menu. The menu reflects the style and extent of meals. Just as the operations of a manufacturing enterprise are reflected by the type of products manufactured there, so the menu reflects what sort of food service is offered. The knowledge and skills of the chef will also determine what can be offered to set the tone and style of the food-service operation, but the chef will have been selected and appointed to suit the aspirations of the operation. The beverage operation will largely follow the parameters of the food service.

The basic categories of menus are:

- table d'hôte—a set meal for a set price (that is, a selection of soup, main course, and dessert for a fixed price); the word comes the French phrase which means 'from the table of the host' (in other words, the dishes that are prepared for the day);
- à la carte—which lists different dishes separately for the diner's choice, with separate prices (that is, dishes especially cooked when selected by the guests from the 'carte', or menu); and
- a combination of the above (that is, a degree of selection of fixed-price dishes).

Menu schedules can be fixed—as is the case with fast-food outlets and chain restaurants. In these cases, the same dishes are presented day after day. Alternatively, menu schedules can be cyclical. A cyclical menu allows some variation, especially for consumers who use the food service for a number of

'Rules of thumb' for kitchen equipment purchases

In all decisions regarding the purchase of capital equipment, there are some basic rules of thumb.
- Usually, the simpler the equipment the easier it is to operate.
- Be wary of equipment with add-on features or built-in additions that will be little used.
- Do not buy equipment designed for a domestic kitchen to use in a commercial food & beverage operation.

days in succession—such as in a long-stay accommodation property or a remote mining catering operation. In these cases, the cyclical menu must take into account the overall nutritional needs of the consumers.

Menus are typically designed around three meal periods—breakfast, lunch, and dinner.

- Breakfast menus are usually fairly standard, simple, quick, and limited in choice.
- Lunch menus are usually more extensive, although still relatively simple, and feature such items as soups and sandwiches.
- Dinner menus are usually more extensive—offering a wider variety, with suggestions for appropriate wines and liqueurs with each course. There can also be speciality menus—such as selections of vegetarian dishes, or dishes catering for those with special dietary requirements (such as religious or health requirements).

Activity 5.3 *The issue of tipping*

Melanie Uczen worked as a server in a restaurant–nightclub in Chicago called 'The Leg Room'. A visiting British software engineer added a tip of US$10 000 (AUS$17 000) to the bill that Melanie brought to his table. The restaurant owner checked with the customer to ensure that he really wanted to tip the server that amount of money. He confirmed that he did and signed a declaration to that effect. Melanie no doubt went home happy and the restaurant's owners reported the mammoth tip to the media. The euphoria was dimmed when the engineer's credit card payment was processed, and dishonoured. However, the restaurant owners paid Melanie the tip themselves because the publicity had brought them so much new business.[4]

As a group, discuss tipping and share the attitudes of group members to the whole question of tipping.

Then consider and answer the following questions:

- Should someone who receives a tip from a customer in cash declare the tip to others?
- Should a waiter who receives a tip share that tip with others who are not in direct contact with the customers but who nevertheless make good service possible (such as kitchen staff)?
- If a tip is shared among all the staff, should the highest-paid members of the staff, such as the chef or the *maître d'*, receive the same share as the others?
- Would you vary your attitude about sharing tips, or putting tips in a common pool, if you received a tip of $17 000?
- Does the practice of tipping encourage restaurant owners and managers to pay lower wages than other industries?

Menu planning

Menu planning revolves around selecting an attractive and cost-effective selection of menu items. Such a selection has to be done in close consultation with the chef, and must take into account the general standard and theme of the food service, the established preferences of guests, and certain cost restraints. As a result of these factors, the dishes on offer will usually share common items and reflect the skills (and labour costs) of the kitchen personnel. For example, the food service will not be economical if all the dishes are of such complexity that every one of them must be prepared by the chef alone.

The ingredients must be costed into the preparation of the menu, and standard quantities (and therefore costs) should be predictable. This means that each dish has a list of its ingredients, and the quantities of ingredients to be used. Preparers must keep to these quantities. This is generally called 'portion control', and the practice enables the manager or the chef to cost the dishes accurately.

Having determined the cost of the ingredients, the cost of the time involved in preparing the dish by the chef and assistants is then added. Then a further amount is added for the cost of overheads such as power, rent, and so on. Finally, a further percentage is added for profit. The sum total determines the price of the dish. Often, for simplicity, the dish can be costed by taking material costs and adding a 'mark-up'. This is a percentage estimate of what the other costs will be—say three times the cost of the ingredients. (The subject of restaurant revenue and pricing is also touched upon in Chapter 8 on accounting aspects of hospitality; see page 224.)

The purchasing function is of great importance—to ensure that ingredients of the correct quantity and quality are available to the kitchen personnel. It is also important to ensure that waste is reduced by the correct use of portions.

Once the items on the menu have been determined by the food-service manager and the chef, the carded selection that will be presented to the guests is designed to be as attractive (and factual) as possible. Menu design and wording, as well as the physical presentation (that is, the folding into single panel or multi-panel) is important. It is a mistake to give a guest a menu that looks cheap and unattractive. On the other hand, it is also inappropriate to present a menu that is too large and complex for easy handling. In some places, to reflect the type of eating establishment, the menu can be written on a chalk board.

Menu popularity

To help with menu planning and design, food & beverage managers use a research technique called 'menu popularity'. This system involves the manager's listing of all of the various dishes for each meal at each restaurant or food outlet, and recording how often the different dishes are selected. This ongoing process is made easier by the use of computerised point-of-sale systems that can automatically track such information. At the end of a set period the management then knows, in percentage terms, how popular each dish has been. Armed with this information, the manager can then delete the least-popular dishes from the menu while retaining those that the customers selected most often.

An astute manager can analyse this information further, and attempt to ascertain the flavour, texture, and food types that are most popular with customers. Meals of a similar type can thus be added to the menu and their popularity tested by the method.

Wines

Hospitality managers should have a basic knowledge of the wines of their local area, and of wines in general. They should also understand licences and wine service.

Full-service restaurants are licensed to serve alcohol sold by the establishment. More limited licences are usually known as BYO ('bring-your-own') licences, or sometimes as BYOG ('bring-your-own-grog').

A full-service restaurant usually offers a 'house wine' (sometimes called a 'jug wine' or a 'table wine'). These house wines are usually offered for sale by the glass or carafe.

Operations that also offer wine lists of bottled wines must ensure that serving staff are knowledgeable about the products being offered, and the correct ways in which to serve wine. Simply put, this involves:

- presenting the wine to the guest so that the guest can read the label for approval;
- opening the bottle and offering the cork to the host to examine—to ensure that the wine is not 'corked' (that is, that the wine has not reacted chemically with the seal);
- wiping the rim of the bottle and pouring a small sample of the wine (unless invited to fill all the glasses at the table directly);
- upon receiving the host's approval, pouring glasses for all those present (a 'full' glass usually being one that is one-half to two-thirds full); and
- placing the bottle in a bucket with a napkin (in the case of white wine) on the host's right; or in a wine holder on the table beside the host (in the case of red wine).

Providing the material—purchasing food & beverage stocks

Effective food-service managers must be knowledgeable about their suppliers, and the quantity and availability of products. If costs are to be controlled, the food-service manager must be directly responsible for the purchase of all products, or be in frequent, direct contact with a designated supply manager.

The largest food services in the United States[5]

Organisation	Product	Outlets
McDonald's	hamburgers	10 513
Kentucky Fried Chicken	chicken	7 761
Pizza Hut	pizza	6 662
Burger King	hamburgers	5 793
Dairy Queen	sweets	5 122
Domino's Pizza	pizza	4 943

Apart from the question of cost control, the purchasing of food and equipment has a direct bearing upon the standard of an establishment's catering. The most common cause of unsatisfactory catering is bad buying—sometimes due to ignorance, although more often due to laziness. It should be a firm rule to purchase only from manufacturers and wholesalers who specialise in supply to the catering trade. Purchasing from such outlets provides first-hand prices, continuity of supply, and variety of choice. In a fluctuating market, day-to-day purchasing is very important.

Once policy is set, all purchasing should operate to a prearranged formula without resort to 'snatch buying'. Whenever practicable, orders should be confirmed in writing only when the agreed price has been rechecked, and all invoices should be properly audited before payment.

The purchaser must know exactly what is being purchased. In the case of perishables, it is essential to see the food before the deal is confirmed. With dry stores, once price and quality are agreed, deliveries and orders become routine, but constant checks of quality and price must be maintained to ensure that the supplier is maintaining standards.

Those who control inventories and order goods and services should have only limited authority, and be subject to the close direction and supervision of more senior management. This limited authority should be clearly defined in job procedures. Such staff members should have written purchase orders, and should be permitted to enter into contracts for the supply of goods and services only in accordance with such purchase orders. To ensure the safe arrival and storage of goods ordered, the person receiving the goods should be present from the arrival of the delivery vehicle and remain until all items have been unloaded, checked for correct quality and quantity, and taken into store. Periodically, the conducting of a stocktake of inventory should be done according to a form which provides assurance that the count is systematic, and which also provides a written history of the exercise.

CASE STUDY

A *purchasing fraud*

Two senior buyers for ITT Sheraton were arrested for taking 'kickbacks' from wholesale companies that supplied food to several Sheraton hotels on the eastern seaboard of the United States. The main charges related to 'kickbacks' from a single supplier, and the scam went on for seven years until the supplier went out of business in late 1994. The buyers then entered into a 'kickback' arrangement with another supplier until the end of 1996.

The scheme was a simple one, but the amount taken was large—amounting to 3% added to food purchased through the supplier. The Sheraton chain used a computerised tendering system whereby the lowest tenderer who met certain quality standards received the contract to supply food and produce to the hotels of the region. The two men involved passed on information about the lowest current tender price to their partners in the supplier, and the supplying company then submitted a bid lower than any of its competitors.

The maximum penalties faced by the two men were five years' imprisonment and a fine of US$250 000.[6]

Food-production procedures will be designed, and then revised as necessary, according to the results of quality-control surveys and cost-reporting systems. There must always be a balance between a high quality of service and a reasonable expenditure on that service. Food-production records must be kept, and regular reports must be prepared for a proper ongoing assessment to be made. 'Portion controls' (see page 138) must be utilised. Quality-control surveys should be part of a quality-assurance program that monitors food quality and presentation. Arrangements must be made to ensure feedback from guests and customers, and this feedback must be regularly and properly assessed—and taken seriously.

The people—food & beverage staff

Kitchen people

The centre of operations in the kitchen is the food-preparation area, and the undisputed general commanding the operation is the chef. The chef is in charge of food preparation and production, and in charge of all personnel involved in the task. In a larger kitchen, the chef might be termed an 'executive chef', who can be assisted by *sous chefs* (principal assistants) and by chefs with particular responsibilities (such as the *chef garde-manger* (who is responsible for the preparation of cold foods).

A pioneer of a pioneer of food services— Auguste Escoffier

August Escoffier was born in France in 1846, and learnt his skills in his uncle's restaurant. His talent was such that he was employed as a chef at such hotels as the Place Vendome in Paris and the Savoy in London, opened in 1898 by Cesar Ritz.

Escoffier designed dishes that were simple yet brilliant, and many of his recipes were original. He had a grand eye for detail and reorganised the way in which kitchens were run, establishing the various grades and positions of the 'kitchen brigade' and a tradition of discipline in the kitchen. He prepared meals for English and German royalty, but always remained a simple man himself.

Escoffier retired to Monaco, where he died in 1935.

Next in status to the chef is a cook. (Never ever call a chef a 'cook' unless you are in the armed forces!) Cooks can prepare some individual dishes, or sauces, and also carve and cut meats. Cooks fall into a number of different categories—such as pastry cook, sauce cook, roast cook, and so on. Assistant cooks prepare the foods—being responsible for peeling, cutting, trimming, slicing, mixing, and making-up portions of food. Sometimes they also do some of the initial cooking.

Bakers and baker's assistants prepare bread and bread rolls, pies, and cakes.

Apart from the food-preparation people, other staff members fill valuable support roles. These include:

- store people who receive and store the food products;
- pantry assistants who set up the utensils; and
- stewards (usually under the supervision of a chief steward) who supervise the removal and cleaning of the many and varied utensils used in the kitchen.

In a very large kitchen, with extended operations, the staff can be structured into shifts, with each shift being responsible to a shift leader.

Dining-area people

The personnel who serve the guests are usually distinct from the kitchen personnel. Just as the chef is the general controlling the kitchen, the diningroom also has its general—the *maître d'*, sometimes also referred to as

French	English
Chef de partie	Head station server
Chef de rang	Station server
Demi chef de rang	Assistant station server
Commis chef de rang	Trainee food server
Executive chef	same
Saucier	Sauce chef
Entremetier	Vegetable chef
Pâtissier	Pastry chef
Rôtisseur	Roast chef
Tournant	Relief chef
Garde manger	Larder chef
Sous chef	Morning (Evening) shift leader/function chef

Figure 5.1 *Chef titles in French and English*

Kevin Baker

the host, or diningroom 'captain'. The *maître d'* has full responsibility for the guests' dining area, greets and seats guests, and supervises the servers (food and beverage) who take orders and serve the dishes.

Bartenders have a separate role in that they have charge of the bar areas—be these service bars or public bars. They mix and prepare drinks, and also serve guests directly. The American term for those who set up the tables in the diningroom and remove dishes is 'buspersons'.

Personal profile—a food & beverage manager

Nick Brunner is a food & beverage manager in a large, four-star hotel in Rio de Janeiro. He gained his food-service skills during his national service in the Brazilian air force when he was trained as an assistant, and then as a cook, in an officers' mess in a large air base near Sao Paulo. He served for two years, and then, on leaving the air force, took a kitchen assistant's job in a full-service city restaurant, where he rapidly advanced to the position of chef.

Brunner specialised in Creole food and developed a range of sauces of his own devising. He featured in a television show on cookery and built up a following among the local epicures. When a new hotel opened on the Copacabana strip, he was asked to set up the food & beverage function, and is now responsible for five outlets, including two restaurants and a bistro called 'Nick's Place'.

In addition to staff who fill the above roles, there might be a separate role for a checker or cashier to record reservations, issue checks, and collect payment. There can also be a separate role for a functions or banquet host (or coordinator). An operation with a cafeteria-style service might have a cafeteria manager.

In a large hotel, the overall responsibility for food services might come under a food & beverage director, with the *maître d'* and the chef reporting to this person.

Because of the range of duties and personnel, there are many different career paths in food & beverage. Career paths might not necessarily progress from one level to the other in the kitchen—because some duties are very specialised and require years of training. For example, in undertaking career progression towards the position of chef, an aspirant might start as an apprentice to the chef. Once qualified, the person might find placement as a *sous-chef*. In the serving area, it is more usual to progress up the various levels from food server to *maître d'*.

Activity 5.4   Kitchen staffing

Contact two hotels of different sizes in your area, and compare their kitchen and restaurant staff against a typical 'full brigade' (as described above).
    Can you explain the differences?

Personal profile—a food & beverage employee

In her eleven years at the Comfort Inn, Carol Jackson has worn many hats: roomkeeper, laundry attendant, assistant housekeeper . . .

General Manager Charles A. Howell praises her warmth and dedication. 'Whether it is pouring coffee, or delivering a newspaper to an elderly guest, or heating a baby bottle for a young mother, Carol has a true passion for personalised customer service and satisfaction,' he says.

Repeat guests often ask at check-in if Carol will be serving breakfast in the morning, and comment cards single out her 'famous coffee' and warm smile.

The 71-year old Jackson defines customer service simply: 'Just being friendly and being there for people—saying good morning, having a smiling face'.

The ultimate testimony comes from Howell: 'Guests are thrilled with her hospitality, co-workers admire and respect her, and management acknowledges that our hotel is a much better place because of Carol,' he says.[7]

Skills and knowledge for food services

Food-handling practices

Food-poisoning

Every year, hundreds of thousands of Australians suffer from serious food-poisoning, and some die. Usually the victim has no indication that the food is contaminated. By sight, touch, and smell there might be no indication that the food is anything but normal. Good food-handling practices are thus of great importance. It is no exaggeration to say that they can be a matter of life and death. Hospitality managers should therefore be well aware of common hazards in food-handling.

There are two broad kinds of food contamination—organic contamination and chemical contamination.

Organic contamination

Organic contamination involves living microorganisms—commonly known as 'germs'. Not all microorganisms are harmful to humans (for example, the 'helpful' organisms that produce vitamins in the human digestive system are important to good health), but other microorganisms produce toxins (poisons) that can cause severe illness.

Essentially, germs require warmth, moisture, and a source of energy to live and reproduce. They are especially likely to thrive in certain foodstuffs, including high-protein foods such as milk, eggs, poultry, and fish.

Examples of well-known dangerous microorganisms include the following:

- salmonella bacteria—which are especially likely to grow in poultry and eggs;
- staphylococcus bacteria—which thrive in the noses and throats of people, and on the skin, often without people knowing that they are carrying the bacteria;
- clostridium bacteria, one strain of which causes botulism—a form of toxic food-poisoning associated with canned foodstuffs, and especially dangerous because a tiny amount of toxin is deadly but difficult to detect (the affected food usually tasting and smelling perfectly normal).

These different microorganisms (and others not mentioned above) all have their individual characteristics. However, it is not necessary to be an expert in microbiology to be aware of two important factors common to all forms of organic food-poisoning.

- Microorganisms cannot cause problems if they are not introduced into food in the first place. Although the hospitality manager cannot be responsible for contamination that occurs before the foodstuffs reach the hospitality establishment, it *is* the manager's responsibility to ensure that any such contamination does not take place in the food-preparation area.

- Microorganisms usually require an opportunity to reproduce to large numbers in the food if they are to cause problems, and this reproduction usually occurs only in a certain range of temperature (about 10–60 degrees Celsius).

If these two points are kept in mind, most organic food-poisoning hazards will be avoided. Hospitality managers must thus be aware of certain measures that should always be followed:

- foodstuffs should be purchased only from reputable suppliers, and should not be purchased until as close as possible to the time when they will be cooked and consumed;
- foodstuffs should be handled as little as possible before and during cooking, preparation, and presentation;
- good personal hygiene should be observed by all staff members in the food-handling areas—see 'Personal hygiene', page 148, for more on this;
- all utensils and surfaces should be kept scrupulously clean;
- meat juices must be prevented from touching other foodstuffs, utensils, or cooking surfaces, and meats should not be left sitting around at room temperatures; and
- all foods (including meats and salads) must be kept refrigerated to avoid possible multiplication of bacteria, and refrigerator temperatures must be maintained at 5 degrees Celsius or lower.

CASE STUDY

The consequences of food contamination

A tragic case that apparently involved food contamination ended in a Sydney courtroom.

A family went to a suburban restaurant for a meal. The mother of the family was extremely allergic to peanuts and peanut oil, and advised the restaurant management of the fact. The management assured her that only one dish on the menu contained peanuts and that they would take great care that there were no peanuts in any dish served to her.

Unfortunately, soon after finishing her meal, the woman suffered a severe allergic reaction and collapsed. Despite medical attention, she suffered brain damage that left her completely dependent. The restaurant owner was sued for $10 million and settled out of court. His only explanation for the event was that food from another dish must have inadvertently splashed onto the woman's meal as it was being served—thus causing her tragic allergic reaction.

In general, commonsense demands that foodstuffs be kept clear of any potential contamination and not be allowed to remain at room temperature for any length of time.

Another good rule based on commonsense is never to taste food that you think might be bad. Apart from the personal risk, taste is not a good test for contamination anyway.

Some 'rules of thumb' for food-handling

- Wash hands before handling food.
- Do not accept delivery of partially thawed frozen foods.
- Do not leave food out overnight to thaw; always thaw in a refrigerator.
- Do not re-freeze food that has thawed.
- Keep everything clean.
- Check the grading of food (including 'use-by' dates and handling requirements).
- When in doubt, throw food out.
- Avoid cross-contamination by ensuring that food is covered.
- Keep hot food hot and cold food cold.
- Use a meat thermometer to ensure that meat being cooked reaches and is maintained at a temperature greater than 60 degrees Celsius.
- Monitor the temperature of refrigerators and ensure that it is always below 5 degrees Celsius.
- Always apply commonsense and good practice in all aspects of food-handling and preparation.

Chemical contamination

Food can also be contaminated by chemical agents. This can occur before foodstuffs reach the food-preparation area. For this reason, food should be purchased only from reputable suppliers, and never from people who come to the kitchen door with 'special deals'. Such product might have been contaminated by chemicals such as pesticides while being grown or harvested or, in the case of meat, might have been affected while being slaughtered.

Once foodstuffs have reached the hospitality establishment, the manager is obviously responsible for proper storage and preparation. Cleaning chemicals should never be stored where spills or leaks could touch foods. Care must also be taken that staff can read and understand labels on chemical containers lest someone inadvertently allows a toxic chemical to come into contact with foodstuffs. Chemical contamination can also occur if packaging has reacted with food or if cans have rusted.

All containers should be thoroughly washed and cleaned before use. Care must be taken when spraying for pests in kitchen areas to ensure that pesticides do not contaminate any food, or any surface where food will be prepared. Care must also be taken to ensure that food is not contaminated by broken glass—from shards of broken containers, or by a broken splinter from the neck of a bottle or container.

Cleaning, garbage storage, and maintenance

Insects and rodents can quickly contaminate food products. Food and garbage should always be sealed with tight-fitting lids. Work surfaces should be thoroughly washed down with hot water before beginning work—microorganisms of many types can be carried in dust and in the invisible residues left by pests overnight. Containers should not be crammed full, but should emptied often enough to prevent a build-up. Garbage containers should be cleaned and disinfected regularly and frequently. Outside garbage collection areas must also be kept clean.

Personal hygiene

As noted above, personal hygiene is very important in food-handling. The following are some essential rules.

- Nails should be short and clean.
- Hands and forearms should be washed before and during work, and after going to the toilet or nose-blowing.
- Clothing should be laundered and clean.
- Hair should be kept short or tied, and be well groomed, and kitchen staff should always wear hair covering (many jurisdictions mandate this). Hair can contaminate food directly (by hair itself falling into food), or indirectly (by allowing microorganisms to fall into food).
- Gum should not be chewed on the job.
- Pencils should not be stowed behind the ear.
- Money should not be handled. Money has been described metaphorically as 'filthy lucre' (1 *Timothy* 3:3), but it really *can* be filthy and full of harmful bacteria.

An individual's health can also have implications for the safe handling of food. If a person has any unhealed injury, care must be taken to ensure that open wounds are covered with a waterproof dressing that will not allow blood to seep out. Any illness, especially sore throats, stomach upsets, and skin rashes should be reported to a supervisor. If food & beverage staff are ill, especially if they are sneezing or coughing, they should not be on duty.

Staff must also take special care if assisting another person who has been injured and who is bleeding. The possibility of transmission of bloodborne viruses (such as hepatitis B and C) should be taken into account. Avoid coming into contact with blood from a bleeding wound or injury. Always wear disposable gloves when assisting an injured person. Such gloves should always be available to be used in an emergency.

Occupational health & safety

A dangerous environment

Dangerous tasks

The hotel kitchen is one of the most dangerous areas of a hospitality operation in which to work. Food & beverage employees have to work quickly and efficiently, often under time constraints, and in cramped areas with projections that can cause bruises and other injuries. They have to handle heavy items in these cramped conditions, and use sharp utensils (knives and automated cutting tools). They work with hot cooking equipment, hot oils, and hot food. The work area is prone to spillages that can leave the floor slippery and dangerous—even after cleaning up, if fats and grease are involved.

Electrical equipment

Food & beverage employees use different types of electrical equipment, and there is always the risk of electrocution if equipment is not properly used and maintained. The rules for using electrical equipment are the same as for all staff—ensure that equipment is in good working order and used in accordance with proper procedures, and that there is no damage to plugs and leads (which should not be extended in a dangerous fashion).

Lifting

When lifting heavy objects such as full pots and pans, the usual lifting rules apply—keep the back straight, and lift using the thigh and leg muscles. In addition, due to the cramped areas in which they work, kitchen staff must be careful not to twist their bodies or overreach.

Machinery

Various types of machinery are used in the kitchen—including cooking, slicing, cutting, grinding, and mincing machines. Staff members must be competent in the use of these machines, understand and respect the hazards, and have all appropriate guards and shields in place. If equipment becomes overheated, it is a sure sign that it is operating outside the manufacturers' design specifications. No matter what the demands of the moment, any overheated machine should be switched off at once, and a supervisor informed.

Burns and scalds

Burn and scald injuries are especially common in kitchen areas. Be aware of this risk, and follow these rules.
- Check that the pilot light is on when lighting gas.
- Keep your face and body well back when opening an oven.
- Tell others who are working in the area if you know that a plate or pot is hot. Although this might seem trivial, just a quiet word of warning

('hot there') whenever another person goes near something that you know is hot might save an injury.

- Turn a steamer off when opening it, and use the door as a shield against a surge of steam.
- Never use a wet cloth to lift a hot container. The wet cloth conducts heat quickly, provides no protection, and the moisture in the cloth can, itself, quickly become heated and cause scalds.
- Never leave pan handles over a heat source, or protruding from a stove or other surface where it can be knocked by persons passing by.

Some other safety rules

Several other safety rules are especially important to food & beverage staff. Some of these include the following.

- Use gloves when washing dishes.
- Beware of hot plates. Always assume that a hot plate is, indeed, hot.
- Spillages and breakages should be cleaned up immediately. Any food possibly contaminated with broken glass or ceramics *must* be thrown away. The area of a spill or accident should be indicated with warning signs (especially on floors).
- Beware of sharp surfaces and implements.
- Never use equipment that you have not been trained to use.
- Use your commonsense and never rush. Plan properly and be aware of the need for teamwork.
- When finishing your shift, see that food is properly stored and everything is shut down completely.

Finally, there is one very simple rule for the kitchen, that might appear to be rather odd. It is, however, extremely wise.

- If you hear an unusual sound, stop what you are doing and be alert.

Knife safety in the kitchen

The following precautions should always be followed in working with sharp instruments in the kitchen.

- Keep knives sharp and handles clean.
- Always carry a knife with the point down.
- Never pass a knife blade-first.
- Cut away from your body.
- Lie knives flat, not overhanging an edge, and never with the blade uppermost.
- Never try to catch a falling knife.
- Always return knives to their usual places.

> ## Safety blunder
>
> When a Swiss hotel chef lost a finger in a meat-cutting machine, he submitted an insurance claim. The company, suspecting negligence, sent an expert to see for himself. He tried the machine out to prove it was safe—and lost a finger too! The chef's claim was approved.[8]

Safety of the guest

One additional aspect of food & beverage safety of which staff should be aware is the need to be conscious of the guest who has had too much alcohol to drink.

Do not serve any more alcoholic beverages to a person who is inebriated. The signs of inebriation are slowed reactions and poor coordination. Hospitality managers have a duty of care in refusing service to guests who are drunk.

Of course, staff members should not drink alcohol while on duty.

Activity 5.5   *Checking-out the property*

Do a tour of kitchen and surrounding service areas specifically watching out for hazards on the floor. These might include: slippery floors, items or obstacles placed in traffic areas, or steps or stairs in poorly lit areas. List any hazardous areas and the steps that should be taken to remove the hazards.

Issues in food services

Changing practices in food-service management

The scope of food-service management has changed steadily over the past decades, and ongoing change and challenge are to be expected.

New management techniques

As in other areas of modern management, the food-services sector has seen an increasing emphasis on progressive management techniques aimed at the accomplishment of more clearly defined goals. As staff in the industry become better educated, and as expectations and demands of proprietors become more exacting, better management techniques and more sensitive labour relations will become even more important.

Increased accountability

In today's more competitive world, management faces increased account-ability through more stringent budgetary controls, and through the practice of allocating costs to those areas (or managers) who incur them. This practice of allocating costs to individual operations or parts of an operation (whose managers are able to control those costs and are therefore responsible for them) is commonly called 'cost centre control and reporting'.

Labour costs and other costs in the food & beverage department will continue to be subject to tighter controls and tougher standards—as they are in other sections of the hospitality industry. Internal controls—such as inventory-control programs, budgetary controls, production controls, wastage controls, and breakage controls—will be increasingly implemented, often in association with computerised systems.

Sharper purchasing practices will also become the norm as goals for improved price and quality buying practices are developed.

All of these programs are necessary if the food-service department is to be economically successful as part of the overall hospitality enterprise.

Automation and specialised equipment

Automation and specialised equipment generate greater efficiency and pro-ductivity in food & beverage departments. Automation will continue to expand in the ongoing search for decreased labour costs and increased efficiency. Computer-assisted programs and automated equipment produce faster meal assembly, superior temperature retention, and more efficient delivery systems—all of which contribute to enhanced food-service quality for guests and customers.

More qualified personnel

Staff in food service are becoming increasingly better educated and trained. Those who come through practical restaurant experience are increasingly well trained and skilled, and those who come through tertiary management colleges are similarly educated to more exacting standards.

Nutritionists are becoming increasingly more important in the industry as guests gain greater knowledge and make more demands for healthy and nutritious food.

The increasing expectation of guests is also leading to greater emphasis on outstanding service. In-service education is gaining greater emphasis as managers strive towards goals of increased effectiveness and efficiency.

Interpersonal relationships in the kitchen

The tradition of the 'kitchen brigade' has produced a strict hierarchy within a disciplined and efficient kitchen operation. However, in some quarters, it has also resulted in bullying and discrimination in the workplace. Although this issue has been ignored or downplayed in the past, it is now receiving increased attention, and food-service management must be aware of the adverse implications if problems in this area are not addressed.

Certainly there is a need for discipline. When staff members are required to work quickly with hot equipment and sharp, dangerous utensils, there is no room for carelessness. However, discipline cannot be enforced by verbal or physical abuse.

English chef Gordon Ramsay featured in a television documentary that highlighted, on the one hand, the high standards he demanded in his kitchen but, on the other hand, also showed the verbal and physical abuse to which he subjected his staff. Despite the difficult interpersonal relationships in his kitchen, Ramsay has been a respected chef and a successful businessman.

Such a threatening milieu can become institutionalised if chefs who have been treated in the same way during their own apprenticeship and training see it as being 'the way that things are done'. The traditional hierarchical structure in large kitchens (which places staff at various levels in a 'pecking order') tends to produce an ongoing tradition in which various staff members are bullied by those above in the accepted 'pecking order'.

Whatever the practices in the past, this style of management is no longer acceptable, and has been made illegal under anti-discrimination legislation. The following practices are unacceptable and must be eliminated in any modern management scheme:

- shouting at, or threatening, staff junior staff members;
- derogatory or abusive remarks;
- using kitchen implements in a threatening way;
- any form of sexual innuendo or abuse;
- making unreasonable demands—such as excessive speed in working;
- requiring long periods of work without breaks; and
- physical violence—including pushing or poking junior staff members.

Any organisation that chooses to ignore these sorts of issues is at risk of legal action, and individuals perpetrating this sort of behaviour could be at personal risk of criminal charges.

Controlling food & beverage operations against fraud and theft[9]

Problems

Food & beverage services are subject to fraud, theft, and embezzlement in a number of ways.

On delivery, there are opportunities for embezzling part of the cash payment. On receipt of payment for meals or beverages, there are opportunities for stealing cash, and this is a major concern. In the words of one restaurateur:[10]

> We had an 'unannounced' promotion (giving away a drink for a better tip); a 'creative' promotion (taking the customer's cash and not ringing

the sale), and an 'off-premise promotion (taking liquor from the storeroom and walking out with it).

Point-of-sale systems are useful for keeping track of every scrap of food, but there are gaps even in such systems. There is also the problem of preventing theft by staff consumption on the job.

The food & beverage department is different from any other area of stock control because the stock is of a perishable nature—which means that there will be frequent 'write-offs' (or losses of goods). Also, food & beverage operations are often conducted in areas that can be crowded, and not well lit, with customers who might not take careful notice of the amounts they are proffering and the change they are receiving. Finally, the retail sales are comparatively small, frequent, and have to be conducted in a short period of time—which means inevitable rush and possible confusion.

One thief exploited the busy working environment by wearing cowboy boots to work every day, then changing into work shoes. At the end of his shift, he put on his cowboy boots, with the addition of a bottle of liquor in each, and so walked out past the security check.

Principles of internal control

The two crucial principles of internal control, as far as the food & beverage operation is concerned, are:

- separation of duties; and
- ensuring authorisations.

Separation of duties should take place all along the chain of food preparation and service. In general, the principle means that several people should be involved in any chain of activities—thus ensuring that no single person is allowed to have unsupervised control (and hence the opportunity for fraud).

Authorisations are necessary at every stage of cash receipt, goods receipt, and goods write-off. Good document control can offset some of the particular problems of control, especially through the use of electronic point-of-sale systems. Such point-of-sale systems also provide good audit trails and independent revenue checks that in themselves are useful as preventive control measures.

Special problems in bars

There are special control problems in bars, and definite rules should be applied to bartenders. These include:

- no complimentary drinks permitted and no free drinks allowed to other employees;
- no acceptance of drinks from guests, and no drinking while on shift;
- standard recipes for drinks, and no authority to make special prices;
- tip receptacles to be kept well away from cash registers; and
- bartenders not to meet regularly with sales or distribution staff of supplying companies.

Even the tightest controls will not be foolproof. One private investigator found that a bartender was using a magnet strategically attached to the computerised liquor dispenser to interfere with the electronics and make the device record zeros instead of the cost of the drinks. Other scams on point-of-sales systems include routinely spilling drinks down the terminal to put it offline, or voiding checks or sales items.

Managers and fraud

Some of the research on fraud indicates that even managers can be involved in theft from food & beverage areas, and some even encourage employees to steal by suggesting that fiddles are a 'fair' way to get an added 'perk' and beat the tax office.[11]

One manager used an innovative (although radical) way to solve the problem of employee theft. On taking over a bar, he sacked all the staff and started again, but hired only people who had no experience whatsoever of bar operations!

Activity 5.6 *Ethical consideration*

You are the food & beverage manager of a restaurant in a hotel. For some time, you have been concerned that on totalling the cash register at the end of shift, there have been many instances of the cash being a few dollars short. The discrepancy is not great—only a few dollars—but it appears to be happening often. You keep a close watch on operations, especially the cash register, and you notice that one staff member gives change to a customer for $10, even though the customer gave a $20 note. The customer does not notice and, in fact, leaves the restaurant before you have the opportunity to go to the register.

You take the staff member aside for an urgent interview in the back office. The person admits that he might have given wrong change, but insists that it was an honest mistake due to distraction at the time.

QUESTION

- What action would you take, bearing in mind that you have nothing else to suggest that this staff member is responsible for the cash shortages?

Environmental awareness in food & beverage operations

Energy conservation

Although they do not use as much energy as some industrial processes, hotels are nevertheless high users of energy in airconditioning and other services, and they have a high profile in the community. Hotel management has a role to play in energy conservation, not only by saving energy themselves, but also by encouraging education in this important area.

Environment Australia has recorded case studies of energy conservation and environmental education in large hotels in Sydney (the Hotel InterContinental and the Regent) and in Melbourne (the Parkroyal). Conservation measures included reassessments of efficient peak and off-peak energy usage, a review of the efficiency of airconditioning (even extending to the use of swing doors to retain warmth or cool air), and the dimming of lights when not needed.

Staff members in hotels should be trained to be aware of the importance of energy conservation in all aspects of their work, and they should be encouraged to present energy-saving ideas related to their particular areas of responsibility.

As equipment is renovated or replaced, and as new constructions are planned, energy conservation should be an important factor in making decisions on various equipment alternatives.

Activity 5.7 *Recycling*

An unexpected advantage of comprehensive recycling and waste-reduction programs is the recovery of lost items in the material being recycled. For example, the Hyatt Regency in Chicago, USA, reported that they had salvaged silverware items valued at US$120 000 from waste sorted for recycling.[12]

QUESTIONS

- Contact a recycling operation in the local area and ask for details of the odd and valuable goods that have turned up in garbage or waste being sorted. List the items and estimate their value.
- Consider the different types of items, such as silverware or utensils, used in hotels that are likely to be included in garbage as it is removed.

The Australian Hotels Association conducted a study of thirteen hotels in 1994 and examined a large number of ways that hotels could conserve energy and contain costs (in all departments, not just in food & beverage). Examples of some of these practices were:

- reducing the temperature of stored hot water to 60 degrees Celsius (but not lower due to the risk of bacterial growth);
- using high-efficiency long-life light bulbs;
- insulating roof and wall areas; and
- shading northern walls.

In relation to chilling and refrigeration, some low-cost control measures included checking door seals on coolrooms, and shifting ice-making machines out of direct sunlight. Refrigerators should always be defrosted regularly (according to the manufacturers' recommendations) to ensure that they are operating efficiently. Another means to reduce energy costs in relation to chilling and refrigeration is to use a chiller to cool foods to recommended temperatures before placing them in cool rooms.

Some energy-reducing practices are as simple as closing windows and doors when ventilation fans are operating. Even simpler is a regular check of airconditioning settings. One of the authors did research into the use of air-conditioning in several Hong Kong hotels and found that in all cases the properties ran at least 5 degrees Celsius too cool, and in one case 9 degrees too cool. In investigating, he found that the hotel management had set the ambient temperatures for the comfort of staff who had to wear jackets and ties, and so on. Guests and the visiting public who wore lightweight summer clothes were not consulted.

Environmental performance benchmarks in the hotel kitchen

InterContinental Hotels and Resorts have developed a number of benchmarks for energy and water usage in kitchens.[13] The benchmarks are based upon energy and water usage per 'cover' (that is, per guest meal).

Energy used in cooking

Good performance	Less than 3 kilowatt hours
Fair performance	Between 3 and 4.5 kilowatt hours
Poor performance	More than 4.5 kilowatt hours

Energy used in lighting

Good performance	Less than 1 kilowatt hour
Fair performance	Between 1 and 1.5 kilowatt hours
Poor performance	More than 1.5 kilowatt hours

Hot and cold water used

Good performance	Less than 35 litres
Fair performance	Between 35 and 45 litres
Poor performance	More than 45 litres

Apart from energy usage within the hotel, consideration should also be given to energy usage in associated functions, such as transport. The hotel should assess whether its vehicles are causing undue pollution, and whether there are cleaner and greener alternatives. Consideration should be given to converting petrol-powered or diesel-powered vehicles (buses or courtesy cars) to gas.

Water usage

In kitchens, water usage can be minimised by:

- running dishwashers fully stacked with dishes (rather than half-empty);
- using bowls to wash vegetables (rather than running water); and
- natural defrosting (rather than using water).

Waste-water minimisation and recycling

The two issues associated with waste water generated at a hotel are:

- the volume of waste water produced; and
- the quantity and nature of pollutants in the waste water.

The quantity and nature of the pollutants discharged into the sewerage system depends upon:

- types and quantities of kitchen fats and oils;
- types and quantities of soaps used in guest rooms and staff rooms;
- types and quantities of cleaning agents used in the cleaning of bathrooms;
- types and quantities of kitchen surfactants and disinfectants; and
- other chemicals used in the hotel (such as pesticides and insecticides).

Through the installation of appropriate systems (such as grease traps and filters) and education of staff in appropriate waste disposal, considerable amounts of pollutants can be prevented from entering the waste-water effluent system. In addition, by the careful selection of chemicals such as shampoos and cleaning agents, the pollutant loading (such as sulphates and phosphorus) can be reduced.

Solid-waste reduction and recycling

Even smaller-scale projects such as a restaurant should take into account environmental benefits when auditing their operations. A comprehensive survey of six Canadian food-service operations found that substantial benefits to the environment could be achieved by reducing polystyrene waste.[15]

The Banff Springs Hotel, Canada

The Banff Springs Hotel made significant savings by purchasing heavy-duty, permanent rubber gloves for kitchen staff instead of using disposable gloves (which added to waste-removal and waste-disposal problems.[14]

The main components of solid waste generated by food & beverage operations are:

- glass waste—most of the glass waste generated in restaurants, bar, and conference areas can be separated and recycled;
- aluminium—comprised mainly of cans in food-service and conference areas, bars, and kitchens, aluminium can be easily separated and recycled;
- putrescible wastes (wastes liable to rot)—generated in considerable amounts by kitchens, organic putrescible waste can be composted or worm-farmed; landscaping and maintenance crews also generate quantities of vegetable matter that can be composted or mulched.

Activity 5.8 Saving corks

A busy food & beverage outlet generates a large quantity of waste material—including containers and wrapping. Corks (natural and plastic) and bottle tops are particular problems in such establishments.

QUESTIONS

- How many alternative uses are there for corks, bearing in mind the nature of cork as a soft but flexible material?
- Are there any alternative uses for bottle tops? Bottle tops are small and round with a roughened edge that could be useful for scraping, but are often bent while being taken off full bottles. Although it takes initiative and imagination to come up with alternative uses, using such initiative and imagination is what recycling programs are all about.

Chapter review questions

1. List five roles in the kitchen and dining area and describe their functions.
2. Describe some different types of food service. List and briefly describe some menu items appropriate to each.
3. Why are different sorts of food stored separately?
4. Why do you think it is inadvisable to allow serving staff to consume alcohol while on duty?
5. For small operations, hotels and motels are big consumers of energy and pollutants. List at least three initiatives could be taken to change this.

CASE STUDY

The HB Hotel

The restaurant in the HB Hotel is a limited operation of fifty seats. However, there is a growing demand for functions, and the function centre is booked-out for some periods of the year. There is a high demand for wedding functions in spring and autumn, peaking in October and May respectively.

The owners of the HB Hotel would like to expand the functions operation, but have the problem that demand is seasonal. They have the opportunity to quote for a contract involving the supply of meals to the 100-unit retirement village called Blossom Park that will be opening soon in the area. There is likely to be a daily demand for approximately eighty hot meals to be supplied at lunch, and the same number at dinner, to the diningroom of Blossom Park.

Discuss the issue of whether the HB Hotel should tender for this contract. Consider the positives and negatives of supplying these catered meals from the kitchen of the HB Hotel to the Blossom Park retirement village.

Part II

Specialised Areas of Hospitality Management

Chapter 6

Hospitality Law

In 1315, King Louis X of France decreed that if any innkeeper was shown to have stolen the property of a guest, the innkeeper would have to make restitution of three times the value of the goods stolen.

Synopsis of chapter

This chapter commences with an examination of the sources of law in Australia. The chapter then considers several areas where either legislation or legal tradition has established the rights and duties of parties involved in hospitality contracts. The rights and duties of hoteliers as hosts, as traders, and as employers are considered in turn.

What is law? Sources of law in Australia

The term 'law' refers to a system of rules of behaviour and the enforcement of those rules. National laws have developed from a number of sources, including written law, unwritten law, historical circumstance, and rulings of administrative agencies. Australian law, like that of many countries of the former British Empire, has mainly developed from the English common law system, which largely relies on precedent. These precedents go back many years and English common law has complex roots dating back to the Middle Ages. It was then called the 'Law of the Land' and was first codified by William of Normandy, who defeated the native King Harold at the Battle of Hastings in 1066 and seized the English throne.

The Law of the Land was composed partly of the customs and traditions of local people, but included many features of Norman law. The principles of law continued to develop during the eleventh and twelfth centuries until, by the reign of King Edward I (1272–1307), what we understand as 'common law'—that is, all accepted laws, written and unwritten—had been for-malised. However, additions continued to be made, and still continue to be made, by judges.

It is important to note that *common* law does not include *statute* law—which is law enacted by parliament. The House of Lords and the House of Commons, the major features of the English parliamentary system, had evolved by 1414. From that date, all laws passed by either house were entered in the statute books and became a part of the law. Any statute can be repealed or modified by succeeding parliaments, and any statute overrules any section of the common law that is inconsistent with the statute.

In Australia, English common law arrived in 1788, and the first bodies to have legislative powers were the colonial governments. These colonial governments later became the state governments of Australia following federation of the colonies to form the Commonwealth of Australia. At the time of federation in 1901, these legislative bodies, through referenda of their citizens, ceded certain of their powers to the federal parliament.

Merchant law developed along slightly different lines from English common law. It was largely influenced by the mercantile practices of the Romans and Venetians and was developed among the merchants and traders themselves as their markets expanded—rather than being enacted by a parliamentary body or sovereign. Later, the British parliament enacted statutes relating to merchant law. In the Middle Ages, separate traders' courts were set up in market towns such as London and Plymouth. However, by the reign of Elizabeth I (1558 to 1603), the rapid expansion of English trade necessitated the establishment of the Court of Admiralty. This was responsible for the creation and administration of merchant law. Another body that dealt with financial disputes was called the Court of the Exchequer (simply because it sat at a table that was covered with a chequered cloth). This system of merchant law was adopted in Australia, and adapted to Australian conditions.

The topics discussed in this chapter are intended as general discussions of areas of legislation of importance to hospitality managers. The matters discussed are not intended to be exhaustive descriptions of every variation of law in every state and territory in Australia, or in other countries. Rather, we will concentrate on areas of law that hospitality and tourism managers should note and consider for application to their particular situations.

Rights and duties of hoteliers as hosts

Rights and duties in relation to the supply of accommodation

The terms 'inn' and 'public lodging house', refer to an establishment where the proprietor provides, for a fee, accommodation, food, and drink to all travellers without necessarily any prior arrangement (reservation). An innkeeper is a person who accepts the responsibilities of operating an inn on an ongoing basis.

An inn is different from a 'private lodging house'. In the latter, residents enter into an agreement to stay in the house, and the relationship is that of 'landlord and guest'. In contrast, a '*public* lodging house' caters for residents whose stay is generally short-term and the relationship is that of 'innkeeper and guest'.

There is a range of accommodation properties on offer—including rooming houses, boarding houses, serviced apartments, and the like. Neither the style of the building nor the range of services it offers affects its nature as an accommodation property. Unless local state law extends innkeeper legislation to cover these accommodation properties, they do not fall within the definition of the innkeeper–guest relationship as it has developed in English common law.

For legal purposes, the word 'inn' is synonymous with 'hotel' and 'motel'. Bed-and-breakfast establishments also fall within the definition of an inn. The size of the 'inn' can be large or small—although the legislation in some jurisdictions defines how large the property must be to fall within the definition of an 'inn'. The rating publication *Dawsons Property Guide* considers properties with four rooms and more to be large enough for such classification. Does the minimum size of the property matter? One sector of the industry where it might matter caters for the 'backpacker' market. There are fears, especially in New Zealand, that small unlicensed operators (that is, fewer than five beds) might give the whole industry a bad name. In the backpacker market, news travels fast by word-of-mouth and over the Internet, and a few operators with substandard accommodation or poor service can leave an unfavourable impression that affects the wider industry. Standards count, and are more difficult to ensure if there is a large number of small operators in the market.

Some interesting definitions of hospitality establishments

Some interesting definitions of hotels and similar properties are offered under the law of Florida, USA.[1] Under these statutes, a hotel is any 'public lodging establishment containing sleeping room accommodations for 25 or more guests and providing the services generally provided by a hotel'. A motel is any 'public lodging establishment which offers rental units easily accessible to guests with an exit to the outside of each rental unit . . . and at least six rental units . . . A "Resort Motel" shall meet the definition and may be classified as a resort if it so requests'.

'Any public lodging establishment' that does not fall within the above definitions of a hotel or motel must call itself a 'rooming house, a guest house, cabins, a tourist camp, or otherwise according to choice . . .'

The operations of restaurants are considered to be outside the operation of the innkeeper–guest relationship. A person can patronise a barbershop, newsagency, or bar located inside a hotel without being a 'guest' of that hotel. Such a person is a 'customer', and not necessarily a 'guest'. Patrons of restaurants are often referred to as 'guests', and there is nothing wrong with this description for everyday use, but it should be noted that such persons do not legally qualify as 'guests' as commonly used in innkeeper's legislation.

Under English common law, the innkeeper has an enforceable obligation to accept travellers as guests, and to provide shelter and refreshment. This obligation arises because it is considered that the traveller is 'on the road' and has nowhere to go, apart from the inn, to find shelter for the night. The traveller thus has need of protection from the 'perils of the dark'. The only conditions are that the guest has to be prepared to pay a fair price and be in a fit condition for reception at the inn.

This requirement to accept travellers is called the 'duty to receive guests'. The duty extends only to those who are travellers and does not extend to local residents. The test as to whether a person is a traveller or a guest depends upon whether they are 'transient'—that is, not staying permanently. A traveller is usually considered to be a person who is staying overnight away from home. The guest can be under eighteen years of age—a legal 'infant'—but the innkeeper, or 'hotelier',[2] is entitled to be assured that even an infant can pay for accommodation. The duty to receive guests also means that guests might arrive at any hour of the day or night and must be able to gain admission. A hotelier may lock the doors of the property, but must be available to unlock the doors to admit new guests, or to allow existing guests to come and go as they please.

Once the guest is accepted at the inn, a contract has been established. This contract means that the guest has the right to occupy a room (subject to being moved to another room) for an agreed period. The hotelier may not enter the room except for good reason—such as to clean it, or to ensure safety, or if the hotelier or the innkeeper's agents suspect that illegal activity is taking place in the room.

The responsibilities of an hotelier are as follows.

1 The hotelier must provide travellers with accommodation in all cases unless there are reasonable grounds for refusal. An hotelier who refuses a guest without reasonable grounds can be fined and/or sued for damages for breaching the duty to receive guests.
2 The hotelier must offer courteous treatment.
3 The accommodation must be clean, and of a reasonable standard, and the rooms must have such necessities as provisions for fire escape.
4 The hotelier must be able to provide food and drink to guests. However, a guest can demand a meal only during the inn's standard mealtimes, and a guest cannot demand that an hotelier go out and obtain food should there be none available in the kitchens.

5 The hotelier must receive other people who might wish to visit the guest without staying themselves at the property.
6 The hotelier has a duty to ensure the safety of their guests' luggage. The hotelier can be liable for its loss, damage, or theft.
7 The hotelier must take mail, phone calls, and messages for guests.

An hotelier does not have a responsibility to go the rescue of a guest who is in danger—unless the hotelier has created the danger. However, this provision (of not having to go to the rescue of a guest in danger) does not mean hoteliers are spared litigation when guests suffer serious injury or death. When deaths occur in hotels or restaurants, be they the result of accident or murder, lawsuits often follow. The legal arguments often revolve around what was the 'proximate' cause of death.[3] The most common causes of accidental death in hospitality operations are water, fire, food, alcoholic beverages, and motor vehicles.

In addition to the above *responsibilities*, the hotelier also has certain *rights* that are recognised in common law. The hotelier may refuse to accept guests when the usual accommodation is completely booked out—although a traveller who has an advance reservation might be able to sue for breach of contract if refused accommodation because the property is booked out. The hotelier may reject guests who arrive in a condition deemed unsuitable—for example, if they are intoxicated or in possession of pets (although there are legislative exceptions for guide dogs). The hotelier can also refuse accommodation to people who are deemed to be a potential irritant to existing guests. An hotelier also has the right to demand payment in advance from guests.

In the case of the hotelier's liability for guest's property—including damage, loss, or theft—there are certain exceptions and limits. For example, the hotelier is not required to make good losses which might have been prevented had the guest exercised reasonable care. The hotelier is thus not necessarily an insurer of a guest's goods. However, the hotelier must act reasonably to look after guests and their goods. The standard of service and skill required is that the hotelier must have 'skill and knowledge that could reasonably be expected of one who occupies that position at that particular location'.[4]

Guests also have responsibilities under various legislation relating to hoteliers. The first responsibility of guests is to conduct themselves in a courteous manner at all times, and not to cause offence to other people. Guests may not conduct themselves in a disorderly manner that could endanger the safety of other guests, and must comply with house rules that are displayed for their notice. Guests may not steal hotel property from the room.

A guest is not strictly entitled to a key to his or her room, and is generally provided with one only—in consideration of the hotelier's liability for property security. The key can be used by the guest to secure the room from other guests and from the public, but not from the hotelier or the hotelier's authorised representative if there is good reason for these persons to enter the room. In law, the hotelier is deemed to have complete control over the room at all times, and this is only reasonable given that the hotelier also has to ensure the safety of other guests.

If an hotelier considers that a guest is behaving offensively, the guest can lawfully be asked to leave. If the guest refuses to do so, he or she may be ejected as a 'trespasser'—although the hotelier must avoid using physical force. An example of a guest being required to leave for offensive behaviour was the case of a hotel guest who disliked the meals served in his hotel, and who therefore went out and purchased some chops of his own—later presenting these to the chef and demanding that the chops be cooked for him. The chef cooked the chops, but then presented a bill for one dollar for the service. The guest loudly and insistently refused to pay the bill, and repeated the performance the next night. The hotel then refused further service. The guest left and sued the hotel. His case was rejected by the courts.[5]

The usual means of removing guests is by a 'lock-out'—removing the guest's luggage and locking the door of the room (changing the lock if necessary). The action of retaining the guest's luggage has sometimes been called the 'hotelier's lien', or means of obtaining a security pending payment. Hoteliers must note that a guest who overstays the time limit for check-out cannot be treated in this fashion. They can be required to leave, but this must be done in a reasonable manner. In the case of lost property, the hotelier should make a reasonable effort to locate the owner. Then, after a period deemed acceptable by the local police (usually six months), such property can be disposed of.

In addition to the rights and duties of a hotelier in supplying accommodation, hoteliers also have a responsibility for what is termed 'the duty of care' towards guests. This means that hoteliers and property owners must be careful that people are not injured through any negligent act or failure to act. Such facilities as swimming pools and play areas on the property must be safe to use. For example, an eleven-year-old guest was injured swimming in a hotel swimming pool when she struck a heavy float in the pool, and her family successfully sued the hotel for damages.[6] Note the discussion below on liability issues (see 'Rights and duties concerning guest safety', page 169).

Rights and duties concerning discrimination by hoteliers

In the hospitality industry, hoteliers may not discriminate against persons on the basis of their race, gender, or marital status. It is illegal to use such grounds to refuse accommodation, to impose special terms and conditions, to defer applications, or to place a person low on a list of precedence. With regard to marital status, the hotelier may not separate two people—married or unmarried. Nor may the hotelier rent only to married or unmarried couples. Nor may they evict guests on these grounds.

Publicans must take special care of anti-discrimination legislation as it relates to racial and sexual segregation. That is, people of a particular ethnic group or race may not be refused access to the public bar. Nor may an hotelier deny women the right to enter the public bar, as was once a frequent occurrence in Australia. These actions are clearly illegal. The law also forbids discrimination against a mother who chooses to breast-feed her child in the bar area or other public parts of the hotel. In cases of alleged discrimination, the complainant bears the burden of proof. The complainant must prove by comparison with a real or hypothetical person, that the complainant was treated differently from what could be considered to be the usual standard of service.

Rights and duties concerning guest safety

It is important for all hoteliers to be aware of their legal obligations to ensure the safety of their guests. Legal suits for damages are not only potentially expensive in themselves, but they could also lead to an insurance company refusing insurance cover in future if the insuring company feels that the suit arose from bad business management.

To avoid such suits for damages by injured guests, hoteliers should take due care in ensuring the safety and cleanliness of their establishment. All staff should be well trained and alert, the premises should be secure and free from defects, and the management should be wary of possible problems.

In English common law, if a hotelier was sued for loss or injury, their defence was in showing that the guest's misfortune came about through one of three causes:[7]

- the guest himself or herself, or someone for whom the guest was responsible, caused the loss or injury;
- the loss or injury was caused by an 'act of God' (for example, a meteor coming in through the roof); or
- the loss or injury was caused by 'an act of the public enemy'.[8]

In cases of litigation, it is irrelevant whether the guest's injury was caused by a staff member, rather than the hotelier. The law makes the hotelier 'vicariously responsible'—that is, even if the hotelier is not personally in attendance at the time, he or she remains responsible for the actions of all staff members during the time of their employment. The hotelier's duty of care applies to all guests and to all parts of the premises that guests might reasonably believe themselves entitled to visit—including outdoor areas, pools, driveways, and other public areas. To avoid legal complications, the hotelier should make sure that *all* parts of the establishment are in fit condition, should a guest inadvertently enter them. Cases where hoteliers have been found liable for breaching the duty of care to provide a safe environment for their guests include:

- a bed that collapsed under a sleeping guest;
- a stool that collapsed when a guest stood on it to adjust the airconditioning;
- a chair that had a hole which staff covered by a cushion, but which a guest fell through;
- a gas heater that exploded (killing a guest who was drunk); and even . . .
- a guest who was bitten by a rat while she slept.[9]

Figure 6.1 *Hotel management might be legally liable for an unusual incident*

Kevin Baker

If a guest is successful in a law suit for damages, it is generally because the guest is able to prove that the hotelier was negligent in carrying out responsibilities under the relevant legislation covering the property. However, the damages claim can be reduced if the hotelier, in turn, can prove that the guest's own lack of care caused, or contributed to, the injury or loss. One factor that can act in the hotelier's favour is the existence of any statements by the hotel limiting their liability—what are called 'exculpatory clauses'.

Rights and duties where food is provided

The provision of food services does not fall directly under the aegis of hotelier–guest relationships. However, because most lodging properties provide food and beverages as well as accommodation, the application of the law as it affects food-service providers should also be examined. Food-service providers include a wide range of facilities, such as drive-in restaurants, lunch counters in retail stores, sandwich shops, golf club food service, counter-meal facilities at small hotels, and so on.

With regard to admitting guests and patrons, there is a distinction in English common law between hoteliers and proprietors of taverns or restaurants. Travellers have the right to demand shelter for the night, but patrons seeking a meal do not have the same right to demand service. The food-service proprietor can turn away anyone he or she wishes, because the common law does not state that the prospective patron requires protection in the same way as the traveller requires protection. The potential patron must be in a fit condition and must be able to pay for the food and services. House rules can be applied. For that reason, it is lawful to turn away people who are not dressed according to the house rules, provided that the house rules concerning dress codes are clear and consistently enforced. It is also lawful to turn away people with bare feet for health reasons.

Under common law, whereas the hotelier has to admit those under eighteen years of age—that is, legal 'infants' or 'minors'—a restaurant does not have to do so. The food-service manager can turn away children if he or she wishes to do so. However, it is *not* lawful to turn people away if the restaurant house rules are framed so as to exclude certain *groups* of people—for example, on the basis of race.

In Australia, all states have instituted Food Acts—which generally state the responsibilities of the food provider, and the penalties should these responsibilities not be observed. Food-service managers are directly responsible to patrons for meeting regulations regarding safety of food. If food is unfit to eat and causes illness among patrons, the food-service operator might be liable if there is negligence in the storage, preparation, or serving of the food. There is an implied contract between restaurant and patron that the food will be of appropriate quality. The provider warrants that the food is safe. This applies even if there is foreign matter in the food—such as glass or stone. It does not apply to something that is usual in the food—such as a fish bone. Note that this legal provision that the food be 'fit to eat' means that it must not make a patron ill; it does *not* mean that the food must be nutritious, or tasty, or even attractive. It means that a reasonable person must be able to eat it without falling ill.

There are other areas where regulations apply to food services. Such practices as the false advertising of food are prohibited. This means that an advertiser may not present a product in a false or misleading way to the consumer. For example, a food-service operation must not advertise that the food is prepared in the Jewish orthodox kosher manner if this is not the case. Also, the operation must not use adulterated food or provide false descriptions—for example, a false description that fails to mention that food products are mixed with other substances that are not specified on the packaging or in the product description. Claims that a particular food is healthy must be able to be substantiated. Furthermore, the legislations provide for a system of analysing and inspecting food by authorised inspectors or police officers.

Activity 6.1 *The case of the flaming cherries*

Consider and discuss whether there is any liability in the following case.

A restaurant serves flambé dishes as a speciality, and the chef is a show-man who takes delight in displaying his skills in tableside cooking. On one occasion, he is preparing a dessert dish of cherries, using rum from a bottle to flame the cherries. For the fourth time, he has splashed liquor onto the pan with the cherries, but has not noticed a small flame still burning in the pan. The flame catches the liquor as it is coming out of the bottle, and a patron is burnt.

Is the chef liable for damages?

(The answer is at the end of the chapter; see page 182.)

There are additional requirements laid upon food-service operators by common law. One such is the obligation to take reasonable care to provide safe premises for all who enter them—whether they be children or adults. Another requirement is the duty to take care of goods entrusted into the care of the operator—such as clothing checked into a cloakroom, or a car (if the restaurant parks the patrons' cars for them).

How far does the hotelier's liability extend? Does it extend to visitors? Does it extend to the environs of the hotel such as the car park and entrance ways and footpaths outside the hotel? The answer to these last two questions is 'yes'.[10]

Rights and duties where liquor is provided

The supply of liquor, or alcoholic beverages, has a number of legal implications.

First, because of the possibility of alcohol abuse, the right to sell liquor is strictly controlled by laws in all Australian states. These authorities control the supply and sale of liquor through the dispensation of liquor licences that are dependent upon the applicants' being of good character. These licences are usually in three categories—a hotelier's licence, an off-licence, or an on-licence. The various licences define trading hours and controls—such as penalties for the provision of alcohol to minors who are not consuming alcohol at a meal accompanied by an adult. It is an offence to supply alcohol at a bar to minors—even to those minors who might appear to be of age. If there is the slightest doubt about the age of a patron in a bar, the staff must ask for proof of age and refuse service if the same is not provided.

Secondly, the supply of liquor to persons can result in those persons becoming intoxicated and causing harm to themselves or to others. Common law excuses operators who supply liquor to those referred to as 'able-bodied' patrons. Examples of those who are not 'able-bodied' are minors or people who are already visibly intoxicated.[11] In these cases, the licence-holder must ensure that service is refused. A hotelier's licence might stipulate that the hotelier may supply liquor for sale by retail only, and that the hotelier is not required to provide residential accommodation as well—as is the case with a tavern. In most cases, the hotelier will also provide accommodation, and the licence will allow liquor to be supplied in rooms as well—that is, through a mini-bar or similar.

An off-licence is available in two categories—retail and wholesale.[12] The difference between these two categories is specified in their names. Those people who wish to sell liquor to other licensees must obtain a wholesale licence. Retail outlets who sell only to the public need possess only a retail licence.

An on-licence is usually divided into specific categories—restaurant, function, theatre, university or college, airport, vessel or aircraft, and public hall. Essentially, an on-licence is necessary for those wishing to sell alcohol in conjunction with meals. Before such a licence is granted, the courts must be satisfied that the proprietor has installed sufficient furniture and equipment, and has employed adequate staff to serve a defined number of customers safely.

Anyone operating a liquor licence must take particular care of the laws relating to the supply of alcohol to minors. Anyone who supplies alcohol to a minor is liable for any injury or damage caused. Most state legislation demands that hotels must contain a restricted area from which minors must be excluded at all times. Other areas of the hotel are termed 'authorised areas'—to which minors may be admitted in the company of a responsible adult. Notices of this classification must be displayed in each area.

The law relating to trading hours differs according to the different categories of licence. The various provisions for trading hours used to be contentious. For example, in some Australian states prior to the 1960s, hotels had to cease serving liquor at 6.00 p.m., and hotel bars were crowded as workers left their place of work at around 4.30–5.00 p.m. and crammed into hotel bars to drink as much as they could in the hour or so before the taps were turned off and the patrons turned out. This was known as the 'six o'clock swill'.

Activity 6.2   A 'bona fide traveller'

Sunday trading threw up an area of contention when a section of the Licensing Acts of some states allowed hoteliers to provide liquor on a Sunday only to those who were called 'bona fide travellers' (that is, genuine travellers).

QUESTION

- Imagine that this Act still applies to your liquor trading licence. A person comes into your bar on a Sunday and asks for a drink. Discuss what you might do to establish, legally, whether or not this person is a 'bona fide traveller'.

Rights and duties of hoteliers as traders

Rights and duties of parties involved in contracts

When working in the hospitality industry, it is important to be aware of the laws relating to contracts. There are several definitions of a contract but, in essence, a 'contract' represents a legally binding agreement between two or more persons. The term 'legally binding' implies that the agreement is enforceable by law.

The main features of a legal contract are:

1 an intention to create legal relations;
2 a genuine offer and its acceptance; and
3 an acceptable form of contract.

These ideas can become complicated. However, in broad outline, here are some notes on what these things mean.

Intention to create legal relations

This is a formal way of saying that a contract involves a definite intention by parties to make a relationship between them 'legal'. If a court should find that this intention is lacking, the contract cannot be enforced.

A genuine offer and its acceptance

A contract involves a legal process of making a genuine offer and its acceptance by the second party. This is signified by the exchange of what is called a 'consideration'. Only by the exchange of such a 'consideration' does a contract become legally binding. (More detail on this is to be found in the discussion on 'Rights and duties regarding reservations', below.)

The form of the contract

A contract can be verbal or written. To avoid later disagreement about what was intended to be included in the contract, it is preferable to have the *contract itself* in writing, or at least written evidence of the *existence* of the contract.

In the hospitality industry, many contracts, such as reservations, are initially made verbally, and then confirmed by issue of a document—such as confirmation of a reservation. This document is not a contract in itself, but is written evidence of the *existence* of a verbal contract.

Rights and duties regarding reservations

In the hospitality industry, evidence of the process of offer and acceptance can be examined by considering in detail an enquiry about a vacant room. Does an advance reservation fulfil the above legal requirements for a contractual agreement, and so constitute a binding contract on the hotelier and the prospective guest?

When prospective guests are advised of the availability, location, and costs of rooms, the hotel's agent (the receptionist, booking clerk, or reservations agent) makes what is called an 'invitation to treat'. This is, in effect, 'an offer to make an offer'.

If the hotel is fully booked on the date in question, and if the traveller is advised that the hotel has no available rooms, there is no indication that the parties can enter the contract. In these circumstances, clearly no contract ensues.

However, if the hotel's agent advises that there *are* vacancies when a traveller makes a definite enquiry in good faith, then there is a response to the offer that the traveller can take up, and to which the traveller can agree or not. In making a booking or reservation, the guest makes an 'offer' (see point 2, page 174), and the hotel accepts the offer when the hotel completes the booking by agreeing to hold a room for the prospective guest. The 'consideration' of the contract (see point 2, page 174) can be made either by paying a deposit, or by the exchange of promises.

Thus, a formal contract is completed (as per the three points made on page 174). This contract is a binding agreement between the guest and the hotel. To avoid problems in the making of verbal contracts on the phone, or perhaps in the mail, hotels should ensure all their advertising material is accurate and can be clearly understood by prospective customers. The contract with a guest or customer must be in plain English.

If a person under the age of eighteen years (a 'minor') is involved, is there a problem concerning the competence of the contracting parties? That is, can a minor make a legally binding contract? The answer is that hoteliers have a legal obligation to provide accommodation for minors under the 'duty to receive'—so there are no legal problems in practice, even if the person seeking a booking is under eighteen.

Because the act of making a reservation completes a contract, what is the legal situation if the hotel should be overbooked when the guest arrives? If the guest arrives before an agreed specified time, the hotel is guilty of a breach of contract. It is usual for the hotelier to use every endeavour to minimise the damages that the traveller might suffer. However, if the guest arrives at 9.00 p.m., having been told that the check-in time is 8.00 p.m. at the latest, then the guest is guilty of breach of contract.

Activity 6.3   *Some interesting legal problems*

What do you think the legal situation would be in the following scenarios?
- Consider the case of the traveller who makes a reservation and does not arrive at all. What if the hotel did not fill the room while holding it for the traveller and, in fact, had refused another traveller's 'offer to treat'. In refusing the second traveller's 'offer to treat', the hotel has

suffered loss by having a vacant room. Discuss whether the first traveller is liable for the hotel's loss.

- Must a hotel guarantee accommodation when a guest has made a reservation and sent a deposit? If a room is not available when that guest arrives, what should the hotel do?

Consider your answers in the light of the principles outlined in the section concerning the rights and duties of hoteliers in accepting reservations (pages 174–5).

NOTES:

(1) For further reading on both questions, refer to case law.[13, 14]

(2) Hint for first case: it is technically difficult for the hotel owner to prove and recover the loss—note American case law.[13]

(3) Hints for second case: consider whether the hotel must make any effort to find alternative accommodation for the guest, and whether the hotel must refund the deposit?[14]

A further legal point arises in relation to 'overbooking'—which results in a guest being left without accommodation. It might be that the hotel is also guilty of fraud or misrepresentation in having stated to the guest that there was accommodation when this did not prove to be the case. The act of overbooking, where deliberate, could be construed as an unfair or deceptive act or practice and the hotel could also be liable under consumer protection legislation.[15]

Another area of contract is that of functions, or banquets, where all terms and conditions of the contract must be carefully spelt out, including provisions relating to cancellation or non-performance. For example, there could be a dispute regarding breach of contract if cold entrées are served whereas hot entrées were expected by the patron. Spelling out the menu in detail should ensure that there are no such disputes. Letters of intent in regard to functions and banquets are not contracts unless they are clearly agreements to carry out the services defined, and are so described.

Rights and duties concerning fair trade

All states in Australia have enacted fair trading legislation. The aim of such legislation is to protect the rights of the consumer, who is, by definition, 'a person who acquires goods and services from a supplier'.[16] The administration of such Acts is generally within the jurisdiction of the various state offices of consumer affairs.

Fair Trading Acts seek to ensure that deception is eliminated from trade. In general, they forbid 'misleading conduct' and 'deceptive conduct', and all hoteliers should be aware of the expected standard of conduct. The Acts generally also forbid what is called 'unconscionable conduct'—that is, conduct that is judged to be morally unacceptable. An example of fair trading in the hospitality industry is the provision of guest billing statements that state clearly and fairly the charges that are being made for the services provided for the guest. No charge should be made for any service not actually rendered, or at a higher rate than that specified in the advertised tariff.

It might seem that 'fair trading' provisions, especially as they relate to such areas as advertising, are somewhat loose and open to interpretation. However, the test of 'fair trading' provisions in such Acts is established by asking this sort of question: 'What would a reasonable person understand by what was said or written?' That is, disputes about the wording of the legislation are not interpreted legalistically, but can be considered in accordance with common usage of words, dictionaries, and general reference works.

This sort of 'commonsense interpretation' means that an advertisement that technically *seems* to be in line with legislation in terms of the words that it contains might nevertheless contravene the *intent* of the legislation by what is *not* included. For example, a holiday advertisement might be deemed to have contravened the intent of the Act if that advertisement states a price, but does not include other charges—such as a holiday 'surcharge'. A consumer might reasonably expect such an unexpected 'surcharge' to have been included in the quoted price, and the advertisement might thus be considered to be in breach of the intent of the Act when it stated a price that did not include this surcharge.

Written contracts must be examined carefully, and must meet all legal and fair trading requirements

Courtesy Parkroyal Hotel, Canberra

Advertising ploys that probably contravene Fair Trading Acts include the following:

- representation of goods as 'unique' or 'exclusive' when this is not so;
- failure to disclose the true nature of the goods;
- failure to disclose the nature of the goods as 'seconds';
- false claims of a manufactured product's origin; and
- claims that services will be carried out by qualified staff when, in fact, they will be performed by other employees.[17]

Rights and duties in recovering debts

A working knowledge of the system for debt recovery is vital in the hospitality industry. There is a series of legal steps which must be observed in the carrying out of what is called the 'adversary system'. This system defines the confrontation of the debtor by the person who is owed money, and outlines the right of that person to sue the debtor to recover the money owed.

Before initiating the adversary system, the creditor must decide whether he or she intends to proceed within the formal legal system for recovery of the amount of money owing. In making this decision, there are several important factors to consider. Foremost among these is the debtor's solvency—that is, whether the debtor is likely to have the capacity to pay if ordered to do so by the court. If the debtor is insolvent or virtually so, or is a person whose sole income is apparently social security benefits, there can be no financial advantage in engaging a solicitor to extract payment.

If the creditor does decide to pursue the case through court proceedings, the process involves several steps:

1 making a formal statement of claim to a court;
2 judgment by default (which means that the other party does not contest the claim in court); OR, if the other party *does* dispute the claim, the debtor puts forward a defence at step 3;
3 a hearing; and
4 a judgment.

In a case where the debtor is ordered by the court to repay the money owed, and fails to do so, a writ of execution might be served. The debtor might be required to reappear in a summons hearing. Finally, the sheriff of the relevant legal jurisdiction might be empowered to seize the defendant's belongings for sale at auction—the money thus raised being used to satisfy the debt. Alternatively, the court might order the debtor's employer to 'dock' the debtor's wages for payment of the debt. Should these methods fail to end the case, the creditor can commence bankruptcy proceedings.

To avoid costly (and often protracted) legal cases, claims of up to $10 000 can be referred to the small claims tribunals that operate in most jurisdictions. These are bodies established to resolve smaller cases referred to them by the courts, or brought directly by those seeking to recover debts.

Activity 6.4   *What can you do?*

A guest at your restaurant has eaten a large meal of several courses and consumed a bottle of a very expensive vintage wine. He then declares that he has no money to pay for his meal.

QUESTIONS

- What would you do?
- Have you the right to demand that he work off the meal washing dishes in the kitchen?
- Survey a small sample of local restaurateurs and ask them what their policy is with regard to such incidents.

Rights and duties of hoteliers as employers

Rights and duties as a manager

A person who aspires to a position of responsibility in the hospitality industry also needs to understand the various pieces of legislation that affect employment in hospitality organisations. All employment decisions—such as hiring and firing, promoting, and providing access to training programs—have to be made in compliance with all pertinent regulations.

There are six main players in Australian industrial relations:

- governments (state and federal);
- tribunals (state and federal);
- employers;
- employer associations;
- employees; and
- trade unions.

Governments make and enforce procedural and substantive rules for the workplace, directly determine some aspects of working life through legislation, and determine work conditions (for example, pay levels and structures). Much of the regulation is enforced by the tribunals, which have the power to intervene in disputes and settlements. However, the Australian Industrial Relations Commission, a federal agency designed to oversee labour-relations issues, has taken responsibility for arbitration proceedings.

There are state and federal trade unions (depending on whether the union conforms to state or federal legal requirements). To have legal status, unions must be registered according to relevant state legislation and/or the federal *Industrial Relations Act* of 1988. Only a registered union can participate in negotiation and arbitration practices.

Employment laws in Australia fall under three categories:

- laws that establish tribunals and courts (which enforce industrial awards and laws and decide upon industrial disputes);
- laws that determine the rights and duties of employers and employees; and
- anti-discrimination laws to ensure that all employees are treated fairly.[18]

Rights and duties in relation to employees

Employee wages and conditions are generally set by collective bargaining, and the employee contract as negotiated. Collective bargaining is a process by which representatives of the employing organisation meet with representatives of the workers, and the parties attempt to work out a contract. The employees' representatives can be a union or a group of unions. A union can exist only if workers prefer to be unionised. A typical employment contract is divided into sections and appendices. A major part of the contract is concerned with such issues as wages, hours, fringe benefits, and overtime. In general, the contract spells out the authority and responsibility of both the union and management.

Day-to-day compliance with contract provisions is an important responsibility of front-line hospitality managers who work closely with contracted employees. The most important issue with respect to contract administration is developing a clear understanding of the contract provisions. Many labour-management contracts are filled with details and legal jargon that is difficult to interpret. In addition, the range of provisions can be quite broad—covering everything from probationary periods and performance requirements for new employees to severance pay allocation for displaced workers. Given the complexity of so many contracts, it is vital that training is provided to both managers and employees such that all individuals gain a complete understanding of the employment requirements that are outlined in the labour-management contract.

Ongoing communication and sensible discussion is essential if disputes are to be handled properly. The most common issue that managers face is the question of discipline. It must be realised that there are various levels of disciplinary problems—for example, simple errors, breaches of the employment contract of varying degrees, incompetence, misconduct of various types, carelessness, negligence, and so on. Grievance-handling procedures are needed for assessments and resolution of these various matters.

Rights and duties in regard to workers' compensation

There are compulsory aspects to the provision of workers' compensation insurance of which every employer must be aware. Aspects of this topic are covered in Chapter 9 Personnel Management (see pages 255–9).

Other legal issues

The above discussion does not exhaust all the legal issues that can arise in the course of a hotelier conducting business. Other legal issues that can arise might involve the law of leases, the law of trespass, the law relating to principal and agent (as it affects parties booking services on behalf of others), and the law relating to corporations (relating to the establishment of businesses). For these and other important topics, the reader is referred to the relevant references and textbooks such as Vermeesch and Lindgren (1995), and Gillies (1988).[19]

Activity 6.5 *Ethical consideration*

See the ethical problem outlined in Activity 3.4 (page 93). You will recall that the general manager has stated that you will just have to 'bump' (that is, cancel the prebooked room of) one or more of the prebooked guests to make room for the general manager's preferred VIP guests. She suggests that you choose from the casual visitors or vacationers—who are unlikely to come back to the hotel anyway.

You now have no option. The prebooked guests who were 'bumped' have now arrived and are standing at reception. There are no rooms of any standard that you can offer them.

QUESTION

- What will you say to the 'bumped' guests to explain the situation? Will you lie to the guests, or will you say (simply and truthfully) that more important clients have been given priority?

Chapter review questions

1 Do the laws that apply to the hotel and catering industry favour (a) the hospitality business or (b) the customer?
2 Given that it is necessary for hoteliers to maximise a room's revenue, and a way to do this is by overbooking the room, what steps should a hotelier take if he or she does not have a room for a guest who has made a proper booking?
3 Would a bar attendant be liable for serving alcohol to a person under the minimum age if that person appeared to be old enough to be served?
4 Why should hoteliers always exercise a 'duty of care'?

Answer to Activity 6.1

THE CASE OF THE FLAMING CHERRIES

(See page 172 for details of this activity.)

Yes, the chef would be liable. In a real-life episode, he was found negligent in the case of *St Petersburg Sheraton Corp. v. Stuart.*[20]

CASE STUDY

The HB Hotel

The back carpark of the HB Hotel stands between a sports park and a transport depot. On days when there is a popular sporting event, many people take shortcuts across the carpark and there is now a well-worn path from one fenceline to the other where the path crosses bare earth.

The manager is concerned that some of the people who cross the carpark might damage guests' cars. The manager would like to stop the practice. He therefore erects a fence all around the car park.

One sports fan objects and delivers a formal letter stating that he (the fan) has crossed the carpark on his way to the sports park for more than five years. The writer asserts that, by now, the path across the car park has become a public thoroughfare—because the owners of the hotel have never, in memory, taken any steps to assert their private ownership of the carpark area.

What are some issues involved in this dispute?

Chapter 7

Marketing Hospitality Enterprises

> . . . what wilt thou do to entertain this . . . stranger? Is this the best thou canst bestow?
>
> Richard Crashaw, *Hymn of the Nativity* 1:37

Synopsis of chapter

This chapter commences the discussion of hospitality marketing by looking at the basic concepts of marketing. The chapter then considers marketing segmentation in detail, the marketing environment, and marketing research, including sources of marketing information.

What is marketing? Basic concepts[1]

Marketing is more than advertising and selling. Advertising and selling are the more visible aspects of marketing, but much more goes on 'behind the scenes'. Marketing involves a close examination of all the activities and operations of the marketplace, so that an enterprise can provide products and services that can be sold to customers at prices that result in long-term profits for the enterprise.

For its ongoing financial health and wellbeing, every business has to conduct its operations in such a way that the main focus is on satisfying customers' needs and wants. If customers are not satisfied, they will not return to purchase goods or services from the business in the future, and the business will decline and eventually fail.

Hence, customer satisfaction is at the heart of any marketing strategy and that satisfaction is achieved by examining exactly what the customer is looking for. The marketing professional must ask some basic questions. What are we to sell? How are we to sell? To whom are we selling?

In regard to this first question, in considering what to sell to meet customers' satisfaction, marketing theorists suggest that customers will be satisfied if five basic product requirements are met. These product requirements are commonly called 'utilities'.

What is being sold—the five basic utilities

The five basic utilities in marketing a product or service are:

- form;
- task;
- time;
- place; and
- possession.

Some thoughts on each of these are offered below.

Form

Form relates to the attributes of a product, or the 'shape' that it takes. The term refers to the fact that the product is designed, manufactured, and packaged in such a way that it will satisfy customers' needs. For example, wine can be offered to a customer in various forms—by the glass (in a bar), in a carafe (with table service), in a bottle (in a bottle shop), or in a miniature bottle (as part of an airline meal).

Task

Task relates to services. A service cannot be prepared in a package because it is not a tangible thing that has a physical shape. The term 'task' refers to the service being designed and performed in such a way that it will satisfy customers' needs. For example, if you attend a theatre performance, you can choose from a variety of shows, and you can select tickets for different types of seats at different prices.

Both the *form* and *task* utilities are created by the production function (department) in an organisation. In a hospitality operation this is either the rooms division (creating the accommodation product), or the food & beverage department (creating meals, drinks, and so on).

Time

Time refers to having the product or service available when customers want it. For example, a hotel must be able to accept guests at any time during the day or night, 24 hours per day, every day of the year (provided there are rooms available).

Place

Place refers to having the product or service available where customers want it. For example, a service provider would not open a lodging property on an isolated road where people seldom go.

Possession

Possession refers to the right of the consumer to use or consume the product. In the case of a physical product, the consumer clearly can do what he or she chooses to do with it. For example, the purchaser of an apple can eat it, or give it away, or plant it in the ground in the hope that an apple tree will grow. However, in the case of services, the consumer never *owns* the service as such. The contract that the consumer enters into with the service provider, and the price that the consumer pays, entitles the consumer to use the product for an agreed period of time. For example, when you pay for an airline ticket, you are buying *the right to occupy* a seat on the aircraft while it travels to the place that you want to go. You are not buying *the actual physical seat*. You are not allowed to take it away and do with it what you will. If you want to travel to another place on another day, you must enter into a new contract for a new service.

When an enterprise can provide all of these five utilities to a customer, in a fashion that the customer demands, marketing theory states that the customer will be satisfied. For a physical product such as an apple, meeting the demands of the five utilities is straightforward—sell the apple to the customer to eat at a time and place that the customer wants. The creation of these utilities is more complex for businesses that are selling a product that is a combination of a physical good and service—such as a meal in a restaurant. These companies must create the utilities of *form* and *task*, and then must also create the other three utilities (of *time*, *place*, and *possession*) in a way that meets the requirements of the customer or consumer for both a physical good *and* a service. These requirements are even more complex for a service such as a hotel room for a night, or an airline seat for a flight—both of which are highly 'perishable', in that the product can no longer be sold once the day or the scheduled flight time has passed.

Activity 7.1   *Why our product will sell*

In small groups, decide upon a product that you would like to create and sell—considering details of form, task, time, place, and possession. Then say why your product would work. Organise and present your reasons in such a way as to be able to convince other groups that yours is the best idea.

NOTES:

1. Each person in each group should rank the products on offer from 1 (the best) downwards. The group with the most first votes is the winner.
2. This Activity is continued in Activities 7.2 (page 188) and 7.3 (page 203) as we continue to explore marketing in greater detail. This Activity should therefore be treated as a developing teaching exercise.

How the product is being offered—the marketing mix

Once the business has determined that its products or services have been designed and prepared so that they meet the five basic utilities required to satisfy the needs of their customers, the business managers need to refine how they will *present* their range of products or services in the marketplace. In marketing terms, the business must consider its *marketing mix*.

Just as there are five *utilities* in designing and preparing the product, so there are five aspects involved in how the product is offered for sale. This marketing mix can be referred to as 'the 5Ps'—product, place, promotion, price, and people.[2]

Some thoughts on each of these are offered below.

Product

As previously noted, the *product* is a physical good or service (or a combination of the two) that the enterprise offers to the market. The first two utilities, *form* and *task*, outline the basic nature of the product. In the context of considering the 'marketing mix', the business reviews exactly what it is offering. For example, if a restaurant offers a fast-food product, should that include hamburgers, purchased separately or as part of a take-away meal? How should the hamburgers be made? How can they be made differently from those of the competition?

In the hospitality industry, because the product is a service it has certain characteristics that a physical product does not have. A hospitality product is:[3]

- intangible (it cannot be touched);
- inseparable (it cannot be removed from the hospitality property and remain the same product);
- variable (it is never exactly the same in all respects); and
- perishable (once the day has passed, the opportunity to offer hospitality for that date also passes).

Given these special characteristics of the hospitality product, it is difficult to design the hospitality product such that it is exactly what customers want.

Place

The concept of *place* refers to the distribution of the product to the consumer. In other words, how will the enterprise get its product from producer to consumer in the marketplace? For physical products, this involves the use of transport networks or agencies to retail or deliver. The concept of place is also relevant to the provision of products that are services, for the service must be provided where the consumer wants to receive it—hence the emphasis upon 'location' as the key to a successful service.

Promotion

Promotion concerns how the business communicates the attractiveness and benefits of what it offers to those who will make the purchase. For example, the business could advertise on television, in newspapers, in trade journals, through associated businesses, and so on. Promotion can be linked with related entities, such as hotels in other regions. In the hospitality industry, personal selling (through telephone calls, word-of-mouth, and so on) is an important factor—because the product being offered is, after all, a personal service or experience. The linking of personal selling with advertising, other promotions, and merchandising makes up the 'promotional mix'.[4]

Price

The *price* of the product is crucial. The price must match the sacrifice that the consumer is prepared to make to receive the benefits of the product on offer from the enterprise. Usually, but not always, this involves the exchange of products for money. Sometimes benefits can be bartered. In the hospitality industry, accommodation for airline staff is often bartered for air travel for hotel employees. The ability to price a product to meet a market is a skill required of all managers, if they are not to be short-term administrators.[5]

People

The nature and behaviour of people who will purchase the product must be taken into account. Who are the consumers and where do they come from? In relation to a hospitality enterprise, the management should ask whether the hotel or motel draws its guests from a local, a national, or an international region. A neighbourhood restaurant might have a clientele that lives or works locally. A theme resort might draw its customers from a particular age group. What are the motives of the target consumer group? The business must consider the people to whom it will market its product. To prosper it must satisfy a consumer need.

All of the 5Ps are considered by consumers when they are deciding whether to enter into a contract to purchase the product or service. For example, the quality of the product or service in the right place might influence the consumer's decision more than the price—a 'no-frills' cabin might not attract custom unless it is the only accommodation in a remote but sought-after location. A good promotion might also have an impact upon consumers' decision-making if the promotion makes one service sound more attractive than an alternative.

Activity 7.2 Applying the 5Ps to your product

We continue Activity 7.1 (page 185), and now apply the 5Ps to your product.

In Activity 7.1, you were asked to create and sell a product or service. In small groups, return to the discussion of the product or service that you would like to create and sell as conceived in Activity 7.1. Now apply the concept of the '5Ps'.

Can you make the product more attractive to consumers and revise the comparative ranking of the products of all the groups who took part in Activity 7.1?

Note: This Activity is continued in Activity 7.3 (page 203) as we continue to explore marketing in greater detail. This Activity should therefore be treated as a developing teaching exercise.

Who will buy? Targeting the market

The term 'mass marketing' is used to describe a situation where all possible customers might want to buy the product. For example, everyone needs soap and toiletry products. In these cases, businesses could treat all such customers as being alike for practical purposes. Virtually all possible customers have the same wants and needs in regard to basic hygiene. Although mass marketing has some applications, it is generally not practical for most enterprises. For example, everyone needs accommodation for the night, but not everyone wishes to (or can afford to) purchase that accommodation from a hospitality operator.

The widest possible market is sometimes called the 'generic market'. A 'generic' object is one that is the same as all others of its class. A generic market consists of a group of customers with broadly similar needs and, in such a market, many enterprises can operate offering a range of products or services that satisfy the same needs. Examples of needs (or desirable goods) are the need for food and drink, the need for accommodation, the need for entertainment, and so on. It is important to describe the generic market when examining the enterprise's marketplace because:

- it makes the enterprise focus on the needs that its product can satisfy, rather than turning its gaze inward upon the product itself;
- it provides a starting point for the enterprise to identify the wider markets within which it could conduct its business.

As an alternative to the generic market, there is the idea that customers can be divided into groups that have different tastes and preferences and will make different consumption decisions. This is a valid supposition, for although each of us is an individual, many of us fall into a group that prefers a particular type of product for a purpose. Thus the widest possible marketplace can be divided up into smaller groups. As an example from the hospitality sector, all people need some form of accommodation when they are away from home, but some who cannot afford paid accommodation will stay with friends or relatives. Others will seek a modest style (such as a backpacker hostel), whereas others will prefer luxury accommodation. Some, indeed, even aspire to the 'seven-star' style of the Arab Tower Hotel in Dubai!

Dividing up the marketplace into smaller groups has the advantage that products can be tailored to meet more specific needs. The process of subdividing the marketplace is called 'target marketing'. Target marketing seeks to identify groups of people who have similar needs for a similar product or service. The business then focuses on satisfying the needs of that particular group of consumers and refines the product or service it offers. It is for that group of customers that the business tries to create the utilities of form, task, time, place, and possession (see page 184) that it believes meet the demand. For example, business travellers require accommodation, but they have special requirements such as communication links and business services.

The process by which an enterprise selects its target market(s) is called 'market segmentation'.[6] There are two steps in the process.

- First, the enterprise identifies the product markets in which the enterprise wants to operate.
- Secondly, the enterprise assembles people who might have similar needs from the same product into a market segment.

The enterprise then can make a choice (based on defined criteria) of one or more of these market segments as its target market. By this means, it can concentrate its resources for maximum benefit.[7] The topic of market segmentation will be considered in greater detail in a later section (see page 191).

The marketing strategy

Having considered what their product is, how they will offer it, and to whom, the business then endeavours to put all these considerations together into a marketing strategy. A marketing strategy is a plan that a business draws up to define their target market (who will consume the product) and decide how they can determine the elements of the marketing mix (the type of product and how it will be packaged) to satisfy the needs of that target market through promotion of the product—that is, what do we want to promote and to whom?[8] It is also important to consider the context in which the business operates—its working environment.[9]

Top-quality marketing needs innovation, imagination, and persistence
Courtesy Parkroyal Hotel, Canberra

This can be expressed as an equation as follows:

enterprise resources + target mix + marketing mix =
marketing strategy (in a given environment)

When drawing up their plans in conformity with business objectives, an enterprise has four alternative courses of action in determining its future strategies in seeking market opportunities.

1 *Product development:* This strategy involves developing or offering new services to meet different needs of the enterprise's current customers— for example, developing enhanced facilities such as free use of spa or gymnasium facilities.

2 *Market development:* In this case, the enterprise seeks a new market for the enterprise's existing services—for example, seeking out new users for conference facilities, such as encouraging wedding parties to be held in the facilities over the weekend when there is limited business demand.

3 *Market expansion:* This strategy involves trying to sell more of the enterprise's current service to current customers or, in the case of hospitality services, encouraging its guests to stay a longer period (or to return frequently). This type of marketing can be done effectively through the use of sales promotions (for example, an offer to stay for four days with the fourth day being free).

4 *Diversification:* This strategy involves the enterprise in developing a completely new service for consumers in a new target market—for

example, renovating a wing of a tourist hotel and rebuilding existing single units into business suites with a full range of support services.

In determining which of these strategies is most likely to yield good results in terms of revenue and profit in the long run, the enterprise must carry out research into the chosen market and not seek to rely on 'gut feeling', thus making a decision blindly. It must also carefully match its resources and capabilities to short-term and long-term strategies.

Every enterprise has a limited capability in the marketplace—based upon its resources. These resources can be financial, technical, marketing advantages, and human resources. Depending upon the limits of an enterprise's resources, it will define the objectives (for example, economic growth) that it is able to pursue. The enterprise is also dependent upon the environment for growing its resources—for example, human resources (recruiting managers and staff) or financial (business loans from banks and other financial institutions). If the business cannot acquire the resources it needs from the environment, the pursuit of their objectives will be restricted. For example, if a new enterprise wants to develop a resort for customers from a target market that is geographical (say Japan), it will need some staff with skills in Japanese language and culture. The enterprise could advertise in the newspaper for such skilled interpreters, but what if no one applies? The developers will not be able to open the resort if they cannot find people with special skills to work for them.

The above discussion leads to three important areas that require further exploration:

- the process of refining the target market through market segmentation;
- the process of examining the market environment; and
- methods of researching the marketplace.

Each of these is considered in more detail below.

Market segmentation

Identifying market segments in general

Identifying market segments is the process of aggregating (putting together) all of the customers within a product market who share a similar need for a specific product or service. The separate groups thus formed comprise the market segments.

When identifying market segments, an enterprise must make sure that the segments meet four criteria:

- similarities within a segment;
- differences among segments;
- useful and relevant criteria identifying the segment; and
- size of the segment.

Similarity within a segment

Individuals comprising the customer group within a segment should be as similar as possible. If this is so, their behaviour will be predictable within reasonable limits as they react to a specific marketing mix in a similar way.

Differences among segments

Individuals comprising different segments should be different, and therefore react differently to the same marketing mix. If people in different segments are similar, they should have been placed in the same segment in the first place.

Useful and relevant criteria

The criteria used to segment the market should be useful and relevant in identifying customers, and so able to be used in designing a marketing mix to meet their needs. If this is not so, the exercise will not be cost-effective.

Size of the market segment

The segment must be large enough to yield sufficient numbers of consumers, otherwise the exercise will not be cost-effective.

Once the various segments within the product market have been identified, the organisation can then decide which one or more of these segments is to be its target market.[10]

How to define market segments in the hospitality industry

What factors can be used to group people together in the hospitality market-place? The factors are described under five heads. Segmentation can be by:[11]

- geographic factors;
- demographic factors;
- price factors;
- benefits and needs factors; and
- psychographic factors.

See below for notes on each of these factors.

Geographic segmentation

This factor includes the place of origin of customers, how far they are prepared to travel, and other aspects of their travel patterns. The organisation thus needs to compile a dossier of all customers, noting where they have come from (local, regional, interstate, international), and how they travelled to the destination.

The organisation could then undertake further analysis of trends. For example, what factors have increased or decreased the numbers from a particular origin—perhaps changing transport means (new roads, new trains) or changing economic conditions (exchange rates, economic conditions in the countries of origin, and so on).

This factor also should consider how large is the drawing area of a hospitality operation. Many years ago, the local market area for a hotel was restricted to a walk of one or two hours—a town could have two to three hotels or inns and they constituted the local market area, because prospective guests would find it too far to walk to the next town. Now, however, a discerning traveller can take advantage of readily accessible transport to travel on to another destination. Thus, if services are not satisfactory in one venue, a hotel or restaurant several kilometres away (or even a hundred kilometres or more away) can be a competitor.

Demographic segmentation

The demographic factor includes age, income, sex, number of dependents, stage of family lifecycle (young children, teenaged children, or adult children), occupation, education, and so on.

Not all of these will be relevant in determining the target market. For example, the sex of business travellers is unlikely to influence their need for accommodation. A further stage of analysis is necessary, and this involves determining which of these demographic factors must be examined. Some of the factors will be necessary to group people together (these are called 'qualifying dimensions') and some of these factors will influence the customer's decision to consume the product or service (these are called 'determining dimensions').

A further stage of analysis is necessary, and this involves determining which of these factors is relevant and must be examined. The *family demographic* might be of relevance, for example, because families who are seeking accommodation generally require a large unit.

Price segmentation

There are market segments that can be clearly defined by price. Business travellers tend to select an accommodation product on factors other than price, but vacation travellers (especially families who travel) tend to be more selective with regard to the price of accommodation. Lodging properties design their services to suit the prices of the various price-sensitive segments of the market, and this is usually reflected in the star rating of properties (see page 25). A five-star property publicises its level of services and amenities and, in so doing, indicates that its product is aimed at a certain segment of the market. A budget motel also advertises a level of services that differentiates on price. Generally the targeted segmentation of the market by price is clearly evident in the accommodation sector.

A sound knowledge of how the hospitality market is segmented on price is essential when determining what rates to set for the accommodation product. (Note that 'price' is one of the 5Ps discussed above, see pages 186–7.)

Benefits and needs segmentation

For hotels, resorts, and associated restaurant facilities, the demand for services comes from three main groups—business travellers, conference travellers, and recreation or holiday travellers. These groups can be subdivided further. For example, business travellers can be subdivided into private-sector and public-sector travellers, whereas holiday travellers can be subdivided into travellers on a tourism package, backpackers, and so on. Each subgroup has different spending habits.

In making a decision on which market segment to target, the hospitality operator has to consider the attributes of the property. For example, is the property geared to meet the benefits and needs of business travellers, and/or convention travellers, and/or holiday travellers?

In the conference and convention sector, an enterprise should seek further information on this market segment as it relates to their actual and potential customers. For conference travellers, relevant information to seek out includes the number of conferences held in the market area, the number of participants, the length of stay, and the level of spending of participants. For recreational or holiday travellers on the other hand, an enterprise should seek statistics on their average length of stay, level of spending, and the length of the tourist season (and any potential changes to the season).

Psychographic segmentation

This heading includes people's preferences, their attitudes and preferences, their rate of usage, their recognition of brands, their purchasing habits and frequency, and so on. In hospitality terms, we ask about the preferences of guests who have already stayed with us, and compile a register of likes and dislikes. We might list their preferred transport needs and preferred standard of accommodation. We might also consider the duration and the times of year of their travel. When dividing the market by this factor, we might identify groups with special interests who come for specific events—perhaps a floral festival or a cultural festival, for example.

In addition to this five-fold division of the hospitality market (geographic, demographic, price, benefits/needs, and psychographic factors), the segments can be further segmented. For example, the geographic segmentation can be subdivided into regions, countries, districts, or even cultures within a country. As long as the four criteria for market segmentation are followed—similarities within a segment; differences among segments; useful and relevant criteria identifying the segment; and size of the segment (see pages 191–2)—there are many ways of dividing up target markets.

Target market approaches

When making a decision on the selection of which segments to target, the business might choose to specialise and target just one segment (this is called 'single-target marketing'). This alternative involves the organisation choosing one segment of the market and focusing on satisfying the needs of that segment—for example, backpacker hostels target the lower end of the market. There are advantages and disadvantages in this. The advantage is that the organisation can focus its resources on meeting the needs of only one group of customers, and become expert in looking after that segment of the market. The disadvantage is that the organisation is placing all its hopes for increased sales on one group, and if that group of customers decides that it no longer wants the organisation's product, the organisation is left without a market. Such a decision might be due to factors beyond the organisation's control. For example, if air fares rise excessively, backpackers might not be able to afford to travel to the destination, and backpacker hostels will lose custom.

The second alternative involves the organisation choosing more than one segment and developing separate marketing mixes to meet the needs of the individual segments ('multiple-target marketing'). This also has advantages and disadvantages. The advantage is that the organisation spreads its risk over several markets—thus overcoming the problem of the single-target marketing approach outlined above. The disadvantage is that resources are spread across different products and marketing mixes. They cannot be brought to bear to concentrate on just one market.

The third alternative involves the organisation choosing several segments that have relatively similar characteristics and then combining them to offer one basic marketing mix ('combined target marketing'). In this case, the organisation spreads its risk across several market segments, but can focus all of its resources on just one marketing mix. The disadvantage of this alternative is that in trying to satisfy the needs of different segments with the same marketing mix, the organisation might not satisfy the needs of individual segments very well. If competitors focus on one of the organisation's market segments, they might very well satisfy consumer needs better, thus disadvantaging the organisation that is trying to satisfy several groups with one mix.

To summarise, businesses with a product to offer choose a *target market* and try to satisfy the needs of the consumers within that market (creating appropriate *utilities*) through refining the *5Ps*. Every enterprise is influenced in some way by the environment in which it operates. No hospitality operation conducts its business in a vacuum. Its environment consists of its existing and potential customers, its competitors, and other factors outside its control.

There can be changes in the environment because of changes in:[12]

- consumer desires;
- fashions;

- technology;
- environmental concerns;
- legislation;
- the economic climate; and
- competition.

The operating environment is always changing in one respect or another, and its characteristics will be different from place to place, and from time to time. The operating environment can be monitored by a close examination of its general characteristics, and by a consideration of all the aspects of the business and marketing environment.[13]

The marketing environment

There are four aspects of an organisation's market environment:

- the competitive environment;
- the economic environment;
- the regulatory environment; and
- the cultural and social environment.

Each of these is considered below.

Competitive environment

The competitive environment is determined by the number and type of competitors faced by a business, and how those competitors behave. There are very few organisations that have no competitors. Some government-owned enterprises (for example, postal services) might seem to have no obvious competition in the area of letter delivery, but the real market is *communication*, and there are many ways in which people can communicate. Sending a letter is only one way of keeping in touch, and consumers can use telephone, fax, and email to communicate, or can send hardcopy letters (and packages) by courier. The competitive environment is therefore not as simple as it looks, and must be carefully analysed to determine the true nature of the competition.

Businesses might compete directly with each other in the same target markets—for example, the competition among five-star hotels in a central urban area all seeking to attract the very same target market. However, there are negative and positive aspects to direct competition. On the one hand, competitors seek to attract the targeted customers to their own services and away from others. However, on the other hand, competitive businesses in some cases can benefit one another, through market development activities that indirectly promote *all* the enterprises in that area of the industry. For example, a number of resort properties might market the attractiveness of their area and the increased demand for accommodation in that area benefits all.

When compiling their market strategy, enterprises must detail their competitive environment. In assessing the market environment, competitors need to be listed and analysed to determine their strengths and weaknesses in comparison with one's own operation. A business needs to consider not only existing competitors, but also potential competitors—businesses that might become competitors in the future.

In assessing competitors, the following sorts of questions need to be asked.

- What exactly is the product? Are we offering mainly accommodation, or are we primarily offering entertainment services? Should we consider the backpackers' hostel as a competitor to our new motel?
- What is the market geography? That is, how far afield should an organisation go in listing competitors?
- How do we get detailed information on our competitors? This does not necessarily imply what might be called 'industrial espionage'. One author has suggested that 95% of the information on competitors that an organisation needs to make marketing decisions is available and accessible to the general public—through advertising, agents, simple enquiries, and the like.[14]

An inventory of competitors should list existing or proposed accommodation venues that will be competitive by reason of the type of services, rating (two-star, five-star, and so on), size, location, and rates. The study should include information on whether the competitive properties are independent or affiliated to a chain. Information on the range of services offered (such as restaurants, bistros, entertainment, and so on) should also be included.

Some aspects of the inventory of competitors can be expressed in *quantitative* terms—for example listing number of beds and tariffs. Such information is usually available in hotel brochures and advertising material.

Other factors are more *qualitative* and difficult to assess—for example the benefits of location, or heritage value. These sorts of factors require a qualitative judgment by the appraiser.

Sometimes competitive barriers exist in an industry—barriers that will limit the entry of new competitors. Competitive barriers are operational factors that make it very difficult for new organisations to compete in a market—for example, the heavy financial commitment required for start-up. Such barriers exist when there is domination of the market by one or two large organisations—for example, the two large domestic airlines that dominate the air-passenger market in Australia. Competitive barriers are good for businesses that are already in an industry, because they place practical restrictions on prospective competitors.

Economic environment

The ability of the target market to consume the product on offer is affected by economic conditions—especially if that product is not a necessity of life. High inflation and interest rates reduce the amount of money that people have to spend, particularly on items that involve discretionary spending. The term 'discretionary spending' refers to items that are not essential. For example, spending money on food is *essential* expenditure, but spending money on a holiday is a *discretionary* matter that people can choose or not choose as they wish. Tourism and hospitality spending is largely discretionary for the non-business traveller—which means that if people have less money to spend, or if concern about future conditions causes them to save rather than spend, they will choose to do without a product or service that they see as unnecessary. Economic conditions can change rapidly, and such changes can be the result of events in other national economies.

Apart from deciding whether to spend at all, economic conditions can determine whether consumers will spend small amounts or large amounts. Competition becomes especially important in difficult economic times—for example, a consumer might choose a cheaper product by staying at a three-star establishment instead of a five-star establishment.

The marketing environment will also be affected by local economic trends. The economic environment of a local marketplace can be assessed through a number of sources—including a consideration of building approvals (listings available through local councils), and employment levels. The trend in building approvals over the last five years will be an indicator of future economic growth. Approvals for new infrastructure projects are another indicator of the strength of local economic growth. Large local projects normally reflect business confidence and the likelihood of further growth. An evaluation of general regional characteristics should also consider transport projects, and transport infrastructure—such as planned airport upgrades or highway development. Tourism in the region under evaluation can be seasonal. Clearly a beach resort, or a ski facility, will have clearly defined peak-demand periods based upon climate and holiday breaks.

Even a smaller hospitality operation, such as a restaurant, should take into account the prevailing economic climate and the likely changes in the near future. If interest rates are high, unemployment high, and confidence low, this must at least be taken into account. Niche ventures can do very well in uncertain climates (for example, backpacker hostels tend to increase their occupancy and their income in difficult financial times), but properties operating in the upper range of the market might not necessarily find the same to be true for them.

Regulatory environment

The 'regulatory environment' refers to the effect of political and legal actions of government (federal, state, and local) on the operation of the market.

Governments make laws and regulations that affect many businesses to varying degrees. Most governments have introduced laws to protect competition—which is viewed as beneficial in forcing businesses to make the best use of resources. Governments also introduce laws to protect consumers from unfair business practices. Apart from such competition and consumer law, there is a host of other government laws that affect the market environment in one way or another.

Government can also make subsidies available, both direct and indirect, to support and enhance industry development within targeted areas— although there is a worldwide trend to reduce the role of government intervention in the marketplace.

When designing market strategies, hospitality enterprises must consider where their planned operations might be hindered by the regulatory environment, and where their prospects could be enhanced.

Cultural and social environment

This area of the business environment concerns how people live and why they behave as they do. This, in turn, affects the buying behaviour of the target market. The cultural and social environment changes very slowly, but these changes cannot be ignored by business.

The environment of the tourism and hospitality industries has changed with changing trends in consumer preferences. The term 'trend' can be defined as a sequence of events that have some momentum and durability.[15]

Some identifiable trends in international trade today include:

- the increasing speed of international transportation and communications;
- the growth of global communication;
- the dissemination of global lifestyles;
- the opening of new markets in Asia, eastern Europe, and the Arab countries;
- the increase in product and service branding; and
- the globalisation of business and corporations.

All of these trends suggest that hospitality consumers and their needs have become more complex. These trends have influenced the hospitality product on offer. Few hospitality operations stand alone any more. To meet changing needs, hospitality operations have embraced vertical or horizontal integration of their services. The hospitality product now encompasses travel and entertainment, as well as accommodation and meals. The product is marketed to consumers as part of a package that might be a 'fly–drive' holiday to a resort area, or a business convention booking with two-day side trips. The increase in brand recognition and consumer loyalty schemes means that these packages are often marketed through a preferred carrier, or through a preferred service supplier.

Marketing research

The necessity of market research

An organisation must thus choose a target market, and develop a marketing mix to try to satisfy the needs of the targeted group of people. The organisation must also consider the limitations imposed by the marketing environment. Once a business has considered all of these variables, it then needs to consider how it can identify marketing opportunities and pursue them to their fullest potential. In hospitality, the product on offer is an experience that guests might share. There are always new opportunities in the hospitality marketplace—given the range of possible experiences and the number of places people wish to visit. The task is to identify those opportunities, and to assemble the resources and ability to do something about it.

In assessing opportunities in the market, a business needs to consider certain criteria (that is, certain factors upon which to base judgments). These criteria are based on a business's objectives and take into consideration the resources available and the impact of the environments. The criteria can be:

- *quantitative*—for example, increase sales by 2000 room–nights, or achieve a return on investment of 15%; or
- *qualitative*—for example, focus on better satisfying the needs of the current target market, or focus on better use of current resources, or focus on finding opportunities within the domestic market.

One common method used for evaluating market opportunities and the enterprise's position in the marketplace is illustrated by the Boston Consulting Group Matrix, developed by a leading management consulting firm.[16]

See Figure 7.1. On the *vertical* axis is the market growth rate. A rate of growth of less than 10% is considered low and more than 10% is high. On the *horizontal* axis is the relative market share—considered 'high' or 'low' in terms of the sales volume or share held by the market leader. Both axes must be considered in assessing market criteria. For example, most businesses start with a low market share (horizontal axis), but a high market growth rate (vertical axis). This leads to an assessment (in the top right-hand corner) of a 'question mark' over how to evaluate market opportunities. However, with work, the organisation should challenge the market leader and aim to grow their comparative share. If they have a high market growth rate and a high market share, they are probably fully utilising market opportunities. Then

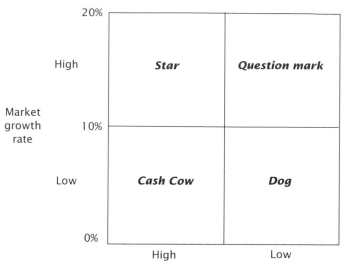

Figure 7.1 *Boston Consulting Group Matrix*

Kotler (1994), pp 56–7

the assessment will be in the top left-hand corner—a 'star', indicating that the business is performing well.

Continuing with an assessment of Figure 7.1, if the business has a low market share and a low market growth rate, the assessment ends in the bottom right-hand corner and can be considered a 'dog'. This business is not utilising opportunities in the market and radical decisions are needed— perhaps selling-off or closing-down the operation. If there is a low market growth rate and a high relative market share (bottom left-hand corner), clearly there will be sales revenue coming in ('cash cow') but the low growth would be a problem. The business should use the cash flow to change tack and grow again in the market.

To make good strategic decisions in the marketplace, good research data are required. All enterprises, including hospitality operations, generate and receive much information through their normal day-to-day operations—for example, sales data, profit data, guest or customer practices, and so on. To make the best use of the information available, it needs to be organised into a logical system so that it can be cross-referenced, and used in analysis of market trends and the nature of the demand in various market segments (with, of course, due regard for the private and confidential nature of any of the material used). The use of information technology (IT) systems, espe- cially database systems such as Microsoft Access, will help the business keep pace with its competitors.

Obtaining marketing research

All organisations receive information from three sources:

- internal data sources;
- external data sources; and
- market research studies.

Existing internal and external data sources should be able to answer many of the questions that managers have when they consider new marketing initiatives or promotions, or changes to the type and level of services provided. If answers cannot be found in existing data, the enterprise will need to undertake specific marketing research projects using some of the techniques described below.[17]

The characteristics of the market within which the business operates or plans to operate can be assessed through quantitative analysis or qualitative analysis.

Quantitative analysis deals with numbers—for example, the total number of guests staying at hotels subdivided among business, conference, or holiday categories.

Qualitative analysis assesses factors that cannot be expressed numerically—for example, the reasons that people give for having visited a region, and their satisfaction/dissatisfaction with their visit.

The information obtained over, say, a previous five-year period can be used for projections for growth over the next five years. If the market is a fast-moving one, such as with some types of restaurant, five years might be too long a time, and three years should be used. In markets where there are long time-spans of development, a longer period might be considered.[18]

We can seek information on general characteristics through a number of sources—which are called 'primary' and 'secondary' sources.

Primary sources

'Primary' information is that relating specifically to an operation and is gathered at first hand by the marketing team. In marketing terms, primary information is that gathered by survey researchers, who seek out original data on attitudes and opportunities for a product or service. 'Primary data' can be defined as '. . . information specifically collected to solve a current problem'.[19]

Primary data can be collected in four ways:[20]

- by direct observation;
- by surveys;
- by focus groups (small groups who discuss a proposal in depth); and
- by experiment (studying responses to proposals by matched groups).

Within these categories, the information can be recorded by questionnaires, by sampling plans, or by direct contact methods (such as mail, telephone, or personal interviewing).

Activity 7.3   *A target market for your product*

We continue on from Activities 7.1 (page 185) and 7.2 (page 188). In those Activities, you were asked to create and sell a product or service, and you were given exercises to carry out with respect to your new product.

Now you are asked to return to you product or service of Activities 7.1 and 7.2, and:

- closely specify the target market; and
- consider where and how you would research that market.

Secondary sources

Other sources of information are existing government, local government, and industry sources. Accessing these sources is referred to as 'desk research'.[21] These sources are termed 'secondary' sources because the information has already been gathered, summarised, and categorised by industry or government organisations. 'Secondary data' can be defined as data that have ' . . . already been collected or published'.[22]

Information from all these sources should include both descriptive (qualitative) and statistical (quantitative) data.

Qualitative research will seek in-depth opinion on services and products, using structured questions in surveys or questionnaires to focus on the needs and wants of consumers. Examples are mail or telephone surveys.

Quantitative research records the absolute number of consumers who use a service, or the number of persons who share certain characteristics as a group.

Interpreting the information

What does it all mean? The information collected through an analysis of the general market environment must always be subject to a review process to ensure that it is interpreted correctly—especially if statistics are used, or sample surveys are completed. Statistics should be cross-tabulated, or subject to referral to a second source of information to ensure that the data are consistent with other studies. Samples used in surveys must be representative of the population from which the sample was taken.

Questionnaires must also be checked, and any inconsistent responses reviewed. It might be that respondents have been biased in their answers—either from personal bias, or from a deliberate motive to mislead the appraiser. Perhaps some people try to be helpful and are too optimistic in projecting trends and possibilities for the future.

The validity of conclusions is dependent upon the validity and accuracy of the information collected. If the information is in doubt, the research should be repeated—if possible with different sources.

Activity 7.4   *Gathering data*

Imagine that you are to open a fifty-bed backpacker-style hostel in a beach-side area.
- Decide upon what form of primary data you would wish to obtain, and what methods you would use to obtain them. Give your reasons for selecting your methods.
- With the collection methods you have chosen, survey other members of your class or educational institute to gather meaningful data on such aspects as the overnight rate you could charge and the likely demand for your product.
- Compare your findings with those of other groups who do the same activity.

For each group that is considered, the operator must then determine the level of existing demand and the likely growth in demand for a five-year period—with estimates divided into low-range growth projections (conservative), mid-range growth projections (moderate), and high-range growth projections (optimistic).

For business travellers, information on the likely growth in the target market could include growth in local airport traffic and growth in office-space occupancy. High demand in each of these areas is often reflected in the demand for hotel and restaurant services.

Possible sources of information on the development of a market include:

- local travel agents and tour operators;
- other local businesses whose business is dependent upon the number of visitors—such as managers of buslines, or agents for car-hire firms; and
- comparable hotels in the area.

With regard to the last of these, note that hotels within a region are usually prepared to share information such as occupancy and average room rate. The information is useful to all the participants—not just to compare their own performance, but to understand regional trends in the industry.

If the demand for accommodation or other services for the target market has been high, how has the market reacted? Have room rates increased, or been higher than the average elsewhere, as a result of the under-supply of the service?

Evidence of a market with an undersupply of a service could be:

- high levels of development in a competing centre;
- the emergence of alternatives such as home accommodation;
- instability in the local economy as a result of tourist-orientated activities operating at less than optimum;
- a distortion in the market whereby visitors are commuting long distances; or even
- a cutback in demand to match the difficulties of undersupply.

Is the quality of the existing product being offered appropriate to the demand? Various studies suggest that matching consumer demand with level of services should be one of the main objectives of management in developing a new hotel.[23] Such information can be obtained from formal or informal surveys of visitors and industry sources. Statistics on repeat visits to a region or area can indicate whether quality meets demand—for if visitors come once but not again, a possibility is that the standard of service that they received was not what they demanded.

Evidence of a 'gap' in the range of services offered can arise if statistics of accommodation by quality level (that is, five-star down) in one area are compared with another. Assuming a similar visitor profile, the demand for each category of accommodation should be broadly comparable.

Activity 7.5   *Ethical consideration*

You are relaxing at a bar with workmates and a friend who works at another hotel offers you a computer disk with details of names and addresses of guests and customers of that other hotel. The marketing potential is, of course, enormous. The hotel where you work can conduct a mailout to the competitors' customers with special offers concerning rates and services tailored to attract them.

QUESTIONS

- Would you accept the disk from your friend?
- If the disk were offered by an employee of the other hotel who was not previously known to you, would you pay for it?

Chapter review questions

1 What role does the marketing department play in an already successful city hotel?
2 What is the difference between marketing and sales?
3 Describe the market segment of a budget motel in a rural area.
4 What are some sources of information on the marketplace?
5 Often marketing is seen as an expensive extravagance with no measurable outcomes. What data can a marketing manager produce to show the department's success?

CASE STUDY

The HB Hotel

The company that owns the HB Hotel has decided to buy another hotel in a coastal resort area. Accordingly, they have asked you, as manager of HB Hotel, to help select an appropriate property and location.

To do this, you are required to look through real estate agents' properties for sale and choose a coastal location you think would ensure good and sustainable business.

Once the property and location have been decided upon you are required to justify your selection through the collection of data—for example, visitor demographics of the region, local competition, the market mix of the hotel, and the infrastructure (that is, road, rail, airport, marina, and so on).

The owners of HB Hotels do not mind what form the hotel will take, but are not prepared to spend more than $4 million on the entire investment.

Chapter 8

Hospitality Accounting

It is likewise to be observed that this society hath a peculiar chant and jargon of their own, that no other mortal can understand, and wherein all their laws are written, which they take special care to multiply.

Jonathan Swift
Gulliver's Travels

Synopsis of chapter

The chapter deals first with basic accounting concepts, and then the uniform system of accounts—the common accounting statement format used in many hospitality operations. Procedures for cash-handling and receipts and payments are detailed. Finally there is a more detailed discussion and models of pricing and budgeting for a restaurant operation, and pricing and budgeting for a hotel or motel.

What is accounting? Basic accounting concepts

Accounting as a diagnostic science

Accounting is a science, a diagnostic science. Like all diagnostic sciences, accounting requires the accurate and timely recording of data based on observable reality, the organisation of these data, and then analysis and diagnosis of the information. Interested parties use accounting information to make decisions concerning the allocation of resources.

There are really only three questions to ask when using accounting information.

- What happened?
- Why did it happen?
- What has to be done about it?

Hospitality managers use accounting diagnosis to make external and internal decisions concerning the operation of the organisations for which they have responsibility.

To illustrate, consider the construction and maintenance of motor vehicles. This has become a science. The design and development of modern motor vehicles has made the diagnosis of mechanical problems more a matter for computer-assisted machines rather than for the backyard tinkerer. Certainly vehicles might have simple and obvious problems that the unskilled can assess and repair—for example, a flat tyre that often seems to happen when you are late for a job interview (although never for a dentist's appointment!). When the problem is more complex (such as a steering difficulty), or near-impossible for unaided human skill to detect (such as ignition timing faults), extra skills are needed to rectify the fault. There are longer-term matters, such as engine wear, that need specialised tools to detect. Even when the vehicle is running smoothly, some questions arise that need engineering analysis. What is a safe speed for cornering? What is a safe load for the vehicle to carry?

The role of accounting is to offer a similar diagnosis and analysis for management. If the organisation has financial problems, accounting systems should make them apparent and offer possible solutions for management. If the organisation needs fine-tuning, accounting should suggest which levers to 'tweak' to improve operations. Various accounting statements provide different sorts of information:

- *balance sheets* reveal the financial situation of the organisation at a point in time;
- *income statements* reveal what has happened over a period in time (in the above analogy of a motor vehicle, being similar to the car's speedometer which indicates how it is travelling); and
- *budget statements* indicate where the organisation (like the car) is likely to go.

Just as the design and operation of a motor vehicle is determined by rules and principles—ranging from design principles to the road rules—that determine how the car should be driven, so accounting statements are subject to conventions, rules, doctrines, principles, and standards that determine what should be included in the statement and what valuations should be used.

Accounting cannot make a diagnosis of non-financial matters. Such *qualitative* matters as the standard of service, organisation behaviour, and the aesthetics of design are outside the purview of accounting. To continue our analogy, we might say that accounting does not consider these qualitative matters just as the design of a motor vehicle cannot take into account qualitative matters such as the behaviour of the driver (the 'nut behind the wheel'), or just as the colour of the car is irrelevant to its engineering.

Accounting for hospitality

Hospitality accounting needs care and diligence
Courtesy Parkroyal Hotel, Canberra

Hotels and restaurants and resorts are categorised as service industries—because the product that they are offering is consumed day by day and is based upon human activity. Within these industries there is a number of different activities. For example, in food services, meals are manufactured either as a single product from time to time, or as a batch. Hence, *some* characteristics of accounting for manufacturing are required—such as recording and allocating production overheads. However, food services seldom keep large inventories of work-in-progress from one accounting period to the next and so the manufacturing accounting techniques of recording raw material, work-in-progress, and finished goods inventories will not generally be applied. It is true that large hotel kitchens prepare desserts, entrées, and pastries in quantity, days before consumption, but these quantities are not large enough to justify the design and use of special accounting systems.

In the hospitality industry, there are extensive retail activities—particularly with regard to beverage sales and merchandising operations. There are also aspects of the hospitality industry involving unique accounting problems—for example, accounting for functions and other large one-off events.

This range of operations means that hospitality managers require comprehensive accounting reports, and three main types of accounting reports—the balance sheet, the income statement, and the budget statement—are considered below.

Activity 8.1   Determining Mr Hunter's financial position

Mr Hunter wants to borrow $100 000. This money will be used for a holiday to Antarctica for six months because Mr Hunter has never been there. You are going to meet him and discuss whether you will lend him the money at 10% interest over ten years.

Mr Hunter is divorced and the father of three grown children who now support themselves. His work as a buffalo-hunter is very demanding physically, and work injuries are common. Moreover, in this activity, every year one worker in twenty loses his job. His workers' compensation insurance is mandatory and costs $2000 per year. The compensation for lost wages is for 90% of the current year's estimated income in the first year following an incapacitating injury, 50% in the second year, and nothing thereafter. Each spring Mr Hunter signs a contract for six months of intensive work in various parts of northern Australia, and each six-month contract earns him $70 000.

Mr Hunter lives in a house that he bought for $90 000 fifteen years ago. The house costs him $3000 per year in expenses (rates, upkeep, and so on). The mortgage has been completely paid and the council valuation shows an unimproved land value of $20 000 for the property. It is insured for $120 000. Recently a neighbour who wanted to extend his own house offered in writing to buy Mr Hunter's house for $125 000. Mr Hunter refused, saying that he liked his home and that it wasn't for sale!

Mr Hunter's furniture has an 'in-use' value of $6000 and an 'antique' value of $16 000.

His car isn't worth much, having been damaged by a buffalo. This has been confirmed by the insurance company (which refuses to insure it) and the garage owner (who doesn't guarantee his repairs of $2500 per year). Mr Hunter still thinks that the car is worth about $1000 because it allows him to save about that much per year (on buses, taxi fares, and so on).

Aside from a dinosaur skeleton that he came across many years ago (and legally purchased) that decorates his garage, Mr Hunter has few other worldly goods. However, he does have an expert's appraisal that sets the value of this skeleton at $500 000, but it's not for sale (and never will be because Mr Hunter thinks it is the most beautiful thing he has ever seen).

Finally, everything is 'going well' for Mr Hunter—except for a $250 000 lawsuit against him that should be settled in a few months. A visitor was hit by a tile that fell from Mr Hunter's roof and is suing him for his injuries.

Unfortunately, Mr Hunter has no insurance covering this kind of loss and his lawyer estimates that the odds of his losing the case are about 60%

Mr Hunter is preparing his case and documents for a loan. He feels that these will be useful in convincing the banker to lend him the money. He does not own any assets of value other than those specified above.

QUESTION

- List all pertinent information and state whether you would lend Mr Hunter $100 000 on the above terms and conditions.

The uniform system of accounts

What is the 'uniform system of accounts'?

The uniform system of accounts was developed in 1925 by the Hotels Association of New York. Since then, it has been adopted by many hospitality organisations, both in the United States and in other countries as well. The system sets out the categories to be used for various expenses (such as linen, glassware, and so on), and its great advantage is that it allows standards and comparisons among properties and the calculation of industry averages in areas such as payroll costs.

The uniform system lists virtually all the different types of receipts and disbursements that come about in the course of operating a hospitality business. It then facilitates the compilation of summary reports—one such summary report being called a 'balance sheet' and another an 'income statement'. The collection of all the different types of receipts and disbursements is referred to as the 'chart of accounts'. These accounts can be either 'debit' or 'credit'.

We have been conditioned to believe that a 'credit' is a good thing, because a credit balance at our bank or shop means that we have funds in hand, whereas a 'debit' must be bad, because then we are 'in the red' and owe money. In fact, 'debit' simply refers to an entry on the left hand side of the ledger, or book of accounts, and a 'credit' is an entry on the right, and every transaction must have both a debit and a credit side.

See Figure 8.1 (pages 212–15) for an example of a large restaurant's chart of accounts that conforms to the uniform system. It is subdivided into categories, and indicates whether those categories are usually debit or credit.

Element	Category	Account Name	Number
ASSETS	**current assets**		
1XX numbers	cash	petty cash	111
(usually debit		cash floats	112
balances except		cash at bank	113
where noted)	accounts receivable	customers	121
		employees	122
		other	123
		provision for doubtful debts (credit)	124
	inventories	food	131
		beverages	132
		other	133
	prepaid expenses	insurance	141
		licences	142
		other	143
	non-current assets		
	fixed assets	furniture and fittings	151
		F & F depreciation (credit)	152
		plant and equipment	153
		P & E depreciation (credit)	154
		leasehold improvements	155
		leasehold amortisation (credit)	156
	other assets	goodwill	161
		goodwill amortisation (credit)	162
LIABILITIES	**current liabilities**		
2XX numbers		accounts payable	211
(usually credit		GST tax payable	212
balances except		accrued wages	221
where noted)		accrued rent	222
		accrued interest	223
		accrued utilities	224
		deposits in advance	231
		current portion of long-term debt	241
	long-term liabilities	bank loan	251
		other	252
OWNERS'	shareholding	ordinary shares	311
EQUITY		share premium reserve	312
3XX numbers		retained earnings	313
(usually credit			
balances)			

Figure 8.1 *Sample chart of accounts—Yass River Restaurant*

Kevin Baker

Element	Category	Account Name	Number
SALES 4XX numbers (always credit balances)		food beverages retained earnings	411 412 313
COST OF SALES 5XX numbers (always debit balances)		cost of sales—food cost of sales—beverages	511 512
OTHER INCOME 6XX numbers (always credit balances)		cash discounts commissions miscellaneous	611 612 613
CONTROLLABLE COSTS 7XX numbers (usually debits)	wages (direct costs)	food-service wages food-preparation wages cleaning wages bartending wages	711 712 713 714
	employee benefits and overheads	public holidays annual leave & leave loading superannuation employee meals employee beverages workers' comp insurance other	721 722 724 725 726 727 728
	other direct costs	tableware (<$200) kitchen utensils (<$200) other kitchen requisites linen paper supplies uniforms menus and beverage lists decorations laundry pest control delivery expenses licences	731 732 733 734 735 736 737 738 739 740 741 742
	entertainment	musicians professional entertainers audio rental royalties agents' fees meals	751 752 753 754 755 756

Figure 8.1 *Sample chart of accounts—Yass River Restaurant*

(continued)

Kevin Baker

Element	Category	Account Name	Number
	marketing	marketing salaries	761
		marketing wage overheads (incl. insur.)	762
		advertising	763
		public relations	764
		complimentary meals/beverages	765
		printing/preparation	766
		travel	767
	administrative costs	administrative wages/ salaries (non-management)	771
		administrative wage overheads (incl. workers' comp. insurance)	772
		stationery/printing	773
		postage & courier	774
		telephone & email	775
		travel	776
		insurance	777
		bank charges	778
		cash short or over	780
		bad or doubtful debts	781
		general insurance	782
		repairs & maintenance (equipment)	783
		repairs & maintenance (other)	784
	utilities	electricity	791
		gas	792
		water	793
		garbage removal	794
FIXED COSTS 8XX numbers (usually debits)	occupancy costs	rent	811
		council service rates	812
	interest	overdraft interest	821
		long-term loan interest	822
	depreciation and amortisation	furniture & fixtures	831
		plant & equipment	832
		leasehold	833
		goodwill	834
	other	management salaries	841
		management benefits	842
		legal fees & charges	843
		miscellaneous	844

(continued)

Figure 8.1 *Sample chart of accounts—Yass River Restaurant*

Kevin Baker

Element	Category	Account Name	Number
TAXES 850 numbers (usually debit or zero)		income taxes	850
		GST	851
CONTRA ACCOUNTS 9XX numbers (debits or credits; must be zero at the end of the accounting period)		customer contras	911
		employee contras	912
		general suspense	999

(continued)

Figure 8.1 *Sample chart of accounts—Yass River Restaurant*

Kevin Baker

The balance sheet

The balance sheet lists all the items of value (assets) that an organisation owns—less liabilities, or legal obligations that are attached to those assets. The remainder is what the owners are entitled to take away—in other words, their equity in the assets, or their net ownership of the business. Ownership can also be expressed as 'proprietorship'. Ownership can take one of three forms—a sole trader, a partnership (which is a formal agreement among two or more parties), or a company. Where the business is a company, ownership is represented by shares in the entity. In the United States of America, the words 'stock' and 'stockholding' are used instead of 'shares', or 'shareholding'.

For a company, owners' equity can be further divided into the profits of the business that have not yet been distributed to the shareholders as dividends (referred to as 'retained earnings' or 'accumulated profits') and other headings that describe various reserves created by the issue of shares or the setting aside of profits for a specific purpose. Examples of these headings include 'share premium reserves', 'capital investment reserves', and so on. The balance sheet therefore is an equation, in which:

$$\text{assets} - \text{liabilities} = \text{owners' equity}$$

This equation can also be expressed as:

$$\text{assets} = \text{liabilities} + \text{owners' equity}$$

The left-hand side of the latter form of this equation is expressed in debit terms, and the right-hand side as a credit. Hence, increasing items on the left (assets) will be reflected by a debit entry in the accounts, and the items on the right (liabilities and owners' equity) will be credits.

The uniform system of accounts provides a guide for how much information and detail to include in the balance sheet. The sheet itself can be presented as shown in Figure 8.2 (page 217), which illustrates a sample balance sheet for a restaurant using the format of the uniform system of accounts. The data for two years can be compared in this format. Note that the data are presented in dollars, and also as a percentage of a significant total—in this case total assets (which, of course, will also be total liabilities and owners' equity, because of the rule of the accounting equation). This balance sheet allows comparisons and analysis of performance between one year and the next.

The assets and the liabilities are subdivided into current and non-current. Current items will be turned over, or converted into cash in the ordinary course of business trading within twelve months. Non-current items generally refer to the longer-term items of the business. Some of those non-current assets that are consumed over several accounting periods are 'depreciated' or 'amortised'—which means that the amount paid for them is distributed as an expense over their useful life. A cynical accountant once said that depreciation is something that you claim happened when you are putting in your tax return, but is something that you claim never happened when you are talking to someone about buying your business!

There will usually be notes attached to the balance sheet, explaining or adding detail to the items. For example, the notes will explain how the amounts recorded for some long-term assets (such as buildings) are being reduced, to take account of how the assets are being consumed in the course of business activity. This reduction is referred to as 'depreciation'.

What is or is not an asset? For an asset (or item of value) to be recorded on the balance sheet, it must:

- be owned by the entity;
- have economic benefit; and
- be capable of having its value fairly recorded (based on evidence of historical cost).

Thus, even intangible items that do not appear to have a physical existence are treated as assets. These could include the value of goodwill, or the value of a brand name, or something that is prepaid (such as rent). The assets are divided into current and non-current. Current assets will be turned into cash normally within twelve months—such as inventory or stock items. Non-current assets (or 'fixed' assets, or 'capital' assets) are assets that are used by the business in the longer term.

Some items can be classed as assets or classed as costs. For example, staff uniforms could be treated as assets (because they are owned by the purchaser) or they could be classed as costs (because of the expense at the time of purchase). The uniform system of accounts generally treats them as an asset.

Liabilities are those items for which the entity has a present legally enforceable obligation to pay, and for which the amount of the obligation can be reliably measured.

	2002	%		2003	%
ASSETS					
Current assets					
Cash on hand	225			270	
Cash at bank	4 590	4 815	1.4	9 000	9 270	2.8
Accounts receivable		34 200	10.2		37 800	11.3
Inventory (food)	18 000			22 950	
Inventory (beverage	41 400	59 400	17.8	36 000	58 950	17.6
Total current assets		**98 415**	**29.5**		**106 020**	**31.7**
Fixed Assets					
Tableware, linen, uniforms		25 200	7.6		25 200	7.5
Furniture & equipment	55 800			55 800	
Less: accum. deprec.	−13 500	42 300	12.7	−18 900	36 900	11.0
Buildings	76 500			76 500	
Less: accum. deprec.	−7 650	68 850	20.6	−9 180	67 320	20.1
Land		99 000	29.7		99 000	29.6
Total fixed assets		**235 350**	**70.5**		**228 420**	**68.3**
TOTAL ASSETS		**333 765**	**100.0**		**334 440**	**100.0**
LIABILITIES					
Current Liabilities					
Accounts payable		7 200	2.2		16 200	4.8
Accrued expenses		2 880	0.9		5 040	1.5
Short-term loan		80 000	24.0		0	0.0
Total current liabilities		**90 080**	**27.0**		**21 240**	**6.4**
Long-term Liabilities					
Mortgage		72 000	21.6		66 656	19.9
TOTAL LIABILITIES		**162 080**	**48.6**		**87 896**	**26.3**
OWNERS' EQUITY					
Shareholding		150 000	44.9		150 000	44.9
Accumulated profits		6 883	2.1		21 685	6.5
Current year's profit		14 802	4.4		74 859	22.4
TOTAL OWNERS' EQUITY		**171 685**	**51.4**		**246 544**	**73.7**
TOTAL LIAB. & OWNERS' EQUITY		**333 765**	**100.0**		**334 440**	**100.0**

Figure 8.2 *Comparative Balance Sheets for the years ending 30 June 2002 and 30 June 2003—Central Tourist Restaurant, The Terrace, Wellington*
Kevin Baker

The income statement

A profit or a loss is the net result of revenue (income being received through trading activity) and expenses (the outgoing related to the receipt of income).

To record what has happened over a period, the first step is to compile a schedule of these items. This schedule is referred to as an 'income statement', although other terms are sometimes used (such as 'profit-and-loss statement' or 'revenue/expense statement'). Whatever name it has, the income statement is intended to show simply whether the operation makes a profit after all the costs of the operation (including taxation) are accounted for.

Figure 8.3 (page 219) is an example of an income statement prepared to conform with the uniform system of accounts.

The information could be presented in a shorter form (see Figure 8.4, page 220), whereby net results from the various departments are reported (instead of showing full details of cost of sales, and direct payroll, and other expenses). The individual departments in this case can be referred to as 'revenue' centres, for they generate their own income and the expenses deducted from that income are what are incurred directly in earning the income.

Income categories

Income, or revenue, results from the sale of goods and services by the operation over a period, and these proceeds are recorded first, before being matched with the expenses of the same period. Note that 'income' does not normally include the proceeds of the sale of assets, say equipment, which is something that occurs only from time to time and does not constitute the usual trading activity of the enterprise. The recording of income is made when the transaction occurs—when the room is sold, or when the meal has been concluded—rather than when the cash for the transaction is actually received. Income is usually recorded when the invoice, or account, has been raised—although income that can be claimed, even if the invoice is not yet raised, can be said to be 'accrued' and therefore can be included in the income statement.

Expense categories

The largest expense category is payroll—labour charges for wages and salaries, and the associated costs such as allowances and benefits, leave provisions, payroll taxes, and superannuation. Because this category (as well as others that follow) is made up of hours worked and rates of pay that are set by common awards in Australia, the overall cost is comparable with other similar operations. Some costs vary with the number of guests, or the volume of business. These costs are termed 'variable costs' and are calculated

TOTAL SALES			1 174 300
INCOME BY DEPARTMENTS			
Rooms			
Sales	638 851.00		
Labour costs	−108 879.50		
Other direct costs	−49 409.50		
Rooms income	**480 562.00**	480 562	
Food & beverage			
Sales	354 121.00		
Cost of sales	−113 783.20		
Labour costs	−140 497.50		
Other direct costs	−33 155.82		
Food & beverage income	**66 684.48**	66 684	
Conference facility			
Sales	123 420.00		
Labour costs	−67 040.00		
Other direct costs	−41 879.00		
Conference income	**14 501.00**	14 501	
Telephone			
Sales	36 018.00		
Cost of sales	−22 198.00		
Labour costs	−5 826.00		
Other direct costs	−1 800.50		
Telephone income	**6 193.50**	6 193	
TOTAL DEPARTMENTAL INCOME			567 940
MERCHANDISING, RENTALS ETC. 21 890.00		21 890	21 890
TOTAL OPERATING INCOME			589 830
UNDISTRIBUTED OPERATING EXPENSES			
Administrative & general		87 217.00	
Marketing		54 521.00	
Property maintenance & operation		55 470.40	
Utility costs		68 416.80	
Total undist. operating expenses		265 625	265 625
Income before fixed charges		324 205	
FIXED CHARGES			
Rates and charges		28 364.20	
Insurance		51 312.40	
Depreciation		52 068.80	
Interest		47 164.40	
TOTAL FIXED CHARGES		**178 909**	178 909
INCOME BEFORE TAXES			145 297
Income taxes			49 811
NET INCOME			95 486

Note the item 'cost of sales' at various points in the above statement. This is also referred to as 'cost of goods sold', but in hospitality we prefer not to speak about food products as 'goods' that we sell. The term 'cost of sales' means the direct cost of the materials that are used to produce the product.

Figure 8.3 *Income Statement for the period 1 July 2002 to 30 June 2003—
Baker's Seaside Hotel and Motel*

Kevin Baker

INCOME BY DEPARTMENTS		
Rooms	480 563.00	
Food	35 582.00	
Beverage	31 102.00	
Conference facility	14 501.00	
Telephone	6 193.00	
Merchandising, rentals, etc.	21 890.00	589 831
Total operating income		**589 831**
LESS UNDISTRIBUTED OPERATING EXPENSES		
Administrative & general	87 217.00	
Marketing	54 521.00	
Property maintenance & operation	55 470.40	
Utility costs	68 416.80	265 625
Income before fixed charges		**324 206**
LESS FIXED CHARGES		
Rates and charges	28 364.20	
Insurance	51 312.40	
Depreciation	52 068.80	
Interest	47 164.40	178 909
INCOME BEFORE TAXES		**145 297**
Less income tax		49 811
NET INCOME		**95 486**

Figure 8.4 *Summary income statement for the period 1 July 2002 to
30 June 2003—Baker's Seaside Hotel and Motel*

Kevin Baker

on the basis of total sales—which measures the economic activity of the operation.

Payroll costs do not easily fit within this description—because some payroll costs vary with the number of guests (such as casual cleaning hours) whereas some are fixed (for example, the enterprise must still pay full-time staff regardless of how many guests are in the establishment). Payroll costs are best treated as 'mixed' costs—containing both variable and fixed elements.

For food & beverage, there is an item termed 'cost of sales' (also referred to as 'cost of goods sold') which is the material cost of the meals and drinks services. Cost of sales can usually be estimated at around 30% of food & beverage revenue (allowing up to 35% as cost of sales of liquor and 25–30% as cost of sales of food). 'Other expenses' include miscellaneous costs that can be directly related to that income heading—such as cleaning materials or the like.

Some expenses are not able to be allocated directly to income headings, and these expenses are therefore referred to as 'undistributed' expenses in the sense that the amounts included there cannot be divided up among the income headings—because the proportion of expense that should be divided and allocated is unclear. For example, marketing for the restaurant or hotel is an expense that is clearly difficult to divide up and allocate to rooms income or to food & beverage—so it is left as one total and shown under a separate section of expenses.

Expenses need not include just those items that have been paid in cash. There are non-cash expenses that are included on the income statement—such as depreciation. There are also expenses that have not yet been claimed by the creditor by the submission of an invoice, but for which the organisation has incurred the cost—such as telephone or utility accounts. These non-cash expenses are said to be accrued, in a similar fashion to the accrual of revenues that are not yet invoiced.

The financial statements for other types of hospitality enterprises (for example, restaurants) will differ from the above examples, especially in the income statements. Balance sheets will not vary as much (and that is why the example of a restaurant was offered as an example of a balance sheet above). However, to illustrate some differences found in income statements, Figure 8.5 (page 222) is given as an example. The format is that of a comparative income statement—that is, it compares the data for two or more years, expressing the differences in both percentage and absolute terms.

Journals

The daily transactions of the business are recorded in a source document referred to as a 'journal', the word being derived from the Latin for 'day'. The source document can be hardcopy or electronic. It can be one general document, a general journal for the business, or it can be subdivided into sales journal, wages journal, debtors journal, and so on—depending upon the volume of transactions. The subdivision is intended to make the handling of a large volume of transactions of a similar nature (for example, sales) easier to handle. Periodically, the entries in the journal are transferred (or 'posted') to the ledger accounts. Computer accounting systems usually carry out the posting function automatically and distribute the data into the appropriate financial statements. Journals can come in more than one form.

Procedures for cash-handling

Accounting for cash

The word 'cash' comes from the French word casse (and from Italian cassa, Latin capsa) meaning a 'case' or 'box'.[1] The etymology refers to coins kept in a safety box. Today, the definition of 'cash' includes not only coins and paper

	1/7/2002–30/6/03	1/7/2001–30/6/02	% difference	$ difference
Sales				
Food	883 174.70	945 188.00	−6.6	−62 013
Beverage	298 497.20	314 207.80	−5.0	−15 711
Total sales	**1 181 671.90**	**1 252 572.21**	**−5.7**	**−70 900**
Cost of Sales				
Food	372 669.58	382 029.40	−2.5	−9 360
Beverage	81 107.20	83 479.00	−2.8	−2 372
Total cost of sales	**453 776.78**	**465 508.40**	**−2.5**	**−11 732**
Gross profit				
Food	510 505.13	563 158.60	−9.3	−52 653
Beverage	217 390.00	230 728.80	−5.8	−13 339
Other income	6 837.00	6 027.00	13.4	810
Total income	**734 732.13**	**799 914.40**	**−8.1**	**−65 182**
Controllable expenses				
Employee wages	250 697.00	275 288.00	−8.9	−24 591
Employee benefits	25 707.65	28 334.80	−9.3	−2 627
Marketing	21 465.30	20 670.00	3.8	795
Music & entertainment	11 198.80	9 860.00	13.6	1 339
Utilities	30 816.40	30 224.30	2.0	592
Maintenance	12 833.60	16 890.00	−24.0	−4 056
Administrative costs	56 973.20	55 822.00	2.1	1 151
Other direct costs	67 599.40	66 789.25	1.2	810
Total controllable expenses	**477 291.35**	**503 878.35**	**−5.3**	**−26 587**
Income before fixed charges	**257 440.78**	**296 036.05**	**−13.0**	**−38 595**
Fixed charges				
Rent	61 060.20	61 060.20	0.0	0
Insurance	17 738.00	17 082.00	−3.8	656
Depreciation	29 181.60	30 097.00	−3.0	−915
Interest	6 294.40	5 874.65	7.1	420
Total fixed charges	**114 274.20**	**114 113.85**	**0.1**	**160**
Income before taxes	**143 166.58**	**181 922.20**	**−21.3**	**−38 756**
Income tax	55 834.96	70 949.66		
Net income	**87 331.61**	**110 972.54**	**−21.3**	**−23 641**

Figure 8.5 *Comparative income statements for the two years 2001/02 and 2002/03—No Riffraff Restaurant*

Kevin Baker

money, but also cheques, money orders, and funds kept on deposit at a bank. Accounting principles relating to cash-handling include the following:

- the person responsible for the handling of cash must not be the same person who records the cash transactions in the accounts;
- all cash receipts from an operating area must be deposited intact in the bank each day;
- as far as possible, a double record of cash-handling should be maintained and be reconciled regularly (for example, cash-register tapes should be reconciled to bank deposits); and
- all major payments must be made by cheque or direct bank transfer, and the only cash payments should be minor ones, controlled from a petty-cash fund.

Cash should never be drawn from registers or floats for small purchases, but a separate petty-cash fund should be held and kept in a secure locked receptacle (such as a tin) under the control of one person and one person only. Expenditure from the fund should be backed up by numbered vouchers signed by the person making the expenditure and the person responsible for the fund.

Receipts

The responsibility for receiving and dealing with cash in an operating area should be nominated to just one person (or a group of people working under the direct supervision of an authorised person) who should not also have responsibility for writing up the cash book, nor have responsibility for preparing bank deposits. An example of the duties of cashiers include the issuing of cash float and the receipt of cash from registers. Where cash is received other than through a register (for example, by post) cash-receipt dockets should be immediately issued. These dockets should be numbered and kept secure and issued as needed. Duplicate receipt dockets should be issued only on a manager's authorisation. Cash received through the post should be controlled by having two people open mail as it is received.

Payments

Payments should be made by cheque (with the exception of the small payments made by petty cash). The issue of cheques should be controlled by maintaining a register of cheque numbers and maintaining the blank cheques under lock and key until they are issued in a reasonable quantity shortly before they are required for use. Because of their nature as legal documents, the cheques themselves need to be secure. There should also be controls over the signatories (that is, those required to authorise the payments).

Controlling stock—Pareto's Law

Pareto's Law refers to statistics and frequency distribution curves, and discusses instances where the significant members of a group are only a small portion of the total number of the group.

Pareto's Law is behind a shortcut to control of stock where there is a large number of items held in inventory. In many food & beverage operations, 10% of the items might constitute 70% of the total value; a further 10% of the items might be a further 20% of the value, and 80% of the items might constitute just 10% of the value. Instead of spending staff time to stocktake all items every time a count is done, the following more efficient system is suggested:

- keep regular and detailed records of every item of the 10% that make up 70% of the value;
- keep records of the total and make periodic counts of the next 10%; and
- make infrequent counts and rely on estimates for the last 80% of stock that constitute 10% of the value.

Pricing and budgeting for a restaurant

Projected restaurant income statements for pricing and costing

The first step in preparing a budget to be used in pricing product or services is to prepare an estimate of forward earnings. Revenue figures are based on estimates for seat turnover and average check for each meal period as well as the number of seats and days of opening. Food & beverage revenue for a restaurant can be calculated by using a basic calculation:[2]

$$\text{revenue} = \text{number of seats} \times \text{seat turnover rate} \times \text{average check} \times \text{days open each year}$$

The number of seats in each venue and the days open each year can be readily determined, but clearly the seat turnover rate and the average check are subject to estimate. The calculation should be repeated for each meal period, even for interim breaks, because the pattern of usage will vary.

For example, assume that an operator has a 60-seat coffee shop and an 80-seat restaurant, both open every day of the year with average checks of $3.50–$5.00 for the coffee shop and average checks of $12–$15 for the restaurant (although limited patronage on the weekends reduces the seat turnover rate, and some promotional packages might reduce the average check). See Figure 8.6, page 225.

Coffee shop—projected revenue			
Breakfast	$60 \times 0.5 \times \$5.00 \times 365$	$54 750	
Lunch	$60 \times 0.75 \times \$6.00 \times 365$	$98 550	
Other periods	$60 \times 0.25 \times \$3.50 \times 365$	$19 162	
Total Revenue		**$172 462**	**$172 462**
Restaurant—projected revenue			
Lunch	$80 \times 0.25 \times \$12.00 \times 365$	$87 600	
Dinner	$80 \times 0.75 \times \$15.00 \times 365$	$328 500	
Total revenue		**$416 100**	**$416 100**
Total food revenue			**$588 562**

Figure 8.6 *Projected revenue*

Kevin Baker

Projecting expenses

Expense projections can be made:
- by direct calculation (starting from the staffing schedule, for example); or
- by 'rule of thumb' (for example using a common percentage for cost of sales for food and for beverage);[3] or
- by comparison with similar operations.

Restaurant revenue and expense relativities will vary according to the range of services offered. A restaurant such as a burger bar or similar—with a limited menu and no table service, serving food but not alcoholic beverages—will have a different cost structure from that of a full-menu, table-service restaurant serving food and beverages. The burger bar will seek a high turnover and operate on low margins because of the nature of the competition, with a lower cost of sales than a venture offering haute cuisine.

Activity 8.2   *What does it mean?*

This is an activity for those who like to dig out the meaning of words. When travellers arrive in Hong Kong, they see directions to the 'SHROFF'. Find out the meaning and derivation of the word 'SHROFF'.

(The answer is to be found on page 230.)

Another method of compiling revenue and expense projections is to set standard costs for labour and for material cost for each meal, and to set budgets for other items such as entertainment or marketing. In this sector of the industry, it is usual to calculate the selling price of the various items on the menu by calculating a mark-up on the cost of goods sold—for example, by multiplying threefold the cost of the food used in the various dishes that will be produced and sold in the facility. Some employee wages (such as casual wait-staff and cleaners) will vary with the amount of activity at the restaurant. A manager will normally be able to calculate a 'standard cost' of these items—for example, these might total 25 cents out of every dollar of revenue. Other items, such as napkins and laundry of tablecloths, might be 5 cents of every dollar of revenue. In addition to these variable costs, there will be fixed wages costs and other fixed costs (such as rent and depreciation) that must be calculated and factored into the projected income statements.

The first (and perhaps most important) calculation that the entrepreneur must make is to calculate how much revenue the restaurant has to pull in each year to meet the predetermined goals. The restaurant manager then has to recalculate this annual sum to determine what sales must be made each time the restaurant opens for a meal period. The entrepreneur must consider the market and decide whether, for example, the venue will open for lunch and dinner only, and on which days it will trade (say, from Wednesdays to Sundays inclusive, or perhaps for seven days). The manager also has to estimate what proportion of revenue will come from each meal period.

To manage the restaurant closely and keep a check on daily sales, it is necessary to ensure sales meet the desired targets. To do this, the manager needs to know how much each person is spending. This statistic is referred to as the 'average check per person per meal period'.

Another (more complex) meal-pricing tool used in food & beverage operations is referred to as 'menu engineering'. This tool analyses the profitability and quantity sold of each item on the menu so as to determine the most profitable items. These are then featured and marketed.

Pricing and budgeting for a hotel or motel

Estimating hotel or motel income statements: calculating room rates

A common measure of evaluation in the hospitality industry is to use what are called 'rule-of-thumb' methods. One such is the 'dollar-per-thousand' method. The analyst simply assesses whether the project will allow the management to charge one dollar of average daily rate for every one thousand dollars invested in a room. For example, if the hotel has 120 rooms, and has a total cost of $18 million, then divide the cost by the rooms and the answer is $150 000. Charging one dollar for every thousand invested in this room gives an average daily rate of $150.

The alternative is to calculate all the expenses involved in providing the operations, adding a desired return after tax (possibly 12–15% or more), allowing for tax payable so that the desired return is net of tax, and then calculating how many room–days the hotel is likely to sell each year. This procedure is referred to as 'bottom-up' pricing or budgeting because it starts at the 'bottom line'—that is, the profit (or net income) desired.

Both of the above methods of rooms pricing ('rule of thumb' and 'bottom-up') are objective pricing systems—that is, they are based on hard facts and the influence of the market is not taken into account. There are also subjective pricing systems. These include:

- competitive pricing;
- follow the leader;
- intuitive; and
- psychological.

These are discussed below.

Competitive pricing

Competitive pricing is a subjective pricing system under which a room is priced in accordance with the local competition.

Follow the leader

Follow the leader is a subjective pricing system by which a room is allocated a rack rate based on the room rate of another hotel of similar star grade and level of facilities, but not in the local area. This system of pricing usually applies when a four-star or five-star hotel is opened in a city or region that has no other properties of comparable standing.

Intuitive

The intuitive subjective pricing process involves 'guessing' the price that should apply to the hotel room. Again, this is used when a new hotel is opened in an area where there is no direct competition, and usually applies when the hotel has no star rating, or is one or two stars.

Psychological

The psychological system determines a room rate after considering the price that management believes the guest is prepared to pay. For example, if an entrepreneur opened a 30-room hotel that did not have a star rating but had five-star facilities, that entrepreneur might consider that potential guests would be prepared to pay handsomely for the stay. The entrepreneur could make a profit even if the rooms were sold at a much lower price, but decides (successfully) on the higher rate because of the psychological factor. This pricing process is very often applied to resort hotels or to a 'boutique' type of property.

Although the above subjective methods of pricing are valid, the knowledgeable hotelier will always balance them against objective pricing calculations.

Other hotel and motel accounting concepts

There are other important accounting statements—such as management accounting reports and cash-flow statements. The latter record an entity's cash situation and the inflow and outflow of cash—so as to ensure that the organisation always has sufficient funds on hand to meet its liabilities.

The following list briefly describes some of these other accounting tools. For more extensive discussion of other aspects of accounting and finance in hospitality, the reader is referred to specialised texts such as Coltman (1998) and Schmidgall (1995).[4]

Accounting and financial ratios

Accounting and financial ratios are mathematical relationships between items (numbers) on the financial statements that allow detailed comparisons between different time periods or different enterprises.

Yield management

Yield management is a pricing process that varies the price charged to different customer groups depending upon market decisions regarding the likelihood of selling the rooms at higher or lower rates to other customers. It thus allows revenue to be maximised.

Responsibility accounting

Responsibility accounting is a system of dividing activity areas within a hospitality organisation and their related accounting information so that area managers can take responsibility for operational decisions that impact upon the area's financial performance. Associated concepts are 'cost centres' and 'profit centres'.

Variance analysis

Variance analysis refers to processes of identifying and analysing significant differences between budgeted results and actual results.

Elasticity of demand

Elasticity of demand refers to comparing the changes in occupancy (that is, rooms demanded) with changes in prices (that is, room rates) through increasing prices or discounting them. An associated topic is sensitivity analysis, which compares changes in dependent variables (for example, occupancy) with independent variables (for example, variable costs of room occupancy).

Time value of money calculations

Time value of money calculations refers to methods of determining present values of future income, expenses, and cash flows in order to make valid comparisons and aid decision-making.

Activity 8.3   *Ethical consideration*

You are assisting the financial controller of a large tourism enterprise. While helping with the end-of-year financial statements, you note that the asset register still has assets recorded that have been disposed of by the enterprise. These are for large items of equipment (such as a bus and generators) that were destroyed in a fire. The controller jokes that maintaining the assets on the register is a shrewd move because the enterprise can claim a depreciation expense for them.

QUESTION

- What would be your reaction, bearing in mind that the controller is a strong-willed personality and will certainly have you sacked for questioning their practices and could even sue you for defamation if you make accusations that cannot be proved in court?

Chapter review questions

1 What are the principal accounting functions that are most relevant for a general manager?
2 What are the primary financial statements?
3 Describe and give examples of assets and liabilities.
4 Why is accurate pricing vital for food & beverage operations?
5 To quote the English writer Charles Dickens' fictional character Mr Micawber: 'Annual income twenty pounds, annual expenditure nineteen nineteen six, result happiness. Annual income twenty pounds, annual expenditure twenty pounds ought and six, result misery.'[5] Is this also true of commercial enterprises at all stages of their development?

Answer to Activity 8.2

WHAT DOES IT MEAN?
(See page 225 for details of this activity.)
Who or what is a 'SHROFF'? They are cashiers, and when the traveller arrives at Hong Kong airport, the signs will direct him or her to the car park cashier. The word is of Indian origin.

CASE STUDY

The HB Hotel

The owners of the HB Hotel decide to open an associated venture—a 60-seat seafood restaurant in the centre of the local town. They plan to invest $100 000. This investment is comprised of $80 000 for equipment and $20 000 for working capital (for example, purchasing stock, advertising, employing staff, and so on). The owners seek a return of 15% on this investment (similar to the return their hotel is achieving). They therefore plan to price the menu items so as to achieve this result, after paying a tax liability based on a rate of 31.5%.

Calculate the average check per meal that is required, if the following information also applies:

* the cost of food will be 40% of revenue;
* variable payroll costs will total 25 cents out of every dollar of revenue; other items will be 5 cents of every dollar of revenue;
* in addition to the above costs, the owners will also have to pay a chef a regular salary that totals $35 000 a year (including all benefits);
* rent for the harbourside venue is $1500 each calendar month;
* all other costs not described so far come to $4000 a year;
* the owners calculate that the equipment will last for five years and after that time will be worn out and worthless, so the purchase price of the equipment will be depreciated over the period (that is, at 20% per year);
* the restaurant will be open for lunch and dinner from Tuesday to Sunday; the amount of revenue from lunch and dinner will be about the same amount, but twice as many people will come for lunch as for dinner.

Chapter 9

Personnel Management

The experienced business manager knows that his employees will include neurotics, self-seekers, incompetents and prima donnas. His success as a business manager is measured by his ability to take this unpromising amalgam and get the job done with the least amount of mayhem.

Anonymous

Synopsis of chapter

This chapter first considers what personnel management is all about.[1] This is followed by an introduction to planning for personnel management, which includes determining staffing levels, aspects of selection procedures and processes, and staff training. It concludes with a discussion of performance appraisal, and introduces a method of performance appraisal especially developed for hospitality operations.

The importance of personnel management

In this book, the term 'personnel management' is used in preference to the more common term 'human resource management' because the latter has an implication that employees are just another resource—like materials. In reality, people are absolutely central to hospitality operations.

Knowledge of personnel management is important to all hospitality professionals, regardless of their career aspirations, because the hospitality industry is all about service. Service is something that is mainly dependent on the behaviour of employees. Therefore, an effective manager must understand how to manage this most important asset. In addition, all hospitality managers are involved in personnel management activities. The objectives of personnel management are to help the organisation achieve its objectives (guest satisfaction, profit, and so on) by influencing employee attitudes (job satisfaction, loyalty) and behaviour (absenteeism, turnover, service delivery).

A typical workforce in a large hotel has certain features:

- first, the typical tenure of employment in the hospitality sector involves a significant level of casual and part-time employment;
- secondly, many employees are young (and a large proportion is female); and
- thirdly, not all employees are committed to hospitality as a career—for many have more than one job.

The nature of the hospitality workforce offers special challenges to managers, and requires good personnel management skills across a range of activities. These activities include:

- planning personnel needs;
- recruitment and discipline ('hiring and firing');
- training and development; and
- performance appraisal.

Each of these will be considered below.

Planning personnel needs

The process of planning

An organisation must ensure that it has sufficient people with appropriate skills to carry out its mission.

Personnel management planning is the process by which an organisation anticipates its needs and arranges the movement of people into, within, and out of the organisation. Such planning involves not only a determination of the appropriate number of employees needed for adequate staffing, but also the types of people needed. A term often applied to this process is 'skills inventory'. The skills inventory of an organisation thus identifies the number and skills of its current employees, and the number and skills of employees required in the future—including the longer-term needs for recruitment, training, and selection.

Associated with the skills inventory is the 'replacement chart'—which summarises present job duties and office-holders, and identifies potential movements and replacements. Planning for internal promotions in this way is also called 'succession planning', whereby employees who perform and show potential are offered training and development and a career path through higher levels of the organisation.[2]

Consider the following scenario. A new hotel is in the pre-opening phase. After a review of staffing needs in all departments it has been determined that the hotel needs 400 employees. Does the hotel simply hire the first 400 people who apply for jobs? Of course, it does not. The hotel does not need 400 'generic' employees. It needs personnel with specific skills (or aptitude to develop those skills). Thus, the hotel requires (perhaps) 70 with the skills to be room attendants, 50 with the skills to be front-office personnel, 65 with the skills to be servers in food & beverage outlets, 70 with the skills to work in the kitchens, and so on. There is a clear need for well-planned and well-implemented personnel policies to employ sufficient numbers trained in the required skills categories.

All personnel management decisions must take into consideration these internal requirements, as well as considering the effects of the external environment, and the overall mission of the organisation.

Steps involved in planning for personnel management

The first step in planning for personnel management is to formulate the mission statement of the personnel management department, and to establish how this mission ties in with wider corporate goals and objectives.

Having established this wider 'philosophical' direction, the practical steps involved in planning for personnel management are:

- assessing current personnel resources in the organisation;
- estimating the supply and demand factors for labour in the organisation; and
- matching the demand with the supply of labour through recruitment or retrenchment.

Determining staffing levels

There is no 'magical formula' for determining staffing requirements. However, certain information can be used to reach an estimate that is less prone to error than one based on 'instinct' or 'gut feeling'. This involves collecting information on job specifications and descriptions—that is, what needs to be done, where, and how.

An existing property will have numerous sources of data in job records and files, diaries, questionnaires, reports, plans, and information systems. If the property is part of a chain, there should be information on staffing levels for similar properties within the chain. If the property is independently owned or operated, a search for other properties that are similar should result in the acquisition of relevant information.

None of this historical information is 'absolute'. Just because another (similar) property has 482 employees does not mean that a new property should have the same number. Each individual property should be analysed to determine its own staffing needs. The information received on similar properties merely serves as a 'baseline' or starting point in determining the staffing needs of the new property.

Certain specific characteristics of the property, and certain general 'rules of thumb', taken together, will result in additions or subtractions to the historical information already obtained—thus allowing appropriate decisions to be made in relation to personnel issues. These characteristics include the following:

- size of property and configuration;
- quality level;
- projected rooms occupancy;
- special facilities or amenities;
- seasonality;
- 'rules of thumb' for staffing levels; and
- matching jobs with skills.

Each of these will be considered below.

Size of property and configuration

The first factor to consider is the size of the property. Note that size should not be based solely on the number of rooms, but on the total floor area of the property as well. Two properties, each with 750 rooms, might require entirely different staffing levels. For example, one might be a high-rise tower, and the other might be an 'apartment-style' establishment spread out over a hundred acres. Obviously, it will be more difficult for the room attendants at the latter property to get from room to room than for those at the high-rise property. Therefore, the 'apartment-style' property will probably require more room attendants than the high-rise tower—even though they have an equal number of rooms.

Quality level

Another factor to consider is the type and level of service that is or will be provided. Higher levels of service require a greater number of employees. All other things being equal, a five-star luxury property needs more employees than a three-star, three-diamond property.

Projected rooms occupancy

Guest room occupancy levels will also help to determine whether any adjustments in the staffing levels is necessary from that suggested by the historical information. If the new property is likely to have higher levels of occupancy than the comparison property, additional employees will be required. Lower occupancy will obviously require a downward adjustment in the staffing levels.

Special facilities or amenities

It is wise to examine the level of amenities offered by the new property as compared with the property used in assembling the historical data. The two properties might have the same number of rooms but, if the new property offers special facilities (a health club, special food & beverage facilities, shops, and so on), the new property will obviously have a need for additional employees to staff these facilities.

Seasonality

At some properties, particularly resorts, seasonality must be taken into account. Obviously, more employees are needed during peak times than during slow times.

'Rules of thumb' for staffing levels

There are some useful 'rules-of-thumb' regarding staffing levels. These provide a guide to the number of employees required per room in the establishment.

Table 9.1 Staffing levels 'rules-of-thumb'

Type of establishment	Example of establishment	Ratio of employees to rooms
high-service luxury	Ritz-Carlton, InterContinental, Four Seasons	1.0 employee per room
middle-market	Hyatt, Marriott, Hilton	0.5–0.8 employees per room
economy market	Budget Motels, Motel 6	0.2–0.5 employees per room

A few too many?

During the 1990s, many Asian hotel groups believed that increased staffing levels meant enhanced customer service. This was particularly so with those hotels that are in the five-star category. In fact, at one stage one of the authors noted that the world-famous Peninsula Hotel in Hong Kong had a staff to room ratio of 4.2 employees per room. (Compare this with the ratios suggested by the 'rules of thumb' given in Table 9.1.)

It has subsequently been found that quantity is no substitute for quality. After all, what is the point of having four or five staff asking about your problem if it never gets fixed?

Matching jobs with skills

As previously noted, skills are just as important as absolute numbers in determining staffing requirements. The personnel planner must be conversant with all aspects of labour supply and demand, including:

- changes in the population;
- changes in the nature of work (for example, the 'casualisation' of the workforce);
- changes in regulation;
- changes in modes of work (for example, the growth of telecommuting and outsourcing of functions); and
- the implications of skills shortages.

The competent planner will be able to use quantitative and qualitative tools to forecast the matching of supply and demand.

Recruitment and discipline

Determining policies and procedures

A policy is a statement of purpose and content relating to an area or activity. A procedure is a step-by-step list of action to achieve the purpose—what action is to be taken, by whom, and how. The area of employee selection and dismissal must have its own policies and procedures to ensure fair and just treatment for all concerned.

With respect to recruitment, it is not always possible to fill skilled (and even unskilled) vacancies in hospitality operations. A survey of hospitality operators by the Bureau of Tourism Research revealed that respondents experienced a number of difficulties in recruiting employees. The survey found that 18% of all establishments in the hospitality industry experienced some difficulties in recruiting staff. Also, more than 50% of establishments that experienced recruitment difficulties felt one reason was 'too few people with the right skills/experience'.

Recruitment is therefore crucial in most hospitality organisations. An organisation should first look for available labour within itself—with an examination of the skills possessed by current employees. Those who possess the skills necessary to do a higher-level job should be given an opportunity at the position. A 'promotion-from-within' policy serves to increase the satisfaction, motivation, and loyalty of current employees. It also produces decreased employee turnover, increased guest service and satisfaction, and increased profits.

Assuming that there are not enough current employees with the skills needed to fill any vacancies, a search outside the organisation is warranted.

The success or failure of these external searches in the wider population depends on several factors, including:

- demographics;
- economic conditions; and
- the local labour market.

Some thoughts on each of these follows.

Demographics

Demographics refers to the characteristics of a group of people—age, gender, educational level, and so on. The demographics of the local area will affect the availability of staff. For example, if a property is in an area where there is a disproportionate number of young people, there will be a large pool of labour for trainee positions.

Economic conditions

When the economy is weaker, unemployment increases and the chances of finding skilled labour increases (and vice versa). During times of high unemployment, it is also easier to find employees with particular skills.

The local labour market

A labour market is the area from which employees are to be recruited. It varies depending on the skills needed. For example, the relevant labour market for low-skilled positions (room attendants, dishwashers, bellstaff, and so on) is most likely to be the local area surrounding the property. However, for a high-skilled position (general manager, executive chef, controller, and so on) the relevant labour market will most likely be national or even international.

Activity 9.1   *Choosing your personnel*

You own a cruising yacht that requires a crew of six including the captain. You will be sailing on the vessel to remote stretches of the Pacific Ocean. You have qualifications to be captain, but limited experience, so you have not yet decided whether you will command the vessel or whether you will employ an experienced captain. You advertise for prospective crew members and receive ten replies.

However, on the night before you will make your selection for crew members and possible captain, you find a mysterious crystal ball that informs you that the yacht will capsize and sink near a remote, uninhabited island. You cannot change your mind about sailing. It is fated that you will sail with five other crew and be stranded on the remote island within a month. With this forewarning, you can stock up on necessary supplies. However, you must make a choice concerning appropriate crew members who will have the range of skills and attributes necessary to survive on the remote island for possibly several months.

You must pick five out of the following ten applicants:

- an experienced captain;
- a former astronaut;
- a skilled horse rider and animal trainer;
- a doctor;
- a carpenter (who always travels with a complete set of tools);
- a professional weightlifter who can pull buses with his teeth;
- a professional explorer and surveyor;
- a skilled sailor who was once wrecked on a remote island;
- a comedian and entertainer; and
- a long-distance swimmer.

QUESTIONS

- You may choose five and only five. Make an initial selection.
- The first five applicants noted above are women. Applicants six to ten are men. Does this information change your selection?

Selection

Selection of personnel for a position is a difficult task requiring special skills. The employer wants the best person for the job, and the selection process must be a merit process based on personal attributes and characteristics solely related to the duties of the position as defined in a job description.[3]

Most employers prefer to select existing employees wherever possible for promotion or transfer. The employers know these people and the employees know the business. Selecting existing employees also has advantages in terms of staff morale. There are techniques that can be used in large organisations to forecast the availability of internal candidates for selection. One such technique is the 'Markov analysis', which forecasts movements from past data and records. Every organisation can benefit from a form of forecast of labour needs that assesses such factors as turnover and the lead time required to select, induct, and train new appointees.[4]

Of course, the employer might also choose to advertise externally—if the right person is not available from within the organisation. Such job advertisements must meet equal employment opportunity provisions.[5]

After having advertised internally and externally, or having used search agencies to obtain a pool of applicants, the organisation must then try to determine which applicant will be the best person for the job. No selection process can predict with absolute certainty the best person for the job. However, selection techniques are constantly being refined. Some steps in the selection process are described below.

Screening

The first step is the initial screen. At this stage, the employer assesses candidates to assess whether they meet essential minimum qualifications necessary to perform the job. For example, assume that you are searching for an assistant director of the food & beverage department. Through job analysis, you have determined that this person must have a tertiary management qualification (to at least TAFE level). Rather than taking applicants without any tertiary qualifications through the process, it is better to 'screen' all applicants against the job specification at the beginning of the exercise.

Application forms

After the initial screening, the next step in the selection process usually involves asking the applicants to fill out an employment application. Such an application serves a number of purposes:

- it provides the organisation with the name, address, telephone number, and other contact details of the applicant;
- it can serve as an early form of assessment of an applicant's basic abilities—although filling out a form might not seem especially difficult, an applicant who fails to complete the form accurately and properly might not warrant further consideration;
- it allows a hospitality organisation to gather information about prior employment, educational background, and other pertinent information which will be useful; it also allows the employer to check the honesty of the applicant by verifying some of the information through references and/or background checks.

There are regulations surrounding certain questions that employers may and may not ask applicants on such application forms. In some jurisdictions it is illegal to discriminate on the grounds of marital status, age, number of children, sexual preference, and so. It might be illegal even to ask questions about these matters.

Interviews

Virtually all employers use some kind of interview when making selection decisions. If there is a very large number of applicants for a position, it might be more cost-effective to have an outside firm conduct these interviews. However, if a hospitality enterprise can conduct its own interviews it will have a better idea of the strengths and weaknesses of prospective candidates.

The process of interviewing requires certain skills. Many interviewers assess the success of the interview based on the rapport established with each candidate, but a successful interview process involves more than this. The overall aim must be to select the best-qualified candidate—not merely to get along well in a general chat.

Careful preparation is required. A set of questions that is asked of all applicants should be established. This allows for direct comparison among applicants. To ensure that these responses are useful and relevant to the job, the questions should be developed with the aid of the job description.

All questions should have a specific purpose. The interviewer should be able to say (to himself/herself): 'I asked this question with such-and-such a specific purpose in mind'. Questions should therefore have a definite aim, and not be raised as part of a general 'chit-chat' with no specific purpose.

Questions are usually of two types:

- specific questions aimed at eliciting specific information from the applicant (for example: 'Do you have any experience in book-keeping skills?');
- general ('open-ended') questions aimed at assessing the applicant's ability to organise and express his/her thoughts (for example: 'What do you enjoy about working in the hospitality industry?')

Other suggestions for improving the effectiveness of the interview are:

- train the interviewer in interview techniques;
- have the interviewer take notes so that the interviewer doesn't have to rely on memory;
- have multiple interviewers to reduce the effects of the biases associated with any one individual.

Figure 9.1 *How to fail an interview*

Kevin Baker

How to fail an interview!

There is a knack in successful interview techniques—both from the side of the interviewer and also from that of the interviewee. Some actions by the interviewee will guarantee he or she has have no chance of selection.

To take a humorous view of the matter, consider the prospects of an interviewee who behaved in the following fashion.

- The interviewee insists upon squatting on the floor in a position suited for meditation—saying that he needs to be able to 'concentrate' on the appropriate answers.
- The interviewee picks up a family photo from the interviewer's desk, smiles, and observes: 'What a hunk! Is he home alone tonight?'
- The interviewee brings in the magazine that he was reading in reception while waiting and flicks through it while answering questions without looking at the interviewer.
- The interviewee takes a razor blade out of her briefcase and holds it over her wrists saying: 'If I don't get the job, I'm slashing my wrists and it'll be your fault'.
- The interviewee takes his mother to the interview and asks her advice on how to answer each question as it is asked.
- The interviewee takes her dog to the interview and asks its advice on how to answer the questions.
- The interviewee takes off his shoes and proceeds to trim his toenails while the interview proceeds.

As an interviewer, would you be impressed? Perhaps you might give the interviewee some credit for daring to be different! Then again, perhaps not!

Employment tests

A number of employment tests can be used as an aid to selection decisions in the hospitality industry. The benefit of employment testing is that it should reduce the chance of error in employment selection. For example, an applicant for a position dealing directly with guests can be asked to attend a test where existing personnel take the role of guests and pose problems, thus testing the applicant on how he or she would address these problems and perform under the pressure of dealing with the public. Other examples include assessing applicants on keyboarding skills (for a front-desk clerk's position), or on the ability to carry a tray loaded with dishes safely (for a food-service position).

The reliability of such employment tests depends upon their design. If the test does not accurately reflect the work situation, it will not be useful as a tool to aid the selection decision.

Some employers request an applicant to attend work for a period without pay, and use this trial period as a form of employment test. However, this practice is unfair to the applicant (in effectively asking them to work without pay), and might not be a good guide to their work performance. Such a practice can also create difficulties in the areas of insurance coverage, workers' compensation, and so on.

Activity 9.2   *Mass interviews*

A large hotel in Macau frequently recruited operational staff in mainland China. The rates of pay being offered (for food servers, room attendants, cleaners, and so on) were five or six times what the recruits could earn in China. Unfortunately, most of the mainland Chinese spoke Putonghua (Mandarin) whereas the language in Macau is Cantonese. Despite the language difference, the Macau hotel frequently received more than a thousand applicants seeking an interview.

To handle this large number, the hotel organised a team of fifteen interviewers. Even with so many interviewers, the large number of applicants meant that each person received about five minutes. Upon this brief time, the person's future was decided.

As might have been anticipated, the hotel had a very poor retention rate among its staff.

QUESTIONS
- Can you suggest why this was so?
- How would you do things differently?

Background reference checks

Background or reference checking is a difficult subject. On the one hand, employers have a responsibility to check certain information about prospective employees who might have sensitive roles to play in their hospitality organisation. On the other hand, many former employers are reluctant to provide negative information about former employees because of the possibility of legal action—for hindering their opportunities of future employment. Many employers, when called upon to provide information regarding former employees, will provide only the dates between which the individual was employed.

But prospective employers must be diligent when hiring people who are going to have access to guests and their belongings, as well as to other employees. It is irresponsible to hire a financial controller who has a history of theft, or to hire a member of the bell staff who has a history of violently assaulting people.

Most organisations ask applicants for references, or at least for a list of referees. Good applicants will be happy to provide such information, and referees will be happy to speak well of good applicants. This is useful and reassuring information for a prospective employer. A failure to provide references or a list of referees, when asked to do so, is a worrying sign.

Medical testing

The last issue in the selection process involves medical testing. This can be a sensitive issue and can infringe against anti-discrimination legislation. Any request of applicants to take medical tests should be made after an offer of employment has been made. The offer can be made contingent on the passing of such tests.

As noted above, employers will need to be aware of anti-discrimination legislation. However, because of the nature of some work in hospitality, particularly in regard to food-handling, issues can arise if applicants for employment have contagious illnesses.

Employment contracts

Once a decision is taken to employ a person, a written contract should be offered. This should describe the work to be done, and the terms and conditions of employment. The contract should specify such matters as:

- hours of duty and overtime;
- salary/wages;

Do you have the right 'bumps'? Phrenology and other tests

In the nineteenth century, the so-called science of phrenology was in vogue. This involved measuring the bumps and curves of a person's skull. Phrenology postulated that, in so doing, conclusions could be reached about the character and criminal inclinations of people.

Such discredited theories have no place in the modern workplace, but there is still a preference by some employers to use psychological testing. S. Tonello of Drake Career Management Services estimates that 50–60% of corporate executive appointments in Australia utilise some form of psychological testing.[6] However, experts caution that such testing should be only a part of the selection process, and should be only an indication of a person's ability and aptitude.

- any other benefits, bonuses, or allowances;
- leave entitlements;
- superannuation;
- place of work and manner of supervision;
- promotion and termination policy; and
- other employee responsibilities (such as confidentiality of information).

Dismissal

There is a rather cynical old adage that 'the secret of good hiring is good firing'. There might be some truth in this saying—suggesting as it does that an employer might have to put off, or 'sack', an incompetent employee in order to recruit a competent one. But there are several problems involved with having such a readiness to fire people.

First, other staff members are likely to feel insecure if the reason for the sacking is unclear. Staff members do not work well under threat of dismissal.

Secondly, the employer still has to find and train another staff person, who might be no better than the person who has been dismissed.

Thirdly, dismissal procedures must be carefully followed to avoid legal ramifications.

For these reasons, dismissal of staff for disciplinary reasons should always be a last resort. Some basic rules, founded on common decency, apply. Staff members should always be treated with dignity, which means that discussions on termination should take place in private, and should never be conducted 'on the spur of the moment' or in anger.

Employees have rights and duties with respect to their employers.

Employee rights include:

- being treated with respect and dignity;
- not having to reveal confidential information about themselves;
- not having to undertake work tasks different from those they were employed under contract to do; and
- not having to make up for losses incurred by their employer in the course of their employment (that is, they do not have to make up for shortfalls in the cash register or pay for equipment that breaks through no fault of their own).

Employee duties include:

- obedience to lawful and reasonable instruction;
- working in a skilful and competent manner;
- cooperating with management and other employees; and
- acting in good faith in their employer's interests (that is, not taking bribes, not disclosing confidential information about the employer, and so on).

As noted above, employees have a right to be treated with respect and dignity. This also applies to relationships between employees. Behaviour such as sexual harassment of one employee by another (which includes any unwelcome attention, advances, or offensive conduct) offends against this right to respect and dignity.

Employees have a right to a safe and secure workplace. Implied in this right is a reasonable quality of work life—with adequate welfare support, and amenities such as change rooms and lockers. Just as employees must treat one another with personal dignity and respect, employees must also ensure that the workplace is physically safe for others. They must not act in a way that threatens the health of others—such as by a failure to observe non-smoking rules in the workplace.

If employees habitually breach these sorts of duties to their employer and to their fellow employees, the employer is justified in terminating their employment. Such termination must take place in circumstances that are fair to all, and which comply with all legal provisions. Generally, employees must be given an opportunity to improve their conduct; hence 'instant dismissals' must be a rarity. Fairness suggests that an employee first receives a warning—with specific deficiencies in his or her conduct being listed. A second warning should be done in writing, and before a witness, with the employee given the opportunity to respond and comment upon the problems. Only after at least two warnings should the employee be dismissed—and even then he or she should be given notice of termination (or have the notice period paid out).

Fair and just termination procedures must incorporate other provisions. Included in those provisions must be a written and publicised grievance and disciplinary policy.

Sometimes terminations are not for disciplinary reasons, but occur when the business goes into liquidation. Different procedures obviously apply, but the central importance of treating employees with respect and dignity still applies. This is especially important because, in these circumstances, employees are losing their jobs through no fault of their own. Notices of termination should always be conveyed personally, not through notes or faxes, and the people involved should be given as full an explanation of the situation as possible.

Training and development

The importance of training

The hospitality industry, in offering a wide range of services, employs labour from an equally diverse spread of occupations. The range of skills possessed or expected to be acquired by the hospitality workforce covers the full gamut of skills utilised in industry generally—although there are differences in the skill composition among various industry sectors and even among firms in the same sector. For instance, the traditional model of a large hotel has a high proportion of unskilled workers many of whom will be employed on a casual or part-time basis. On the other hand, senior managers within a large hotel are usually graduates with formal qualifications, are highly skilled, and occupy career positions within the organisation. The differences in skill needs within these two groups are reflected in their differing education and training arrangements.

In tight economic conditions, training expenditures are usually among the first that are reduced or cut. However, there are many hospitality organisations that recognise the importance of this activity and have continued to spend a significant amount of money on formal employee training and development programs. (Formal training programs refer to those programs that are conducted in an offsite facility that is separate from the immediate work context, whereas informal training programs refer to those that are conducted on-the-job.)

The development of sophisticated information technology systems for hotels and other hospitality enterprises has made staff training even more important. Operators cannot take advantages of technological advances unless they give their staff the skills to use them.[7]

Training should be viewed as a continuous system of development. The training and development function should involve a continuous assessment of needs so that ongoing training and development programs are developed, implemented, and evaluated. This continuous development approach is critical to cope with the dynamic and changing nature of work in the hospitality industry.

In a small hotel, an individual's skills are enhanced principally through on-the-job-training; that is, the employee learns on the job. Larger organisations are more able to incorporate a training objective as part of their organisation goals and are more likely to encourage people to undertake skills enhancement through the improvement of qualifications or participation in 'off-the-job' formal skills-enhancement programs.

Designing training programs

The first step in determining whether training is necessary is to conduct a needs analysis. If a rigorous assessment of needs is not conducted, time, effort, and money can be wasted. Three types of needs assessments must be conducted:

- organisational assessment;
- task assessment; and
- individual assessment

Some thoughts on each of these follow.

Organisational assessment

The first type of assessment is an organisational assessment. This focuses on where in the organisation training might be necessary. Information on safety records, turnover, absenteeism, places where new technology has been incorporated, and so on, can be compared across departments to determine if training is required in certain operational areas.

Task assessment

The second type of assessment is a task assessment. This focuses on possible areas of training in terms of what employees do—tasks, duties, and responsibilities. Information from job descriptions, performance-evaluation forms, and career development systems can be used to assess which work-related functions might be the target of formal training activities.

Individual assessment

The third type of assessment is individual assessment, which focuses on who requires training. Examining an employee's performance against a standard, or compared with the performance of other employees, can help identify strengths, weaknesses, and needs.

Training objectives

Once training needs have been identified, the next step is to translate the needs into training objectives. This involves the development of clearly defined, results-orientated statements. For example, it might be found from an organisational analysis that a new guest-information system (Maxial, Fidelio, and so on) should be installed in the front office. Furthermore, the results from the task and individual analyses show that the current employees do not possess the skills necessary to effectively operate the new system. Therefore the development of training objectives requires a restatement of needs in a results-orientated format.

Training plan

After objectives have been set, a training plan that outlines the logistical details of the training program can be developed. A formal training plan includes:

- a statement of the training objectives;
- a justification for those objectives based on the needs-assessment results;
- an implementation plan describing the administrative and design aspects of the training (who the trainees will be, where they will be trained, the methods of training to be used, and so on); and
- methods for evaluation.

Performance appraisal

The author of this section of the chapter (pages 248–55) is Professor Jamal Feerasta[8]

What is performance appraisal?

Performance appraisal—also known as performance review, merit rating, performance evaluation, employee appraisal, and employee evaluation—is the assessment of an employee's effectiveness in a job. A properly constructed performance-appraisal system is closely linked with all major personnel management functions, including selection. Performance appraisal must be linked to selection in that good measures of employee performance are required to validate selection systems.

With respect to training, certain factors must be assessed by performance appraisal. These include newly acquired skills, knowledge, behaviour, and so on. Without such a system, there is no accountability and no incentive to use training.

Performance appraisal has several important uses.

- First, appraisal outcomes serve as input for conducting the skills inventory that is necessary for effective personnel planning.
- Secondly, performance appraisals can help determine which employees need more training, and can help to evaluate the results of training programs.
- Thirdly, performance appraisals provide input to the compensation program, and can be used for making decisions on pay rises and promotions.
- Fourthly, performance appraisals can be used for motivational purposes. The process of appraisal and feedback can encourage initiative, develop a sense of responsibility, and stimulate efforts to perform better.
- Fifthly, performance appraisals have a useful legal purpose in that the outcomes can serve as a legally defensible justification for making promotions, transfers, rewards, and termination decisions.

Performance-appraisal methods

Graphic rating scales

The oldest and perhaps the most common performance-appraisal method is the graphic rating scale. Using this technique, the appraiser is presented with a set of job-related traits—such as 'initiative', 'responsibility', 'leadership', and so on. The appraiser is asked to evaluate an employee along a rating continuum that measures such things as work quality, work quantity, and other performance-related dimensions. Alternatively, the rating can be more individualised by providing the appraiser with a range of performance expectations—with this range of expectations being drawn up to match the attributes of the employee. The system is adaptable across a large range of jobs, performance can be quantified, and it is relatively easy to develop.

The rating continuum is typically represented by a series of points on a continuous scale. For example, the appraiser places a check above the descriptive words ranging from 'unsatisfactory' to 'outstanding' (or some other scale points)—in which 'unsatisfactory' can be assigned a score of 0 and 'outstanding' be assigned a score of 6. Total scores are then computed.

However, there are problems with rating scales. These include:

- problems of definition;
- problems of personal bias; and
- problems of relativity.

Some thoughts on each of these follow.

Problems of definition

The terms used in the rating scale might seem straightforward enough, but different words mean different things to different people. How exactly does an interviewer define the terms used in the rating scale?

Problems of personal bias

Each rater might interpret the behaviour (or productivity, or performance) of an employee differently. Some people are harsh markers; others are more generous. This leads to problems of inconsistency between two raters with regard to the same employee.

Problems of relativity

The options on the rating scale described above vary from 1 to 6. Note that this is an even number. An odd number scale has been avoided because of the tendency for interviewers to rate in the centre (number 3 on a scale of 1 to 5) when they are unsure of what to put down. Another problem with the rating scale is that it can measure only relativities. A '2' is worse than a '4'—but how much worse? Twice as bad? Probably not, and yet the numbers might suggest that it is so.

Relative rankings

Another type of comparative assessment method is ranking. In their simplest form, rankings ask a supervisor to rank subordinates on one or more performance criteria. Under this system, the evaluator ranks employees from highest to the lowest and only one person can be ranked 'first'. The system brings in an element of competition, but the qualitative differences between various ranks are assumed to be the same.

The disadvantage is that if there is a large number of people to be ranked, the process can become tedious and questionable. Ranking can be very difficult if the supervisor is asked to rank a large number of subordinates (for example, more than twenty persons). It is also much easier for the supervisor to rank the best and the worst in a reliable way, than it is to rank the 'average' ones.

Group order ranking

Another type of comparative evaluation method is a type of forced distribution called a 'group order ranking system'. This approach is similar to grading on a curve. The appraiser is asked to rate employees in some fixed distribution of categories—such as 10% in the 'low' category, 20% in 'low–average', 40% in 'average', 20% in 'average–high', and 10% in 'high'. Alternatively, employees can be placed into a particular group classification—for example, into the 'top 10%', or the 'second 10%', or the 'bottom 10%', and so on. The disadvantage of this system is that it cannot be applied effectively if the number of employees is too few. In addition, if the overall quality of the employees is low, a supervisor might be looking at a case of evaluating the 'best of the worst'.

The essay method

As the name suggests, this is a simple method, under which the assessor writes a narrative describing the performance of the individual over a given period, highlighting the interviewee's strengths and weaknesses. The candidate is really at the mercy of the assessor's pen and the system can be highly subjective, even though certain criteria are chosen beforehand as being essential in measuring effectiveness of performance. The interviewer then uses those criteria in writing the essay. The value of this method is that it enables the interviewer to describe the interviewee's strengths and weaknesses in detail. The major disadvantage is that it can be time-consuming and the accuracy of the essay often depends on the ability of the interviewer to write clearly. Some training in writing skills might be needed.

360-degrees appraisal

This is a system under which performance feedback is obtained from peers, team members, customers, managers, subordinates, and other stakeholders. The information provides management and the individual concerned with a better perspective on how they are perceived by others with respect to their abilities, work performance, skills, attitudes, attributes, and so on. By analysing the information, various training and development programs for the staff can be designed, pay-scales adjusted, and goals set. Involvement of the stakeholders in the process ensures greater commitment towards achieving the corporate and individual goals, minimises subjectivity in the appraisal process, and facilitates the process of empowerment. On the negative side, this appraisal process is difficult and very time-consuming. It can be a difficult exercise to coordinate information among the various stakeholders, and then to interpret the information and provide appropriate feedback.

Management by objectives (MBO)

In most of the traditional performance systems, the appraisers judge past performance and attempt to report their judgments using one of the techniques discussed above. However, because performance appraisals are used for making important decisions that affect employees, the appraiser is placed in a difficult role.

The concept of management by objectives (MBO) was developed to make performance appraisal a collaborative effort between supervisor and supervised. The two work together to link the supervised employee's areas of work responsibility with the results that the employee is expected to achieve. The two parties agree on the objectives of their endeavours. The quality of the employee's work can then be measured according to the extent to which these goals are achieved.

This goal-setting process enables subordinates to exercise self-control and management over their jobs and how they performed them.

Figure 9.2 *Superior performance should be noted for appraisal purposes*
Kevin Baker

Activity 9.3   *What would you do for your boss?*[9]

A boss asks a subordinate to help him paint his house. The subordinate, who does not feel like doing it, discusses the situation with a colleague.

The colleague argues: 'You don't have to paint if you don't feel like it. He is your boss at work. Outside he has little authority.'

The subordinate argues: 'Despite the fact that I don't feel like it, I will paint it. He is my boss, and I can't ignore the opportunity for some extra outside work.'

QUESTION

- Would you choose to paint the house or not?
  (To compare your response with the responses made by people from various cultural groups, see page 260.)

Performance appraisal in the hospitality sector

The hospitality sector has particular problems with regard to performance appraisal. Some of the fundamental characteristics of the service industry are:

- the production, delivery, and consumption of the product are often taking place simultaneously;
- people with different backgrounds and needs interact with each other within a short time;
- the window of opportunity to rectify a service error is very limited;
- every member of the service-delivery team can contribute to product excellence or product downgrade; and
- the product is highly perishable, largely intangible, and heterogeneous.

The customer-contact people are the crucial elements of the organisation. They are the real face of the organisation who make or break the business. Performance appraisal is the anchor that holds the service-production system and service-delivery system together. Therefore, effective performance appraisal is especially crucial for the hospitality industry.

The diary method of performance appraisal

In the hospitality industry, employees at every level are contributing to the guest experience. It takes many people to provide the experience that a customer expects, and it takes just one person to shatter that experience. The 'moment of truth' is lived every hour of every day. The onus is on the manager to ensure that performance appraisal is fair and free of ambiguity. From the above discussion regarding the various approaches to performance appraisal, it emerges that there are numerous potential areas of conflict between management and employees, and the tools of performance appraisal should be updated regularly. This is expensive and often time-consuming, and individuals being appraised are generally at the mercy of the person conducting the appraisal.

It is not uncommon for a situation to arise in which the person under whom an individual has worked for most of the time is no longer around—as a result of the supervisor having been relocated, or having left the organisation. Then a 'newcomer' ends up conducting the appraisal. A newcomer might remember more about complaints and deficiencies in service, rather than the 'good things' that might have been said about the employee. All in all, an employee might feel aggrieved that his or her work is not being properly or fairly assessed.

The individual diary method can be introduced as a performance-appraisal system devised specifically for services industries. The system is simple, unambiguous, updated, and documented. Moreover, the primary stakeholders are involved.

The objective of the diary method is to keep a record of individual performance and behaviour that merit positive or negative feedback from the guests, manager, supervisor, peers, and so on—measured against the job that a individual is assigned to do. However, the focus is on the 'positive' aspects of the tasks performed, the attitude of the employee, and so on.

The diary is given to the individual at the time that he or she starts work and it is maintained by the individual. The diary can take many formats. It is usually pocket-sized, so the employee can carry it about while working. It should have duplicate pages that are be code-numbered to ensure that comments are authentic and can be verified. There should be spaces on each page of the diary to enable incidents to be noted and countersigned by the employee's immediate supervisor, department manager, and personnel manager.

Advantages

From the organisation's perspective, the advantages of maintaining the diary are:

- it prevents litigation with respect to unfair performance appraisal, pay increases, development opportunities, promotions, and so on;
- it provides evidence of management calibre;
- it can assist organisational SWOT analysis (SWOT standing for strengths, weaknesses, opportunities, threats);
- it minimises any disruptions or gaps in performance appraisal brought about by management restructuring (because there is an ongoing record);
- it decreases the risk of bias and different interpretations of performance no matter who the supervisor is;
- it is simple, inexpensive, and takes little time to implement;

```
┌─────────────────────────────────────────┐
│                         A- 0403          │
│   Name:                 Date    Day      │
│   _____      _____  _____     │
│                                          │
│   Dept. _____                 │
│                                          │
│             Highlight Incident           │
│                                          │
│   Date & Day                   Location  │
│   _____        _____  │
│                                          │
│                                          │
│                                          │
│                                          │
│   Reported by                    When    │
│   _____        _____  │
│                                          │
│   Confirmed by               Supervisor  │
│   _____        _____  │
│                                          │
│   Manager                         HRM    │
│   _____        _____  │
│   © PAP/MJ 03/99                         │
└─────────────────────────────────────────┘
```

Figure 9.3 *A sample page from the diary method of performance appraisal*

Jamal Feerasta

- it can easily be integrated to complement the effectiveness of any of the other performance-appraisal systems discussed above; and
- the system can be generic or specific in its implementation by taking into account the productivity standards, performance standards, quality of human resources, and differing attributes of the employees involved.

From the employee's perspective, the advantages of maintaining the diary are:

- it gives the employees active involvement in performance appraisal (because they are accountable for the entries);
- it provides employees with ownership of evidence;
- it reinforces productivity and performance standards;
- it acts as a foundation for identifying areas for individual development;
- it provides unbiased documentation; and
- it provides a record of incidents available for review whenever required.

From the guest's or customer's perspective, the advantages of maintaining the diary are that it encourages better quality of service from all staff members.

From the management perspective, the advantages of maintaining the diary are:

- it provides ongoing monitoring of performance and productivity standards;
- it identifies training needs;
- it rewards the right people;
- it is the foundation for a database in benchmarking and developing standard operating procedures (SOPs);
- it provides information on management performance as well as employee performance; and
- it involves a range of management roles including immediate supervisor, department manager, and personnel manager.

Disadvantages

The diary method also has a limited number of disadvantages. These are:

- there might be difficulties in establishing and defining the parameters of incidents that should be recorded;
- staff members might attempt to manipulate the system—for example by inducing customers to endorse staff actions, rather than relying on spontaneous expressions of approval.

Summary

The diary method is a refinement of 'critical incident appraisal', '360-degree evaluation', and 'peer assessment'. The onus is no longer on the supervisor to record critical incidents. More often than not, such recording by supervisors is limited by the supervisor's willingness and availability to carry out the task. The employee becomes an active participant in his or her performance appraisal. This helps with motivation—which, is after all, one of the main reasons for conducting performance appraisal.

Personnel occupational health & safety issues

Different languages

Hospitality managers must ensure that advice on occupational health & safety procedures, and on safety in general, is available to staff members who come from a different language background. Many of the hotel guests also will not have English language skills.

The system of using warning signs or pictograms for hazards should therefore be utilised. There are many commonly understood symbols for such warnings, and certain colours also have common meaning (for example, red means danger, orange caution, and green indicates safety).

People with disability

The occupational health & safety policies of the organisation should not neglect the special needs of employees with disability. For example, care must be taken to ensure access to and from the property in the event of emergency. The safety audit and analysis should take into account work layout and facilities.

Alcohol and drugs

Alcohol addiction is the fourth most common disease in Australia, and is common in the workplace. The International Labour Organization (ILO) states that 15–30% of all fatalities in the workplace are related to alcohol.[10] Alcoholics also suffer a higher rate of accident injury in the workplace.

The hospitality industry is one of the major providers of alcohol to members of the community, and certainly many of its employees imbibe. The hospitality employer should be aware of the problem of drug and alcohol-dependent employees by ensuring that there are adequate counselling and assistance programs for its workers.

No employee should consume alcohol while on duty.

Stress management

Problems caused by stress

Stress can lead to health problems, and aspects of stress management must be considered in the context of occupational health & safety. Signs of stress in the work area can include irritability and anger (with guests and colleagues), poor work performance, a higher frequency of accidents, and increased ill-health and absenteeism.

If a hospitality manager has indications that employees are under stress, the problems must be properly investigated (see 'Investigating stress' page 257). Apart from a desire to minimise the personal distress of those involved, management wishes to minimise the economic consequences of stress in the workplace. It is expensive to cope with employees whose health is suffering (workers' compensation, reorganisation, retraining, and so on), and the quality of service offered to guests can also suffer.

Stress can be a result of personal circumstances (such as family or money problems, or drug dependence), but it can also come about through work conditions at the place of employment. In the case of the latter, it is the responsibility of management to review the individual's work situation.

Investigating stress

The nature of the work

The first matter to be reviewed should be the employee's actual work. Workplace stress can result from a high workload and high levels of responsibility with which the individual cannot cope. The work itself could be stressful of its nature—for example, if the employee has to deal with members of the public or guests in fraught situations.

Alternatively, stress can also result from the person having too little work and too much spare time, or having work that is boring and repetitive.

Some revision of job design might be necessary if counselling determines that the work itself is a cause of stress.

Relationships in the workplace

The second matter requiring review is the individual's personal relationships within the workplace. This involves relationships with supervisors and relationships with other employees.

Problems in this regard can be due to the difficult personalities of the individuals involved—in which case the remedy could involve personal redirection or even a separation.

Stressful relationships could also be due to a difficult supervisor, or faulty procedures that put the individual under stress. Management has a responsibility to rectify these circumstances—especially if it is apparent that the circumstances are causing more than the one individual to be under stress.

Terms of employment

The third area to consider is the terms of employment. Stress can result from the terms and conditions of work, or from such things as a lack of promotion, lack of training opportunities, or from job insecurity.

Training for occupational health & safety

When staff members are first employed, they should be given a familiarisation session with their working environment and with safety procedures. As a very first step, they must be shown the emergency exits, the routes to those exits, and evacuation assembly points, and they must be informed about procedures to follow in the event of an emergency. New staff members should also be informed about first-aid and accident procedures—including who to call and where to find safety equipment in the event of an accident.

Employees should be familiarised with fire drills and the location and type of fire-fighting devices. New employees should be introduced to the sound of the fire alarms, so that they can identify the various warning sounds used on the alarm systems.

Figure 9.4 *Protect your back*
Kevin Baker

Any familiarisation session should deal with some basic commonsense practices appropriate to the area of employment. In addition, some practices are common across many departments—such as rules for safe lifting (for example, 'save your back'), and safety on stairs and steps.

Back strain is one of the more common causes of injury in the workplace. New employees must be given instruction on the correct, safe ways to lift and carry heavy goods.

Rules to avoid back injury

Use proper lifting techniques as follows:
- check path is clear;
- 'size-up' the shape, size, and type of load to be lifted;
- position feet and bend knees;
- grasp load diagonally;
- strengthen back; and
- lift correctly, pushing chin in, and driving upwards with the thighs and buttocks.
  In cases of difficult lifts:
- do not be in a hurry;
- be careful with hot or liquid loads;
- get help if you need it; and
- use mechanical lifting devices where appropriate.

Some basics of first aid

- Ensure that everyone knows the basics of first aid.
- Ensure that employees know the location of the first-aid station, and where to go for help.
- Ensure that first-aid kits are accessible and properly stocked at all times.
- Ensure that emergency phone numbers are clearly displayed beside all telephones.
- Ensure that all staff know what to do in an emergency.

Finally, the new staff member should be informed of the procedures for reporting accidents or hazards. Employees should be given the name and contact details of the person who serves as a focal point for safety in the workplace.

Other personnel management functions

The personnel manager has a wide range of other duties and functions that cannot be detailed here. These duties include exit interviews and turnover analysis to establish why people are leaving the organisation, and compensation analysis to ensure that people are fairly remunerated for their duties.

Activity 9.4   *Ethical consideration*

You are assisting the personnel officer in the selection process for new administrative staff for your enterprise. The personnel officer says that, as part of the selection screening, she wants you to contact the central police register that has details of criminal offences.

QUESTIONS

- What would be your reaction if you discover that a prospective employee has a criminal record for a shoplifting offence, but ten years have passed since that offence and the person has no record of any further offences?
- What would be your reaction if you discover that a prospective employee had been charged with several offences, but the offences were discharged due to a legal technicality?
- What would be your reaction if, while conducting the check, you inadvertently discover that the personnel officer herself has a criminal record for serious offences?

Chapter review questions

1 What are the main objectives of planning for personnel needs?
2 Why can't hospitality organisations rely solely on historical data to determine their own effective staffing levels?
3 What is the 'relevant labour market'? Is it the same for all hospitality organisations?
4 At an employment interview, what are some questions you should ask, and what are some questions you should not ask?
5 What are some steps you could take to assess whether an applicant is suitable for an employment position in food & beverage?

Solution to Activity 9.3

WHAT WOULD YOU DO FOR YOUR BOSS?

(See page 252 for details of this activity.)
Percentage of respondents who would paint the house of the boss:

China	72%	Hong Kong	34%	Japan	17%
Indonesia	52%	Mexico	30%	Ireland	13%
Kuwait	50%	Spain	29%	Germany	11%
Singapore	44%	Pakistan	25%	UK	8%
Thailand	40%	India	24%	Netherlands	7%
Egypt	38%	USA	20%	Australia	4%

CASE STUDY

The HB Hotel

The executive housekeeper of the HB Hotel has recently promoted you to be his deputy. One of your responsibilities is to train room attendants to work effectively and efficiently. To do this, you have been asked to draw up a 'training plan and training schedule' for room attendant staff.

Using colleagues to assist you, create a plan that lists:

• the tasks to be learnt;
• the time allotted for the training of each task;
• the location of the training; and
• the training format of each task.

Present your detailed plan to the executive housekeeper.

Chapter 10

Casinos and Gaming Operations

The whore and the gambler, by the state licensed, build that nation's fate.

William Blake 1757–1827, *Auguries of Innocence*

Synopsis of chapter

This chapter commences with a description of casinos and gambling generally, with a special focus on Australia. The chapter then examines possible career paths within the sector and concludes with a section on an important issue for management of a casino—the control issue.

Gambling through history

A story from China dating from the fourth century BCE tells of two gamblers who grew tired of the usual games. They decided to bet on which side of a birch leaf would be left facing upwards when the birch leaf fell from a tree. The wager was to be their ears! In due course, the losing gambler cut off his ears and presented them, on the birch leaf, to the winner!

In Greek mythology from the same era, even the gods are depicted as gambling with each other, and with humans, using dice.

All through history, humans have loved to gamble. The reasons for this desire have been debated. Sigmund Freud saw sexual overtones in the movements of gambler's hands and the reaching out of the croupier's rake at the gaming table. Whatever the reasons, gambling has long been a part of the human psyche and, in some people, can become compulsive—a problem of which casino and gaming-room operators must be aware, and for which they must make provision.

In a busy casino

Courtesy Casino Canberra

'Casino' is a word derived from the Italian word *casa* ('house'). The *Concise Oxford Dictionary* defines a casino as 'a public room or building for gambling'.[1] The same source defines 'gambling' as to 'play games of chance for money'.

Casinos and gambling in Australia

In Australia, the gambling sector of the hospitality industry includes not only casinos, but also Totalisator Agency Board (TAB) outlets, Keno gaming, and other gaming activities (such as poker machines) installed in hotels and clubs.

The gambling and gaming sector is important within the tourism and hospitality industry. The Household Disposable Income Survey conducted by the Australian Bureau of Statistics reveals that, of the aggregate household disposable income of AUS$290 billion, approximately AUS$8.2 billion was spent on gambling.[2] Statistics also reveal that gambling revenue is approximately 1% of gross domestic product (GDP)—although the turnover is the equivalent of 9% of GDP, which means that gamblers win back 89 cents on average for every $1 gambled.

There are several casinos in Australia, including properties in the larger cities, which have a strong local market. These include the Crown Casino in Melbourne and Star City Casino in Sydney. These cities also have higher average per capita incomes than other Australian cities, and the highest proportion of people born in Asia. There are also properties in smaller centres—such as Reef Casino in Cairns, Wrest Point in Hobart, and the Darwin Casino—that rely on the tourism market. Most casinos have hotels associated with their operation and, of course, substantial food & beverage operations.

The casino market falls into three categories:

- first, there is the 'grind' market, which includes local players who go to the nearest casino or gaming venue;
- secondly, there is the 'tourist' market, which takes in both domestic and international tourists who make a visit to a casino as part of a package that includes other features and trips; and
- thirdly, there is the 'premium' market, which is composed of the big players—sometimes called 'high rollers'—who can be either local or international.

The casino sector in Australia is extremely competitive in the premium market. These high rollers can wager more than AUS$5 million over just a few days, and casinos endeavour to attract these players by offering free first-class air travel (or sometimes travel in a private Lear jet), limousines, and accommodation.

The Asian tourist markets and premium markets are especially important to Australian casinos, as these markets account for up to 80% of casino revenues.

Despite heavy promotional activities, exclusive licences, and the support of state governments (which see casinos and gambling as attractive sources of tax revenue), few of the Australian casinos have returned profits of 10% (or better) for their operators as yet. This might be due to the very high capital costs involved in establishing a casino, and to the growing competition in the sector.

Ethical issues related to gambling are important in any assessment of gaming in Australia. One such issue relates to 'problem gamblers'. These people have a gambling habit that has become an obsession, to the extent that they sometimes borrow or even steal to finance their gambling habit. They can neglect their family responsibilities—and there have been many instances of parents leaving small children outside casinos or gambling venues while the parent gambles inside. All casinos in Australia recognise these issues and have instituted various responses—including the placing of warnings, the patrolling of car parks, and the establishment of funds for the counselling and support of problem gamblers. Because of these ethical issues, and also because of concerns that organised criminal groups might take control of gambling outlets, all applicants for casino licences have to pass strict criteria and probity checks. All operations, including hotel and club gambling venues, must adhere to detailed regulations.

Australians are the greatest gamblers in the world. Australia has 25% of the world's poker machines and Australians gamble ten times as much per head as does the next-highest gambling nation.

Activity 10.1 *Odds on a payout*

Go to a local club or venue that has poker machines and ask the manager of the 'games room' if it is possible to know the odds of the poker machines. Then quietly observe players and note how often a particular machine makes a payout, and how often players leave a machine without taking a refund of credit. Then try to calculate how much money each poker machine takes after the payouts.

Staffing and career paths in casinos and gaming venues

Employment in casinos has many parallels to employment in other hospitality ventures, but with significant differences. First, anyone taking up a career in casinos has to be prepared for the shift work involved, because most casinos experience activity peaks outside the standard '9 to 5' regimen of office workers. Secondly, employment in casinos means entering a workplace that has very high standards of security.

Where would a person typically start a casino career? Casinos offer a variety of games on which patrons wager. The person who represents the casino ('the house') in these various games must be fully conversant with the rules, practices, and style of play. This person is usually called the 'dealer' or, in some cases, the 'croupier'. The dealer is the face across the gaming table, and the skill of the dealer is crucial if the house is to achieve the proportion of wagers upon which it depends for its gaming profit. The mathematical odds generally favour the house, although many players seek to develop systems to tip the odds in their own favour. The dealer must have a range of skills—including the ability to think quickly (often under stress) and a well-groomed, personable, and pleasant demeanour that encourages patrons to remain and play with them. In addition, dealers must have an ability to concentrate—to memorise the fall of the cards.

Clearly, dealers or croupiers do not chance their luck on behalf of the house on the first day of their employment. A lengthy training period is necessary. This training period can last for approximately six weeks. The training not only includes the basics and finer points of the games they will play professionally for the casino, but also includes:

- how to make the appropriate commentary (for certain announcements are mandatory);
- how to handle and convert chips (chips are tokens representing cash, and chip-handling is sometimes referred to as 'chipping' or 'chip-cutting'); and
- how to handle and calculate wagers.

In the course of training, casino personnel are sometimes required to undertake training in legal aspects of their duties, and to be licensed by the government's regulatory body as an approved employee.

The dealers are obviously closely supervised, to ensure the smooth running of the games and uniform standards of dealing, and to check the handling of large amounts of cash and chips. The person who carries out this supervision is an 'inspector' or 'supervisor', and normally has the responsibility of opening and closing tables, checking that all the equipment is in perfect working order, and supervising the handling of cash. The inspector is also responsible for dealing with any disputes that might arise in the course of gaming.

An additional responsibility of the inspector is to note who is playing in the casino. The casino has an interest in being aware of both inexperienced and experienced players. The casino seeks to welcome novice players to encourage them to return for the entertainment experience offered by the casino. However, the inspector also wants to be aware of the presence of very experienced players. Among these experienced players are high rollers, who are welcomed familiarly and encouraged to play. Very experienced players might also include cheats—who are not welcome and are discouraged. In Australia, as there is still a relatively small number of casinos, it is possible to identify cheats who go from one property to another.

The inspector usually reports to a more senior supervisor—who is sometimes known as the 'pit boss', or perhaps by the French term, *chef de partie*. This person normally has several years experience as a dealer and inspector.

Skill requirements of a dealer or croupier

A dealer of croupier must:

- know all aspects of the appropriate game, especially the table limits and the payouts on wagers;
- be able to concentrate and memorise the fall of cards and tiles;
- be able to convert cash to chips and use mental arithmetic to add up and calculate bets without making mistakes;
- be able to speak clearly and precisely so that all players are aware of the state of play, without being so loud as to disturb the concentration of players of other games close by;
- be able to conduct the game at sufficient speed without making players feel pressured or confused, and
- be organised, neat, and groomed—even in the heat of a game late at night.

Table 10.1 *A typical career path in casino management*

Casino general manager	up to 15 years
Casino operations manager	3 years
Gaming shift manager	4 years
Pit boss	3 years
Inspector	3 years
Dealer/croupier	2 years

Note that the career path illustrated in Table 10.1 can be more extended than that of hotel general management—taking approximately fifteen years to reach top management level. There are several reasons for this. Casino operation is a specialised activity, and there are many regulations of which the manager must be aware and implement. Also, most casinos are medium-to-large operations, and it therefore takes longer to master all the skills and responsibilities demanded, and to give evidence of competence. Small casinos cannot survive because they cannot attract the high volume of wagering that is required to raise a sufficient revenue stream from the low mathematical margins that exist on wagering. Hence, in casino management, an aspirant cannot move quickly to take charge of a small operation and then move to a bigger one—as a hotel or motel manager can do.

Las Vegas—a city built on gambling

The American state of Nevada legalised gambling in 1931, but it remained on a small scale until the late 1940s. A New York speculator named Benjamin 'Bugsy' Siegel had attempted to run gambling operations on ships in international waters off the coast of California, but that state's laws were amended to stop the practice, so Siegel went inland to a rural settlement called Las Vegas (which means 'meadows' in Spanish). Siegel and his backers opened a luxury hotel named the 'Flamingo' in 1946. The Desert Inn followed in 1950 and, by 1956, there were twelve luxury hotels with casinos in the growing desert town. Their revenues soon reached hundreds of millions of dollars.

Big gamblers are fêted with free first-class air travel and chauffeur-driven Rolls-Royces, and are provided with top entertainment. But most of the casinos' revenues come from the small gamblers—millions of ordinary folk who go to the city for a 'flutter' in the glamorous surroundings.

There are alternative career streams in casinos. One such career stream might be through marketing of the casino's operations. The entry position for this stream can be at the level of 'valet'—people who are trained to assist patrons around the floor of large gaming venues.

The provision of security is a major and specialised task. Personnel commence as security officers after a period of training in all aspects of the casino operation—including outlines of games, cash-handling, identification of cheating and fraud, and dealing with disputes. Security personnel also deal with such procedures as emergency evacuation and first-aid training. Security officers can aspire to supervisory status and then responsibility for security over a property. A related area of duty to security is surveillance—which does not have the same potential for physical confrontation, but has the intellectual challenge of spotting cheating or fraud, and identifying one of the known 'rogues' gallery' of cheats.

Another career path in casino employment is through cash-handling—which has its own challenges and specialisations. These personnel have titles such as 'chip-changer' or 'cashier'. Chip-changers require good mathematical skills, and also the ability to deal with people. The initial employment position in cashiering has a title such as 'front-window changer', and the training for this position includes:

- techniques for dealing in chips and the role of the 'chips bank';
- cash-handling procedures related to the movement of cash and chips from tables (each gaming table having a drop box for cash to avoid too much cash or chips accumulating on the playing area); and
- currency exchange rates and the practices of currency exchange.

From front-window changer, employees might advance to a supervisory position—with responsibility for the cash-handling of a shift, including bank deposits and reconciliations. The next step up is to 'cash-desk manager'—with responsibility for all cashier staff, as well as control of procedures and the chips inventory.

Activity 10.2 Job descriptions

Through the use of publications, the Internet, or a site visit to a gambling venue (with observation of the various activities), write up job descriptions for:

(a) a dealer;

(b) an inspector; and

(c) a pit boss.

Casino games

The games that the dealer plays for the house can include:

- card games (such as blackjack, five-card stud, draw poker, and so on);
- games involving two or three dice (such as sic-bo);
- games dependent upon the random fall of a ball (such as roulette); and
- tile games such as the ancient Chinese game of pai gow.

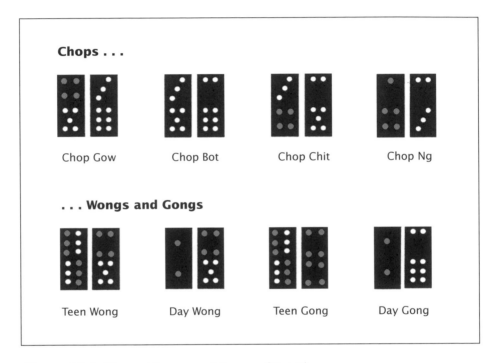

Figure 10.1 *Chops, Wongs, and Gongs of Pai Chow*

Kevin Baker

For games such as pai-gow, the dealer must know the rules and be able to play the game quickly and skilfully, and also has to be fully conversant with such terms as 'wongs', 'gongs', and 'highs' and 'gee jun' jackpots.

It is usual for a novice dealer to play only one game until that dealer has become fully conversant with all its aspects. Some of the more common casino and gaming-room games are described below.

Roulette

The word 'roulette' comes from the French word for a small wheel. The wheel is divided into a number of slots with different colours (alternating red and black) and numbers (usually 37 in Europe and 38 in America). A small ball rolls from a ledge in the middle to fall into one of the numbered and coloured slots. Provided the wheel is perfectly horizontal, and spinning freely, pure chance directs where it lands. The game might have originated by being played on a horizontal spinning chariot wheel. The game became well known when European royalty and nobility began to patronise a small barn in the principality of Monaco, where a gaming house had been opened in 1854 by a Frenchman named François Blanc.

Slot machines

Slot machines, also known as poker machines or gaming machines (or 'one-armed bandits'), have reels of symbols that are spun —either electronically or by the pulling of a handle—after coins or credit have been inserted. If there are three reels and twenty symbols on each reel, this makes approximately eight thousand combinations of symbols. The machines are devised to pay out a proportion of the money invested in them when certain combinations of symbols come up. The proportion paid out varies from approximately 80% to approximately 95% of the machine's takings—but strict regulations govern the amount to be paid out. The device was invented by an American named Charles Fey in 1895. Because it is such a simple and low-maintenance means of making money, it has become popular. Because it is a mechanical device, cheats have used mechanical means to steal from it—including inserting wire down the coin slot, or up the payout tray.

Two-up

A well-known Australian gambling game is called 'two-up'. It originated from an English game known as 'pitch and toss', and became common among Australian servicemen during World War I. Normally it is illegal throughout Australia but, because of the service traditions of the game, it may be played on Anzac Day (when Australians and New Zealanders recall the deeds of servicemen and servicewomen). The game involves tossing two coins into the air from a flat piece of wood called a 'kip', the person doing the tossing being referred to as the 'spinner'. Bets are placed as to whether the coins come down as two heads or two tails. If a the coins fall and show a head and a tail, the toss is referred to as a 'no throw'.

Craps

Craps is a game involving the throwing of dice that originated with African Americans in the nineteenth century. A player throws two dice and wins if the dice total 7 or 11 on the first throw, and loses if they total 2, 3, or 12 (which is called a 'crap'). He or she may then throw again according to the total shown.

Backgammon

Backgammon is a game involving a board and fifteen pieces for each player. The player throws dice to advance or restrict the movement of the pieces along parts of the board divided by a bar. It is a common game and variations of it exist around the world. Variations are called pacisi in India, shing kun t'o in China, and sugoroku in Japan.

Blackjack

Blackjack (also known as 'twenty-one', 'vingt-et-un', or 'pontoon') requires a player to take cards from the dealer that total 21 or less than 21—a total of more than 21 meaning the player is 'bust'. The player then wins if his or her cards total more than the dealer's cards, or if the dealer goes 'bust'. Face (or 'court') cards—that is, king, queen, and jack—count for ten, and an ace can be one or eleven. 'Pontoon' is constituted by an ace and a court card.

Poker

The name 'poker' might have come from a similar German game in which a withdrawing player called out 'Ich poche' and tapped his cards to show he was 'out'. Draw poker involves being dealt five cards and, after discarding some as desired, betting on hands such as pairs or threes, consecutive cards, all of the same suit, and so on. Stud poker is the same except that some of the player's cards are left on the table for all to see.

Chance, the odds, and the numbers in various games

For as long as humans have been gambling, they have been assessing their chances of winning. Very often, superstitions come into the calculations. One gambler at the casino at Monte Carlo had a big win after he had been soiled by a pigeon as he was entering the casino. Afterwards, he would wait outside the building, underneath flocks of pigeons, and he would go in to gamble only if he was again a pigeon's target. In some cultures, certain numbers are held to be lucky and others to be unlucky. Some people wear what they consider to be lucky charms—for example, a rabbit's foot. Despite strongly held beliefs by some, only the mathematical odds can be relied upon.

The odds of winning from a slot machine are not high in the long run. Roulette offers odds of 36 to one (considering 36 spaces to bet upon) and, if the true mathematical odds were offered, the gambler would be offered a pay out of $35 for every $1 he or she bet on a space. In practice, the payout is less than this (say $30 for $1)—hence the host of the gaming house makes a profit (and pays taxes) when play is extended over a long period.

A pioneer of gambling casinos—François Blanc

François Blanc was born in Avignon, France, in 1806. As a young man, he speculated on the stock exchange and saved enough to open a small bank with his brother in 1834. The bank prospered, mainly because Blanc used the newly developed telegraph to get early information of movements in stocks and financial news.

By the mid nineteenth century, gambling was booming in Europe and Blanc decided to invest in the industry. However, he was concerned that there was pressure on the French government to ban gambling activities. The answer seemed to be to open a casino in another country that was close enough to the wealthy gamblers of France, and the answer became a reality when Blanc met a German Count who had a small principality called Hesse-Homburg that was on the edge of bankruptcy. Blanc opened his casino there and it became popular and profitable through Blanc's skills in public relations, and in his ability to attract the rich and famous.

At around the same time in the south of France, other French entrepreneurs had built a resort, including a hotel and small casino, in a small principality called Monaco, the property of the Grimaldi family. The principality of only 368 acres (fewer than 150 hectares) was in the south of France. By 1863, the resort facilities were near collapse, and the Grimaldis approached the brilliant and well-known French financier François Blanc to take over the casino concession. Blanc accepted and built a new casino called the Monte Carlo and a luxurious hotel called the Hotel de Paris for the patrons. He also spent large amounts of money on local facilities, including a railway line that was built by 1870. Profits surged despite the large capital expenditure. When Blanc died in 1877, he was worth more than US$14 million.

In the very long run, odds generally favour the house. The house knows the odds of each game from long experience, and then the odds are tilted slightly more in their favour. The house does not seek to tilt the odds too far in its favour—for fear that patrons might not show up to play. The adjustment to the odds (or 'rake-off') is approximately 3%. Of course, in the short run, any patron or punter can make a big win and this fact maintains the hopes and enthusiasm of most. However, the cardinal rule of all gambling must be: *never bet what you cannot afford to lose*.

Like roulette, games involving dice are also ruled by mathematical odds, for each dice has six sides and, when two dice are used, there is a finite number of possible combinations. In the game of craps, for example, there are five ways of getting a six, and six ways of getting a seven. The fall of the dice is dictated by chance and chance alone, unless cheats tamper with the dice. Some cheats attempt to use 'loaded' dice—which have been tampered with to increase the chances of landing in a certain way. Tampering can involve curving sides (dice will land on the flat sides), inserting weights on a side, or boring out a hollow on the opposite side to that desired. The quick and easy way to check for loaded dice is to put them in a glass of water. They will float the same way each time that they are cast into the water.

Card games and games such as backgammon offer some opportunity to use a level of skill—for example, by memorising the fall of cards—such that the odds of a win are increased. For example, a person playing blackjack has slightly better odds than the dealer if all the fives have been played, but slightly worse odds than the dealer if all the aces have been played.

Some card games, such as poker, depend upon psychology as much as upon mathematical odds. These mathematical odds give the player some chance of getting something when the five cards are first dealt (that is, a 1 in 2 chance of receiving a pair of cards), but a limited chance of a really good hand. The chances of receiving four cards of a kind when first dealt are more than 600 to 1, and the chances of being dealt a 'royal flush' (consecutive cards of the same suit, ace high) are nearly 650 000 to 1.

The problem of control in casinos and gaming venues[3]

The importance of control

Casino operations present peculiar problems because of the large amount of cash involved in various gambling segments, and the fact that the cash (or chips) is not easily subject to reconciliation and count in the middle of a session. The same principles apply to casino operations as those that apply to tourism and hospitality operations at large. This means that there should be:

- division of duties;
- authorisation and reconciliation procedures; and
- physical security of assets.

The operations on each table, and on each shift, should be subject to a reconciliation and the use of a count sheet for the cage bank. This sheet should detail not only the amount of cash, but also the totals of each note denomination.

Control of a gaming location

The prime control function in a gaming location is ensuring the correct operation of gaming machines. These can include poker machines, slot machines, other amusement games, interlinked machines, and associated

Notable gamblers

The Roman emperors Claudius, Caligula, and Nero were all passionate gamblers. The writer Seneca portrayed Claudius as condemned to an eternity of trying to throw his dice in a cup without a bottom.

King Henry VIII of England gambled for the bells of St Paul's Church in London and won them; and then lost them again!

The socialite Giacomo Casanova loved the game of faro, and frequently gambled and lost the diamonds of his lady friends—but recouped his fortunes by organising one of the first government lotteries, in France in the 1760s.

The Russian author Fyodor Dostoyevsky was addicted to gambling at the roulette tables and was most often poor, despite his author's royalties.

The American Western sheriff 'Wild Bill' Hickok was shot dead while playing cards, and the final hand dealt to him comprised a pair of eights and a pair of aces—now known as a 'dead man's hand'.

devices (such as coin-dispensing machines). In addition, there are what are termed 'header systems'—such as data-recording systems intended to monitor playing and operations. As well as gaming through machines, there are also non-machine activities—such as bingo, sweepstakes, and so on.

Activity 10.3 Gamblers Anonymous

Contact Gamblers Anonymous and discuss with them the problems faced by people who are addicted to gambling. Prepare a short report on the major issues involved gambling addiction, and steps that can be taken (from a casino management perspective) to minimise the extent of the problem.

Control of cash and physical security

For both machine and manual gaming, there are two crucial control areas:

- control of cash; and
- physical security of employees and public.

With respect to the first of these, control is maintained by the principles of responsibility for the issue of cash and chips, and separation of duties with regard to monitoring. Coin-dispensing equipment must be correctly operated and any faults promptly reported and repaired. Cash reconciliations should be made and cross-checked regularly. Payout summaries must be made and reconciled with cash and machine readings. Payouts over a defined limit must be verified independently, and the payout to winners witnessed. Surprise audits of banks and floats should be conducted.

The security of staff, players, and onlookers is generally ensured by constant observation, and by the use of logs to record unusual occurrences and practices. The logs and reports on breaches of security functions should be reviewed regularly, and action taken to rectify weaknesses in the control systems. The operation should have a dispute-resolution policy. People who are perceived to threaten the security of other players or staff should be barred, and the barring procedures should be determined and strictly followed.

Activity 10.4 *Ethical consideration*

You are a duty manager in a hotel with a gaming room. One of your staff members comes to you to advise that a particular player has won jackpot after jackpot on a gaming machine. You watch carefully, without being noticed yourself, and you cannot see that the player is doing anything untoward or illegal. However, the person is certainly exceptionally lucky.

Work in a casino is usually busy and exciting

Courtesy Casino Canberra

It seems that the player is being rewarded with payouts every second minute. You feel sure that there must be something suspicious. The player has not been in the gaming room before and, although you have studied descriptions of known cheats, this player does not meet any such description.

The staff member who alerted you to the player suggests that the person should be told to leave. An alternative course of action would be to activate the fire alarm and evacuate the gaming room—thus enabling you to end the player's run of luck without being liable for any complaint.

What would you do?

Chapter review questions

1 To what extent does a casino have to have a moral responsibility to the community at large?
2 What steps should gaming management take to ensure that underage players do not join the gaming?
3 'Gambling can bring great benefits to society.' List the benefits, and the problems, of a large-scale gambling venue.

CASE STUDY

The HB Hotel

The owners of the HB Hotel have decided to add poker machines to the lounge and bar areas of the hotel.

As the manager, in conjunction with your staff write a report on the potential benefits and problems associated with this venture, with particular reference to those that are relevant to the HB Hotel and its environment. Remember to take into account that the poker machines are to go into a public area as well as the bar.

Consider what licences and permits will be needed, and how much revenue the hotel might expect to receive from the machines.

Appendix 1

The Multilingual Manager

In the opinion of the authors, hospitality professionals must have some language skills, and a knowledge of some useful phrases and sentences, in languages other than their own. As a courtesy to guests, it is polite to be able to address people with a few words of their own tongue. This does not take a lot of effort, and it is one of the secrets of true hospitality—the art of making people welcome—to take a little trouble for the sake of others. To greet people in their own language is a powerful way of saying: 'You are welcome'. It is also a way of saying that the guest is respected as a person and is not seen as being merely an entry in the reservations system.

The authors do not suggest that every hospitality professional must become fluent in a range of languages. However, hospitality staff should have a grasp of some basic words and phrases such that there can be at least some communication. The foreign guest should not always be placed in the position of struggling for meaning in a strange tongue.

This basic skill, or courtesy, is appropriate for a range of hospitality professionals—including managers, front office staff, restaurant staff, and concierges. Note the example (page 87) of the young commissionaire of a London hotel who learned seven languages in two years.

There is a difficulty in finding basic language material, for there is limited language material compiled from the point of view of service providers—as distinct from the material available from the point of view of service consumers (tourists, guests, and so on). There are many tourist phrasebooks and guidebooks published that have 'handy language tips' or 'essential phrases'. However, hospitality professionals might not find these suitable for their purposes, for these phrasebooks are compiled for the use of people seeking services in a foreign country—not for those offering services and attempting to make foreign guests welcome.

The following short phrases and sentences have been compiled for the specific needs of the hospitality professional. The list is not meant to be comprehensive. It is simply a collection of key phrases intended to reassure guests that their needs and comfort are seen as important and that their hosts have taken trouble to try to make them feel at home, and to comprehend their basic needs.

Each group of words is numbered and there is a concordance between the numbers in all the languages.

Selected words, phrases, and sentences

English

Each phrase is numbered. Note the number of the phrase you wish to translate and look it up under the same number in the language lists that follow.

1 Good morning, sir. Good morning, madam.
2 Good evening, sir. Good evening, madam.
3 Welcome to . . .
4 What is your name?
5 Have you had a good journey?
6 How may I help you?
7 This is reception.
8 Do you have a reservation?
9 May I see your passport?
10 Please fill in the registration form.
11 Do you want a double room? Single room?
12 How long will you be staying?
13 Please sign here.
14 You may park your car . . .
15 Here is your room key.
16 Is this your luggage?
17 The porter will assist you.
18 Your room is on floor number . . .
19 Check-out time is . . .
20 Time: 9 a.m., 10 a.m., morning, midday, afternoon, 6 p.m., evening
21 The elevators are over there.
22 . . . on the left.
23 . . . on the right.
24 We hope you have a good stay in . . .
25 This is your bill.
26 Do you want a taxi?
27 Numbers: one, two, three, four, five, six, seven, eight, nine, ten
28 Meals: breakfast, lunch, dinner
29 Please, thank you
30 Entrance, exit

31 Place, date
32 Excuse me.
33 Hotel staff: manager, porter, room attendant, waiter, receptionist
34 Places: bedroom, bathroom, toilet, dining room, swimming pool, shops
35 Items: telephone, towels, mail, postage, message, window, laundry

Japanese

Transliterated into 'English' characters

1	Good morning, sir. Good morning, madam	1	Ohayo gozaimasu.
2	Good evening, sir. Good evening, madam	2	Kombanwa.
3	Welcome to . . .	3	. . . ni yokoso
4	What is your name?	4	O namae o onegaishimasu?
5	Have you had a good journey?	5	Ryoko wa yokatta desu ka?
6	How may I help you?	6	Irasshaimase?
7	This is reception.	7	Kochira ni furonto de gozaimasu.
8	Do you have a reservation?	8	Goyaku shite arimasu ka?
9	May I see your passport	9	Passupoto o misete kudasai?
10	Please fill in the registration form.	10	Kado ni kinyuu shite itadakema suka.
11	Do you want a double room? Single room?	11	Daburu rumu gahoshii no desu ka? Shinguru rumu gahoshii no desu ka?
12	How long will you be staying?	12	Donokurai tomarimasho ka?
13	Please sign here.	13	Kochira ni sain shite kudasai.
14	You may park your car . . .	14	. . . chuusha shitara kekkoo desu.
15	Here is your room key.	15	Kore ga oheya no kagi desu.
16	Is this your luggage?	16	Onimotsu wa anata no desu ka?
17	The porter will assist you.	17	Potasan wa tetsudai itashimasu.
18	Your room is on floor number . . .	18	Oheya wa . . . kai de gozaimasu.
19	Check-out time is . . .	19	Chekku auto wa . . . ji de gozaimasu.
20	Time: 9 a.m., 10 a.m., morning, midday, afternoon, 6 p.m., evening	20	Ji: asakuji, asajuji, asa, hiru, gogo, gogorokuji, yugata
21	The elevators are over there.	21	Erebeta wa asako de gozaimasu.
22	. . . on the left.	22	Hidari ni.
23	. . . on the right.	23	Migi ni.
24	We hope you have a good stay in . . .	24	Ni tomaru no o tanoshite kudasai.
25	This is your bill.	25	Korewa osei kyusho de gozaimasu.

26 Do you want a taxi?

26 *Takushii ga irimasu ka?*

27 Numbers: one, two, three, four, five, six, seven, eight, nine, ten

27 *Kazu: ichi, ni, san, shi/yon, go, roku, shichi/nana, hachi, ku/kyu, ju*

28 Meals: breakfast, lunch, dinner

28 *Shokuji: choshoku, chushoku, yushoku*

29 Please, thank you

29 *Onegaishimasu, arigato gozaimasu*

30 Entrance, exit

30 *Iriguchi, deguchi*

31 Place, date

31 *Tokoro, hizuke*

32 Excuse me

32 *Sumimasen*

33 Hotel staff: manager, porter, room attendant, waiter, receptionist

33 *Hoteruin: shainin, pota, meido, furonto gakari*

34 Places: bedroom, bathroom, toilet, dining room, swimming pool, shops

34 *Basho: beddor umu, furoba, otearai, shokudo, puru, omise*

35 Items: telephone, towels, mail, postage, message, window, laundry

35 *Mono: denwa, taoru, yubin, yuzi, messeji, mado, sentaku*

Indonesian (Bahasa Indonesia)

1 Good morning, sir. Good morning, madam.

1 *Selamat pagi, Tuan. Selamat pagi, Nyonya.*

2 Good evening, sir. Good evening, madam.

2 *Selamat malam, Tuan. Selamat malam, Nyonya.*

3 Welcome to . . .

3 *Selamat datang di . . .*

4 What is your name?

4 *Siapa nama, Tuan/Nyonya?*

5 Have you had a good journey?

5 *Bagaimana perjalanan Tuan/Nyona?*

6 How may I help you?

6 *Bagaimana bisa saya menolong?*

7 This is reception.

7 *Inilah resepsion.*

8 Do you have a reservation?

8 *Apakah Tuan/Nyonya mempunyai reservasi?*

9 May I see your passport?

9 *Bolehkah saya melihat paspot?*

10 Please fill in the registration form.

10 *Silakan mengisi formulir pendaftaran.*

11 Do you want a double room? Single room?

11 *Apakah Tuan/Nyonya mau kamar untuk dua orang? Seorang?*

12 How long will you be staying?

12 *Berapa hari Tuan/Nyonya akan menginap disini?*

13 Please sign here.

13 *Silakan menanda tangani disini.*

14 You may park your car . . .

14 *Bolen memakir kendaraan Tuan/Nyonya disini . . .*

15 Here is your room key.

15 *Inilah kunci kamar, Tuan/Nyonya.*

16 Is this your luggage?	16 *Apakahini bagasi, Tuan/Nyonya?*
17 The porter will assist you.	17 *Si porter akan membant.*
18 Your room is on floor number . . .	18 *Kamar Tuan/Nyonya di lantai . . .*
19 Check-out time is . . .	19 *Waktu cek out adalah . . .*
20 Time: 9 a.m., 10 a.m., morning, midday, afternoon, 6 p.m., evening	20 *Waktu: jam sembilan pagi, jamepuluh pagi, pagi, siana, sore, jam enam petang, malam.*
21 The elevators are over there.	21 *Elevator ada disitu.*
22 . . . on the left.	22 *Pada sebelas kiri*
23 . . . on the right.	23 *Pada sebelas kanan*
24 We hope you have a good stay in . . .	24 *Kami beri Tuan/Nyonya menyukai waktu di . . .*
25 This is your bill.	25 *Inilah bill, Tuan/Nyonya.*
26 Do you want a taxi?	26 *Apakah Tuan/Nyonya man taksi?*
27 One, two, three, four, five, six, seven, eight, nine, ten	27 *Satu, dua, tiga, empat, lima, enam, tujuh, delapan, sembilan, sepuluh*
28 Meals: breakfast, lunch, dinner	28 *Makanan: makan pagi, makan siang, makan malam*
29 Please, thank you	29 *Silakan, terimah kasih*
30 Entrance, exit	30 *Masuk, jalan*
31 Place, date	31 *Tempat, tanggal*
32 Excuse me	32 *Permisi*
33 Hotel staff: manager, porter, room attendant, waiter, receptionist	33 *manager, porter, pembantu, pelayan, resepsionis*
34 Places: bedroom, bathroom, toilet, dining room, swimming pool, shops	34 *Tempat: kamar tidur, kamar mandi, kamar kecil, kamar makan, kolam renang, toko-toko.*
35 Items: telephone, towels, mail, postage, message, window, laundry	35 *Barang barang: Telpon, handuk, surat, penginman, pesan, jendela, barang-barang pencucian*

German

1 Good morning, sir. Good morning, madam.	1 *Guten Morgen, Herr. Guten Morgen, gnädige Frau.*
2 Good evening, sir. Good evening, madam.	2 *Guten Abend, Herr. Guten Abend, gnädige Frau.*
3 Welcome to . . .	3 *Willkommen zu . . .*
4 What is your name?	4 *Was ist Ihr Name?*
5 Have you had a good journey?	5 *Haben Sie eine gute Reise gehabt?*
6 How may I help you?	6 *Wie könnte ich Ihnen helfen?*
7 This is reception.	7 *Dies ist Empfang.*

8 Do you have a reservation?

9 May I see your passport?

10 Please fill in the registration form.

11 Do you want a double room? Single room?

12 How long will you be staying?

13 Please sign here.

14 You may park your car . . .

15 Here is your room key.

16 Is this your luggage?

17 The porter will assist you.

18 Your room is on floor number . . .

19 Check-out time is . . .

20 Time: 9 a.m., 10 a.m., morning, midday, afternoon, 6 p.m., evening

21 The elevators are over there.

22 . . . on the left

23 . . . on the right

24 We hope you have a good stay in . . .

25 This is your bill.

26 Do you want a taxi?

27 Numbers: one, two, three, four, five, six, seven, eight, nine, ten

28 Meals: breakfast, lunch, dinner

29 Please, thank you

30 Entrance, exit

31 Places, date

32 Excuse me

33 Hotel staff: manager, porter, room attendant, waiter, receptionist

34 Places: bedroom, bathroom, toilet, dining room, swimming pool, shops

35 Items: telephone, towels, mail, postage, message, window, laundry

8 *Haben Sie eine Reservierung?*

9 *Bitte, kann ich ihren Pass sehen?*

10 *Füllen Sie das Registrierung-Formular aus, bitte.*

11 *Wollen Sie ein doppeltes Zimmer? Einzelnes Zimmer?*

12 *Wie lang werden Sie bleiben?*

13 *Unterschreiben Sie hier, bitte.*

14 *Sie konnen Ihr Auto parken . . .*

15 *Hier ist Ihr Zimmer-Schlüssel.*

16 *Ist dieses Ihr Gepäck?*

17 *Der Pförtner wird Ihnen assistieren.*

18 *Ihr Zimmer ist auf Boden-Nummer . . .*

19 *Prüfen Sie, Zeit ist . . .*

20 *Zeit: 9Uhr, 10Uhr, Morgen, Mittag, Nachmittag, 18Uhr, Abend*

21 *Die Fahrstühle sind dort drüben.*

22 *. . . auf der Linke*

23 *. . . auf dem Recht*

24 *Wir hoffen, dass Sie einen guten Aufenthalt in . . . haben.*

25 *Dies ist Ihre Rechnung.*

26 *Mochten Sie ein Taxi?*

27 *Zahlen: eins, zwei, drei, vier, fünf, sechs, sieben, acht, neun, zehn*

28 *Mahlzeiten: Frühstück, Mittagessen, Abendessen*

29 *Bitte, danke*

30 *Eingang, Ausgang*

31 *Stellen, Datum*

32 *Entschuldigung . . .*

33 *Hotel-Personal: Manager, Pförtner, Zimmer-Aufseher, Kellner, Empfangschef*

34 *Stellen: Schlafzimmer, Badezimmer, Toilette, Esszimmer, das Schwimmbad, Geschäfte*

35 *Gegenstände: Telefon, Handtücher, Post, Porto, Mitteilung, Fenster, Wäsche*

French

	English		French
1	Good morning, sir. Good morning, madam.	1	*Bonjour, Monsieur.* *Bonjour, Madame.*
2	Good evening, sir. Good evening, madam.	2	*Bonsoir, Monsieur.* *Bonsoir, Madame.*
3	Welcome to . . .	3	*Bienvenu à . . .*
4	What is your name?	4	*Quel est votre nom?*
5	Have you had a good journey?	5	*Avez-vous eu un bon voyage?*
6	How may I help you?	6	*Comment est-ce que je peux vous aider?*
7	This is reception.	7	*C'est la réception.*
8	Do you have a reservation?	8	*Est-ce que vous avez une réservation?*
9	May I see your passport?	9	*Est-ce que je peux voir votre passeport?*
10	Please fill in the registration form.	10	*S'il vous plaît remplissez la forme de l'inscription.*
11	Do you want a double room? Single room?	11	*Est-ce que vous voulez une pièce double? Une pièce seule?*
12	How long will you be staying?	12	*Combien de jours est-ce que vous resterez ici?*
13	Please sign here.	13	*S'il vous plaît signez ici.*
14	You may park your car . . .	14	*Vous pouvez garer votre voiture . . .*
15	Here is your room key.	15	*Voici votre clef de pièce.*
16	Is this your luggage?	16	*Est ce votre bagage?*
17	The porter will assist you.	17	*Le concierge vous aidera.*
18	Your room is on floor number . . .	18	*Votre pièce est sur le . . . etage.*
19	Check-out time is . . .	19	*Le temps de la caisse est . . .*
20	Time: 9 a.m., 10 a.m., morning, midday, afternoon, 6 p.m., evening	20	*Le temps: 9 hr, 10 hr, matin, midi, après-midi, 18 hr, soir*
21	The elevators are over there.	21	*Les ascenseurs sont là-bas.*
22	. . . on the left	22	*. . . à gauche*
23	. . . on the right	23	*. . . à droite*
24	We hope you have a good stay in . . .	24	*Nous espérons que vous avez un bon séjour dans . . .*
25	This is your bill.	25	*C'est votre billet.*
26	Do you want a taxi?	26	*Est-ce que vous voulez un taxi?*
27	Numbers: one, two, three, four, five, six, seven, eight, nine, ten	27	*Les nombres: un, deux, trois, quatre, cinq, six, sept, huit, neuf, dix*
28	Meals: breakfast, lunch, dinner	28	*Les repas: petit déjeuner, déjeuner, dîner*

29 Please, thank you

30 Entrance, exit

31 Places, date

32 Excuse me

33 Hotel staff: manager, porter, room attendant, waiter, receptionist

34 Places: bedroom, bathroom, toilet, dining room, swimming pool, shops

35 Items: telephone, towels, mail, postage, message, window, laundry

29 *S'il vous plaît, merci*

30 *Entrée, sortie*

31 *Places, date*

32 *Excusez-moi*

33 *Le personnel d'hôtel: directeur, concierge, serviteur de pièce, serveur, réceptionniste*

34 *Les places: chambre, salle de bains, toilette, salle à manger, piscine, magasins*

35 *Les articles: téléphone, serviettes, courrier, affranchissement, message, fenêtre, lessive*

Italian

1 Good morning, sir.
Good morning, madam.

2 Good evening, sir.
Good evening, madam.

3 Welcome to . . .

4 What is your name?

5 Have you had a good journey?

6 How may I help you?

7 This is reception.

8 Do you have a reservation?

9 May I see your passport?

10 Please fill in the registration form.

11 Do you want a double room? Single room?

12 How long will you be staying?

13 Please sign here.

14 You may park your car . . .

15 Here is your room key.

16 Is this your luggage?

17 The porter will assist you.

18 Your room is on floor number . . .

19 Check-out time is . . .

1 *Buongiorno, signore.*
Buongiorno, signora.

2 *Buona sera, signore.*
Buona sera, signora.

3 *Benvenuto a . . .*

4 *Il Suo nome, prego?*

5 *Ha fatto un viaggio buono?*

6 *Come posso aiutarla?*

7 *Questo è il Ricevimento.*

8 *Ha una prenotazione?*

9 *Potres vedere il Suo passaporto?*

10 *Per favore potrebbe riempire*

11 *Vuole una stanza doppia o una singola?*

12 *Quanto tempo ha intenzione di stare?*

13 *Per favore firmi qui.*

14 *Lei può parcheggiare la Sua macchina . . .*

15 *Ecco la Sua chiave.*

16 *È questo il Suo bagaglio?*

17 *Il facchino L'auite rà.*

18 *La Sua stanza è al piano . . .*

19 *Dourebbe lasciare l' hotel all ore . . .*

20 Time: 9 a.m., 10 a.m., morning, midday, afternoon, 6 p.m., evening

20 *Dalle: 9 a.m., 10 a.m., mattina, mezzogiorno, pomeriggio, 6 p.m., sera*

21 The elevators are over there.

21 *Gli ascensori.*

22 . . . on the left

22 *. . . sulla sinistra*

23 . . . on the right

23 *. . . sulla destra*

24 We hope you have a good stay in . . .

24 *Spero che abbia un buon soggiorno . . .*

25 This is your bill.

25 *Questo è il Suo conto.*

26 Do you want a taxi?

26 *Vuole un tassì?*

27 Numbers: one, two, three, four, five, six, seven, eight, nine, ten

27 *Numeri: uno, due, tre, quattro, cinque, sei, sette, otto, nove, dieci*

28 Meals: breakfast, lunch, dinner

28 *Pasti: colazione, pranzo, cena*

29 Please, thank you

29 *Per favore, grazie*

30 Entrance, exit

30 *Entrata, uscita*

31 Places, date

31 *Luoghi, data*

32 Excuse me.

32 *Mi scusi.*

33 Hotel staff: manager, porter, room attendant, waiter, receptionist

33 *Personale di albergo: direttore, facchino, compagno ai piano, cameriere, receptionist*

34 Places: bedroom, bathroom, toilet, dining room, swimming pool, shops

34 *Luoghi: camera da letto, bagno, gabinetto, sala da pranzo, piscina, negozi*

35 Items: telephone, towels, mail, postage, message, window, laundry

35 *Articoli: telefono, asciugamani, posta, affrancatura, messagi, finestra, bucato*

Portuguese

1 Good morning, sir.
Good morning, madam.

1 *Bom dia, senhor.*
Bom dia, senhora.

2 Good evening, sir.
Good evening, madam.

2 *Boa noite, senhor.*
Boa noite, senhora.

3 Welcome to . . .

3 *Bem-vindo para . . .*

4 What is your name?

4 *O que é o seu nome?*

5 Have you had a good journey?

5 *O senhor teve boa viagem [male];*
O senhora teve boa viagem? [female]

6 How may I help you?

6 *Como eu posso o ajudar?*

7 This is reception.

7 *Esta é a Recepção.*

8 Do you have a reservation?

8 *Você tem uma reserva?*

9 May I see your passport?

9 *Eu posso ver o seu passaporte?*

10	Please fill in the registration form.	10	*Por favor preencha a forma de inscrição.*
11	Do you want a double room? Single room?	11	*Você quer um quarto de casal? Singelo quarto?*
12	How long will you be staying?	12	*Quanto tempo você estará ficando?*
13	Please sign here.	13	*Por favor assine aqui.*
14	You may park your car . . .	14	*Você pode estacionar seu carro . . .*
15	Here is your room key.	15	*Aqui está a sua chave de quarto*
16	Is this your luggage?	16	*É este a sua bagagem?*
17	The porter will assist you.	17	*O porteiro o ajudarão.*
18	Your room is on floor number . . .	18	*Seu quarto està no . . . andar*
19	Check-out time is . . .	19	*Tempo de saída é . . .*
20	Time: 9 a.m., 10 a.m., morning, midday, afternoon, 6 p.m., evening	20	*Tempo: 9 a.m., 10 a.m., manhã, meio-dia, tarde, 6 p.m., noite*
21	The elevators are over there.	21	*Os elevadores estão ali.*
22	. . . on the left	22	*. . . na esquerda*
23	. . . on the right	23	*. . . à direita*
24	We hope you have a good stay in . . .	24	*Nós esperamos que você tenha uma permanência boa dentro . . .*
25	This is your bill.	25	*Esta é a sua conta.*
26	Do you want a taxi?	26	*Você quer um táxi?*
27	Numbers: one, two, three, four, five, six, seven, eight, nine, ten	27	*Números: um, dois, três, quatro, cinco, seis, sete, oito, nove, dez*
28	Meals: breakfast, lunch, dinner	28	*Refeiç ões: O pequeno almoço, almoço, o jantar*
29	Please, thank you	29	*Por favor, obrigado*
30	Entrance, exit	30	*Entrada, saída*
31	Places, date	31	*Lugares, data*
32	Excuse me.	32	*Com licença.*
33	Hotel staff: manager, porter, room attendant, waiter, receptionist	33	*Pessoal de hotel: gerente, porteiro, criado de quarto, criado de mesa, recepcionista*
34	Places: bedroom, bathroom, toilet, dining room, swimming pool, shops	34	*Lugares: quarto, quarto de banho, retrete, sala de jantar, piscina, lojas*
35	Items: telephone, towels, mail, postage, message, window, laundry	35	*Artigos: telefone, toalhas, correio, taxa postal, mensagem, janela, roupa suja*

Appendix 2

Sources of Data

Sources of data on the tourism and hospitality industry in Australia

These sources can change names and locations from time to time. This list of sources is intended to be indicative rather exhaustive, and the authors acknowledge there are other sources and industry associations that are not included here.

Commonwealth government sources

Australian Bureau of Statistics (ABS)   Cameron Offices, Chandler Street, Belconnen ACT 2617; <www.abs.gov.au>; published series include: Overseas Visitor Arrivals and Departures (Catalogue No. 3401.0); Accommodation Statistics

Australian Tourism Commission   4/80 William Street, Woolloomooloo NSW 2011

Bureau of Tourism Research   GPO Box 9839, Canberra ACT 2601; 4/20 Allara Street, Canberra ACT 2601; <www.btr.gov.au>; two important registers of information from the bureau (which is located in the Department of Industry, Science and Resources) are the International Visitor Survey and the National Visitor Survey

Commonwealth Department of Foreign Affairs and Trade   RG Casey Building, Barton ACT 2600; <www.dfat.gov.au/geo/eeag/index.html>

Office of National Tourism   PO Box 1545, Canberra ACT 2601

Sport and Tourism Division, Department of Industry, Science and Resources   GPO 9839, Canberra ACT 2601

Tourism Forecasting Council   GPO Box 9839, Canberra ACT 2601; 4/20 Allara Street, Canberra ACT 2601

State and territory government sources

Canberra Tourism and Events Corporation Level 13, SAP House, Akuna and Bunda Streets, Canberra City ACT 2601

Northern Territory Tourist Commission Tourism House, Levels 3 & 4, 43 Mitchell Street, Darwin NT 0800

South Australian Tourism Commission Levels 7 & 8, Terrace Towers, 178 North Terrace, Adelaide SA 5000

Tourism New South Wales Tourism House, 2/55 Harrington Street, The Rocks, Sydney NSW 2000

Tourism Queensland Level 36, Riverside Centre, 123 Eagle Street, Brisbane Qld 4000

Tourism Tasmania Level 15, Trafalgar Building, 110 Collins Street, Hobart Tas. 7000

Tourism Victoria Levels 6 & 7, 55 Collins Street, Melbourne Vic. 3000

Western Australia Tourism Commission Level 6, 16 St George's Terrace, Perth WA 6000

Industry organisations in Australia

Association of Australian Convention Bureaux
Australian Amusement, Leisure & Recreation Association
Australian Automobile Association
Australian Farm and Country Tourism Inc.
Australian Federation of Travel Agents
Australian Hotels Association
Australian Youth Hostels Association
Bus and Coach Association
Caravan Parks' Association
Caravan Trade and Industry associations (various in Australian states)
Ecotourism Association of Australia
Fast Food Industry Association
Inbound Tourism Organisation of Australia
Meetings Industry Association of Australia
motorists' associations (various, in Australian states)
Pacific Asia Travel Association
Property Council of Australia
Registered Clubs Association
Restaurant and Caterers' Association
Retailers' Association
Tourism Training Australia
World Tourism Organization

Subscription trade publications

Australian Hotelier, National Publishing Group, NSW

Convention and Incentive Marketing, Rank Publishing Company, NSW

Hospitality: Foodservice, Beverage, Accommodation, APN Business Publishing, Vic.

Hotel Watch, Blake, Dawson and Waldron, NSW

Inside Tourism, NSW
National Liquor News, National Publishing Group, NSW
Restaurant and Catering Australia, Association of Restaurant and Catering, NSW
Tourism and Hospitality Review, Genesis Multimedia, NSW
Traveltrade, Reed Business Publishing P/L, NSW
Travelweek, APN Business Publishing, Vic.

Sources of international and national statistics

International Monetary Fund (IMF) <www.imf.org>; for international financial statistics on CPI, GDP, daily exchange rates, direct foreign investment
Organisation for Economic Co-operation and Development (OECD) <www.oecd.org>

Other sources

Internet indexing services for example, ABI Inform (which covers approximately 800 major business journals)
stockbroking advisory services, merchant banks, and specialist consultancies for example, Horwarth & Horwarth; National Institute of Economic and Industry Research

Chapter Notes

Chapter 1 The Context of Hospitality Management

[1] *Concise Oxford Dictionary*, 9th edn, p. 656.

[2] Ibid.

[3] Ibid., p. 1590.

[4] Urdang, L. (ed.) 1991, *The Oxford Thesaurus*, p. 201, Clarendon Press, Oxford.

[5] Butkarat, A. & Meddlik, S. 1974, *Tourism: Past, Present and Future*, p. vii, Heinemann, London.

[6] BCE = before common era (equivalent to BC); CE = 'common era' (equivalent to AD).

[7] *The Phaedo*.

[8] This is an example of the humorous aside often attempted by the authors (and occasionally successfully).

[9] Sigaux, G. 1966, *History of Tourism*, p. 67, Leisure Arts Ltd, Geneva.

[10] Ibid., p. 78.

[11] Gross domestic product (GDP), simply defined, is the sum total of all the production of goods and services in an economy or business—that is, a measure of the total economic activity of an entity.

[12] Estimates of the World Travel and Tourism Council for 1999.

[13] Koldowski, J. 2000, 'Beyond 2000: Pacific–Asia Tourism Forecast', *PATA Compass*, May–June 2000, pp 22–4.

[14] Arthur Andersen 1999, 'The Hotel Industry Benchmark Survey', p. 6.

[15] According to 'Travel and Tourism Intelligence', quoted by Koldowski, p. 23.

[16] For a discussion on the definition of 'off licence', see pages 172–3.

[17] Jacobs, J. 2000, 'Out of this World', *Asta Agency Management*, January 2000, pp 26–30.

[18] Horwath International and Smith Travel Research, quoted by Bailey, M. 1998, 'The International Hotel Industry—Corporate Strategies and Global Opportunities', *Travel and Tourism Intelligence Research Report*, 2nd edn, 1998, p. 13.

[19] Carter, R., of the School of Marketing, University of New South Wales, quoted in Stanton, W., Miller, K. & Layton, R., 1994, *Fundamentals of Marketing*, 3rd edn, p. 717, McGraw-Hill Book Company, Sydney.

[20] Statistics from Arthur Andersen 1999, 'The Hotel Industry Benchmark Survey', October 1999, p. 7.

[21] For an extended treatment of B&Bs, refer to Dickman, S. and Maddock, M. 2000, *The Business of Bed and Breakfast*, Hospitality Press, Melbourne.

[22] An extended discussion of the evolution of the ratings system can be found in Salter, S. 1995, 'The Evolution of Australia's Ratings Scheme for Accommodation', *Motoring Directions*, Spring 1995 Issue 4, Vol. 1, pp 13–16.

[23] Ibid. p. 16.

[24] *Dawsons Hotel Guide (Australia)*, 61st edn, 1999.

[25] Cover story, 'The Future is Now', *Hotel Asia Pacific*, Jan/Feb 2000, pp 26–9.

[26] Readers can refer to their website at <www.tourismdotcom.gov.au>.

[27] *Canberra Times*, 17 May 1999.

[28] In addition to Global Distribution Systems, another 12% of worldwide reservations is handled by other computer reservation systems, and 17% by hotel-based reservation departments (1999 figures from *Hotel Asia Pacific*).

[29] Cover story, 'The Future is Now', *Hotel Asia Pacific*, Jan/Feb 2000, p. 27.

[30] Dickey, C., 1996, 'Niche for the Night', *Newsweek*, 9 December 1996, p. 71.

[31] Scoviak-Lerner, M. 1996, 'Market-Driven Design Trends for the Millennium', *Hotels*, May 1996, p. 58.

[32] Hensdill, C. 1996, 'Partnerships in Dining', *Hotels*, February 1996, p. 57.

[33] Described by Ashton, C., in 'Singapore Falls for History', *Australian Financial Review Magazine*, March 2000, p. 16.

[34] Plummer, A. 1992, 'Projected Growth in Technologies Required by a Teleresort', *Pacific Asia Travel Association*, PATA Conference 1992, San Francisco, pp 267–8.

[35] Details reported in the *Australian*, 7 November 2000.

Chapter 2 The General Manager

[1] Guerrier, Y. & Lockwood, A. 1989, 'Developing Hotel Managers—a Reappraisal', *International Journal of Hotel Management*, Vol. 8, No. 2, p. 84.

[2] *A Guide to College Programs in Hospitality and Tourism*, 3rd edn, John Wiley & Sons, New York, 1993, pp 13–14.

[3] Miller, K. & Layton, R. 2000, *Fundamentals of Marketing*, 4th edn, p. 675, Irwon/McGraw-Hill, Sydney.

[4] Knutson, B. J. 1988, 'Ten Laws of Customer Satisfaction', *The Cornell Hotel and Restaurant Administration Quarterly*, November 1988, pp 15–16.

[5] Quoted in Berry, Leonard L. 1995, *On Great Service—a Framework for Action*, p. 74, The Free Press, New York, 1995.

[6] Berry 1995 (as above, note 5) p. 89.

[7] Acknowledgments to Campbell, A. & Featherstone, A. 1995, *How to get a Job in Hotels and Resorts*, p. 3, Hospitality Press, Melbourne.

[8] Hofstede, G. 1993, 'Cultural Constraints in Management Theories', *Academy of Management Executive*, Vol. 7, February 1993, pp 81–94.

[9] Sherwyn, D, Lankau, M. & Eigen, Z. 1999, 'The Good, the Bad, and the Ugly', *Cornell Hotel and Restaurant Administration Quarterly*, October 1999, pp 10–17.

[10] Meade, V. 2000, 'Cultural Tourism, *Lodging*, February 2000, p. 53.

[11] Hall, S. 1992, *Ethics in Hospitality Management*, p. 9, American Hotel & Motel Association, Michigan.

[12] Pitt, H. & Groskaufmanis, K. 1990, 'Minimizing Corporate Civil and Criminal Liability: A Second Look at Corporate Codes of Ethics', *The Georgetown Law Review*, 78, 1990 (1559).

[13] Rogers, P. & Swales, J. 1990, 'We the people? An Analysis of the Dana Corporation Policies Document', *The Journal of Business Communication*, Vol. 27, No. 3, pp 293–307.

[14] Stevens, B. 1996, 'Using the Competing Values Framework to Assess Corporate Ethical Codes', *The Journal of Business Communication*, Vol. 33, No. 1, January 1996, pp 71–84.

[15] Cree, N. & Baring, G. 1991, 'Desperately Seeking Ethics', *Australian Accountant*, July 1991, pp 25–6.

[16] MacCrimmon, K. & Wehrung, D. with Stanbury, W. 1986, *Taking Risks—The Management of Uncertainty*, p. 10, The Free Press, a Division of Macmillan Inc., New York.

[17] Singleton, W. & Hovden, J. 1987, *Risk and Decisions*, p. 3, John Wiley & Sons, Chichester.

[18] Crockford, N. 1986, *An Introduction to Risk Management*, p. 16, Woodhead-Faulkner, Cambridge.

[19] The term 'assets' is here used to cover any severable item with present or future economic benefit.

[20] Crockford, N. 1986, *An Introduction to Risk Management*, p. 6, Woodhead-Faulkner, Cambridge.

[21] Ibid. pp 6–8.

[22] Ibid. pp 25–6.

[23] MacCrimmon et al. 1986, op. cit. (note 16 above), p. 111.

[24] Ibid., p. 125.

[25] Ibid., p. 247.

[26] Ibid., pp 249–65.

[27] Singleton & Hovden 1987, op. cit. (note 17 above), p. 7.

[28] Thompson, C. & Mooney, M. 1998, Waiariki Institute of Technology, 'Is it all Rubbish? Incentives and Impediments for Waste Minimisation in the Accommodation Industry', paper at New Zealand Tourism and Hospitality Research Conference, 1 December 1998.

[29] Reported in the *Green Hotelier*, Issue No. 17, January 2000, p. 10.

[30] Enz, C. & Siguaw R. 1999, 'Best Hotel Environmental Practices', *Cornell Hotel and Restaurant Administration Quarterly*, October 1999, p. 77.

[31] Ibid. p. 74.

[32] Ibid. p. 76.

[33] Reported in the *Green Hotelier*, Issue No. 17, January 2000, p. 11.

[34] Ibid., p. 10.

[35] Gill, T. & Satyanarayan, S. 1995, 'Critics See Downside to Thai-style Ecotourism', *Nation*, 12 February, quoted by Dowling, R. K., 'Ecotourism in Southeast Asia: Appropriate Tourism or Environmental Appropriation', paper at the Third International Conference, 'Tourism and Hotel Industry in Indo-China and Southeast Asia', 4 June 1998.

[36] This scenario was inspired by a real-life event at Cairns in May 2000, when a crocodile capsized a seaplane while trying to mount its float.

Chapter 3 The Front Office

[1] Author not noted, 'Presenting Lodging's Best', *Lodging Hospitality*, April 1996, p. 97.

[2] Obituary column, *Daily Telegraph*, 31 May 2000.

[3] This and the following checklists based on self-test exercises in 'The Art of Handling International Visitors', National Tourism Industry Training Committee.

Chapter 4 Housekeeping, Laundry, and Maintenance

[1] A reasonable workload for a room attendant or housekeeping aide is 2.5 to 3 rooms per hour, but this is dependent upon the size of the room and the standard of the work demanded.

[2] A benchmark for the American situation is 6.6 minutes of labour for every occupied room in the hotel, or US$1.10 for every occupied room. (As quoted in Walker, R. 1996, *Introduction to Hospitality*, p. 121, Prentice Hall, New Jersey.)

[3] C. Leeman 2000, *Executive Housekeeping Today*, p. 15, January 2000.

[4] Martin, R. 1986, *Professional Management of Housekeeping Operations*, p. 325, John Wiley & Sons, New York.

[5] Some synthetics have a tendency to 'pill'—that is, form small lumps, with wear.

[6] Blackhall, S. 1999, *The World's Greatest Blunders*, p. 57, Octopus Books, London.

[7] Such dogs are trained by a British charity called 'Canine Partners for Independence' and one dog was awarded the title 'Dog of the Millennium' by a national magazine.

[8] The 'Holidaying with Cats' directory was authored by Kate Harte.

[9] The Sebel Hotel of Sydney accommodated a pelican in one of its suites with a spa. Housekeeping brought up a bucket of fish four times a day. The pelican had starred in the film 'Storm Boy', and was in Sydney for publicity functions. The incident is noted by S. Kurosawa in the *Australian Magazine*, 19–20 September 1998, p. 42.

[10] One of the authors was asked by a German guest if he could bring his pet crocodile to the hotel, and whether it could be kept in the bath.

[11] Baker, K. 1984, *Handicapped Employment: Contracting Hospital Services*, p. 11, Shield Press, Canberra.

[12] Author not noted, 'Presenting Lodging's Best', *Lodging Hospitality*, April 1996, p. 99.

[13] Davis, G. 1993, 'Environmentally Responsible Housekeeping: How to Begin', *Executive Housekeeping Today*, May 1993, p. 32.

Chapter 5 Food & Beverage Services

[1] Although, perhaps unexpectedly, studies suggest that only 20% of guests choose to eat in hotel restaurants.

[2] *Red Dwarf*, episode 'Future Echoes', copyright BBC, 1993.

[3] *Star Trek*, episode #60, 'And the Children Shall Lead', copyright Paramount Pictures, 1968.

[4] Reported in the London *Daily Mirror*, 10 June 2000.

[5] *Restaurants and Institutions*, 10 July 1989, pp 73–9, 1988 statistics.

[6] Baker, K. 1999, *Internal Control and Fraud Prevention in Hospitality Operations*, Hospitality Press, Melbourne, 1999.

[7] Author not noted, 'Presenting Lodging's Best', *Lodging Hospitality*, April 1996, p. 98.

[8] Blackhall, S. 1999, *The World's Greatest Blunders*, p. 57, Octopus Books, London.

[9] For a complete treatment on all aspects of control of fraud and theft in food-service operations, refer to Baker, K. 1999, *Internal Control and Fraud Prevention in Hospitality Operations*, Chapter 14, Hospitality Press, Melbourne.

[10] Reported by Sherer, M. 1989, 'Inside Job', *Restaurant and Institutions*, 3 April 1989, 99(10) p. 40.

[11] A 'perk' is a slang term for 'perquisite'—an extra payment or benefit, over and above normal remuneration of employment.

[12] Enz, C. & Siguaw, R. 1999, 'Best Hotel Environmental Practices', *Cornell Hotel and Restaurant Administration Quarterly*, October 1999, p. 73.

[13] Reported in *Green Hotelier*, Issue No. 17, January 2000, p. 18.

[14] Ibid. p. 19.

[15] Menzies, D. 1990, 'From Big Mac Boxes to Yo-Yos: Group to Determine Viability of Polystyrene Recycling', *Canadian Hotel and Restaurant*, January 1990, p. 24.

Chapter 6 Hospitality Law

[1] Florida Statutes Chapter 509 Public Lodging and Public Food Service Establishments, quoted in Ellis, R. 1986, *Security and Loss Prevention Management*, pp 198ff, American Hotel & Motel Association Educational Institute, Michigan.

[2] The more modern word 'hotelier' will be used from this point on in preference to the archaic 'innkeeper', even in cases where legislation, regulations, and so on refer to 'innkeeper'.

[3] Lee, R. 1995, 'Liability of Hospitality Firms for Deaths on Premises: Recent Court Cases and Methods for Prevention', *Hospitality Research Journal*, Vol. 19, No. 3, 1995, pp 45ff.

[4] Goodwin, J. & Rovelstad, J. 1980, *Travel and Lodging Law Principles, Statutes and Cases*, p. 254, Grid Publishing, Ohio.

[5] Sherry, J. 1993, *The Laws of Innkeepers—for Hotels, Motels, Restaurants and Clubs*, 3rd edn, p. 146, Cornell University Press, New York.

[6] Cournoyer, N., Marshall, A. & Morris, K. 1994, *Hotel, Restaurant and Travel Law: A Preventive Approach*, p. 221, Delmar Publishers Inc., New York.

[7] Stauber, A. & Ohlin, J. 1994, 'Exculpatory Clauses: Legal Environment and Implications for the Hospitality Industry', *Hospitality Research Journal*, Vol. 17, No. 2, 1994, p. 78.

[8] A notorious criminal on the loose might be declared a 'public enemy' by the king. The term survives in pulp fiction by references to a criminal being 'public enemy number one'.

[9] Cournoyer et al. 1994, op. cit. (note 6 above), pp 179ff.

[10] Jefferies, J. 1990, *Understanding Hospitality Law*, 2nd edn, pp 95–6, American Hotel and Motel Association Educational Institute, Michigan.

[11] Sherry, J. 1984, *Legal Aspects of Foodservice Management*, p. 53, National Institute for the Foodservice Industry, New York.

12 Simons, M. 1988, *Hotel, Restaurant and Catering Law*, 4th edn, pp 83–4, University of New South Wales Press, Sydney.

13 Goodwin, J. 1987, *Hotel Law, Principles and Cases*, p. 419, Publishing Horizons Inc., Columbus, Ohio.

14 Refer to discussion in Jefferies 1990, op. cit. (note 10 above), p. 52.

15 Wilson, R., Enghagen, L. & Sharma, P. 1994, 'Overbooking: The Practice and the Law', *Hospitality Research Journal*, Vol. 17, No. 2, 1994, pp 93ff.

16 Quotation from s.5 of the *Fair Trading Act 1987* (NSW), in Simons 1988, op. cit. (note 12 above), p. 139.

17 Simons 1988, op. cit. (note 12 above), p. 147.

18 Cordato, A. 1999, *Australian Travel and Tourism Law*, 3rd edn, p. 392, Butterworths, Sydney.

19 Vermeesch, R. & Lindgren, K. 1995, *Business Law of Australia*, 8th edn, Butterworths, Sydney; Gillies, P. 1988, *Concise Contract Law*, Federation Press, Sydney.

20 Quoted in Cournoyer et al. 1994, op. cit. (note 6 above), p. 205.

Chapter 7 Marketing Hospitality Enterprises

1 The marketing concepts discussed in the chapter are not the original work of the authors, but are widely discussed and used by many experts and writers. For one such specialised marketing text, refer Kotler, P., Chandler, P., Brown, L. and Adam, S. (1994), *Marketing: Australia and New Zealand*, 3rd edn, Prentice Hall, Sydney.

2 Some authors leave out 'people' and describe only four 'Ps'. The present authors prefer to add the fifth 'P'. Note also Wise, B. (ed.) 1991, *The Business of Hotel and Restaurant Management*, pp 200ff, Hospitality Press, Melbourne.

3 These characteristics are discussed in more detail in Kotler, P., Bowen, J. & Makens, J. 1996, *Marketing for Hospitality and Tourism*, pp 82–4, Prentice Hall International Editions, New Jersey.

4 Morrison, A. 1994, *Hospitality and Travel Marketing*, p. 393, Delmar Publishers Inc., New York.

5 For a discussion of factors involved in pricing products, see Kotler et al. 1996, op. cit. (note 3 above), pp 376ff.

6 Miller, K. and Layton, R.(2000) *Fundamentals of Marketing*, 4th edn, pp 192ff, Irwon/McGraw-Hill, Sydney.

7 Nykiel, R. 1983, *Marketing in the Hospitality Industry*, CBI Publishing Inc., New York, p. 26.

8 Ibid., p. 114.

9 McDonald, M. 1995, *Marketing Plans—How to Prepare Them and How to Use Them*, 3rd edn, pp 3–4, Butterworth-Heinemann Ltd, Oxford.

10 Miller & Layton 2000, op. cit. (note 6 above), pp 214ff.

11 Adapted from Nykiel 1983, op. cit. (note 7 above), pp 12–22.

12 Nykiel 1983, op. cit. (note 7 above), p. 13.

13 McDonald 1995, op. cit. (note 9 above), p. 4.

14 Robichaux, M. 1989, '"Competitor Intelligence"—A Grapevine to Rivals' Secrets', *Wall Street Journal*, 12 April 1989, p. B2, quoted in Robbins, S. & Mukerji, D. 1994, *Managing Organisations*, 2nd edn, p. 167, Prentice Hall of Australia P/L, Sydney.

15 Nykiel has a good discussion of the use of trend analysis in researching the marketing environment; see Nykiel, R. 1983, op. cit. (note 7 above), pp 182–5.

16 Kotler, P. 1994, *Marketing Management—Analysis, Planning, Implementation and Control*, 8th edn, pp 56–7, Prentice Hall of Australia P/L, Sydney.

17 Miller & Layton 2000, op. cit. (note 6 above), pp 192ff.

18 Lewis, G. et al. 1993, *Australian Strategic Management—Concepts, Context and Cases*, pp 82ff, Prentice Hall, Sydney.

19 McCarthy, E. et al. 1994, *Basic Marketing—A Managerial Approach*, p. 113, Richard D. Irwin Inc., Sydney.

20 Kotler 1994, op. cit. (note 16 above), p. 135.

21 McDonald 1995, op. cit. (note 9 above), p. 351.

22 McCarthy et al. 1994, op. cit. (note 19 above), p. 113.

[23] Pyo, Sung-Soo, Chang, Hye-Sook & Chon, Kye-Sung 1995, 'Consideration of Management Objectives by Target Markets in Hotel Feasibility Studies', *International Journal of Hospitality Management*, vol. 14, part 2, 1995, pp 151–6.

Chapter 8 Hospitality Accounting

[1] *New Shorter Oxford Dictionary*, CD version 1.0.03, Oxford University Press, Oxford.
[2] This calculation is explained in various accounting texts, such as Coltman, M. 1998, *Hospitality Management Accounting*, 6th edn, pp 381ff, Van Nostrand Reinhold, New York.
[3] The phrase 'rule of thumb' refers to a rough method of estimating length (similar to 'foot' and other ancient units of measure).
[4] Coltman, M. 1998, *Hospitality Management Accounting*, 6th edn, Van Nostrand Reinhold, New York; Schmidgall, R. 1995, *Hospitality Industry Managerial Accounting*, 3rd edn, Educational Institute of the American Hotel & Motel Association, Michigan.
[5] Charles Dickens (1812–70), *David Copperfield*, Chapter 12. The monetary units referred to are the (pre-decimal) English pounds, shillings, and pence. There were 12 pence in a shilling, and 20 shillings in a pound. Mr Micawber is thus proposing that an expenditure of sixpence (a small amount) less than income is 'happiness', but that an expenditure of only sixpence more than income is 'misery'.

Chapter 9 Personnel Management

[1] As in Chapter 7, Marketing Hospitality Enterprises, the authors acknowledge that some of the concepts presented are not original, but are used and discussed by a variety of authors. A number of sources of further specialised study are contained in these notes and in the bibliography.
[2] Wheelhouse, D. 1989, *Managing Human Resources in the Hospitality Industry*, pp 177ff, The Educational Institute, Michigan.
[3] Wise, B. 1991, *The Business of Hotel and Restaurant Management*, p. 176, Hospitality Press, Melbourne.
[4] Wheelhouse 1989, op. cit. (note 2 above), pp 45ff.
[5] Wise 1991, op. cit. (note 3 above), p. 176.
[6] Quoted in the *Australian*, 5 May 2000, p. 15.
[7] Cover story, 'The Future is Now', *Hotel Asia Pacific*, Jan/Feb 2000, p. 27.
[8] The authors gratefully acknowledge Jamal Feerasta, Assistant Professor, Hospitality Management Program, University of Akron, Ohio, USA, for this section on performance appraisal, and particularly his development of the 'diary method' of appraisal discussed later in this chapter.
[9] CIBS/ECA Copyright 1993 (13Q) Fons Trompenaars.
[10] Quoted in 'Planning Occupational Safety and Health' (no author noted), CCH Australia Ltd, Sydney 1991, p. 185.

Chapter 10 Casinos and Gaming Operations

[1] *Concise Oxford English Dictionary*, 9th edn.
[2] Australian Bureau of Statistics, 1994 figures.
[3] Elements of this discussion have been drawn from Baker, K. 1999, *Internal Control and Fraud Prevention in Hospitality Operations*, Hospitality Press, Melbourne.

Bibliography

Ashton, C. 2000, 'Singapore Falls for History', *The Australian Financial Review Magazine*, March 2000.

Australian Bureau of Statistics 1994, *Prisoners in Australia 1994: Results of the 1994 Prison Census*, ABS, Canberra.

Author not noted 2000, *Green Hotelier*, Issue No. 17, January 2000.

Author not noted 1991, *Planning Occupational Safety and Health* CCH Australia ltd, Sydney 1991.

Baker, K. 1999, *Internal Control and Fraud Prevention in Hospitality Operations*, Hospitality Press, Melbourne.

Baker, S. & Huyton, J. 1999, *Principles of Front Office Operations*, Hospitality Press, Melbourne.

Berry, Leonard L. 1995, *On Great Service—A Framework for Action*, The Free Press, New York.

C. Leeman 2000, *Executive Housekeeping Today*, January 2000.

Carter, R. 1994, of the School of Marketing, University of New South Wales, quoted in Stanton, W., Miller, K. & Layton, R. 1994, *Fundamentals of Marketing*, 3rd edn, McGraw-Hill Book Company, Sydney.

Coltman, M. 1998, *Hospitality Management Accounting*, 6th edn, Van Nostrand Reinhold, New York.

Dickey, C. 1996, 'Niche for the Night', *Newsweek*, 9 December 1996.

Dowling, R. K. 1998, 'Ecotourism in Southeast Asia: Appropriate Tourism or Environmental Appropriation?', paper at the Third International Conference, 'Tourism and Hotel Industry in Indo-China and Southeast Asia', 4 June 1998.

Enz, C. & Siguaw, R. 1999, 'Best Hotel Environmental Practices', *Cornell Hotel and Restaurant Administration Quarterly*, October 1999.

Gill, T. & Satyanarayan, S.1995, 'Critics See Downside to Thai-style Ecotourism', *The Nation*, 12 February 1995.

Gillies, P. 1988, *Concise Contract Law*, Federation Press, Sydney.

Hall, S. 1992, *Ethics in Hospitality Management*, p. 9, American Hotel & Motel Association, Michigan.

Hensdill, C.1996, 'Partnerships in Dining', *Hotels*, February 1996.

Horwath International and Smith Travel Research, quoted by Bailey, M. 1998, *The International Hotel Industry—Corporate Strategies and Global Opportunities*, Travel and Tourism Intelligence Research Report, 2nd edn, 1998.

Jacobs, J. 2000, 'Out of This World', *Asta Agency Management*, January 2000.

Knutson, B. J. 1988, 'Ten Laws of Customer Satisfaction', *The Cornell Hotel and Restaurant Administration Quarterly*, November 1988.

Lewis, G. et al. 1993, *Australian Strategic Management—Concepts, Context and Cases*, Prentice Hall, Sydney.

Mars, G. & Nicod, M. 1984, *The World of Waiters*, George Allen & Unwin, London.

McCarthy, E. et al. 1994, *Basic Marketing—A Managerial Approach*, Richard D. Irwin Inc., Sydney.

McDonald, M. 1995, *Marketing Plans—How to Prepare Them and How to Use Them*, 3rd edn, Butterworth-Heinemann Ltd, Oxford.

Meade, V. 2000, 'Cultural Tourism', *Lodging*, February 2000.

Menzies, D. 1990, 'From Big Mac Boxes to Yo-Yos: Group to Determine Viability of Polystyrene Recycling', *Canadian Hotel and Restaurant*, January 1990.

Nykiel, R. 1983, *Marketing in the Hospitality Industry*, CBI Publishing Company Inc., New York.

Plummer, A. 1992, 'Projected Growth in Technologies Required by a Teleresort', Pacific Asia Travel Association, *PATA Conference 1992*, San Francisco.

Pyo, Sung-Soo, Chang, Hye-Sook & Chon, Kye-Sung 1995, 'Consideration of Management Objectives by Target Markets in Hotel Feasibility Studies', *International Journal of Hospitality Management*, vol. 14, part 2, 1995.

Robbins, S. & Mukerji, D. 1994, *Managing Organisations*, 2nd edn, Prentice Hall of Australia P/L, Sydney.

Robichaux, M. 1989, '"Competitor Intelligence"—A Grapevine to Rivals' Secrets', *Wall Street Journal*, 12 April 1989.

Schmidgall, R. 1995, *Hospitality Industry Managerial Accounting*, 3rd edn, Educational Institute of the American Hotel & Motel Association, Michigan.

Scoviak, M. 1996, 'The Full Service Business Room of the Future', *Interior Design*, June 1996.

Scoviak, M. 1996, 'Hotels: the Next Generation', *Interior Design*, June 1996.

Scoviak-Lerner, M. 1996, 'Market-Driven Design Trends for the Millennium', *Hotels*, May 1996.

Sherer, M. 1989, 'Inside Job', *Restaurant and Institutions*, 3 April 1989, 99(10) pp 38–68.

Sherwyn,D., Lankau, M. & Eigen, Z. 1999, 'The Good, the Bad and the Ugly', *Cornell Hotel and Restaurant Administration Quarterly*, October 1999.

Simons, M. 1988, *Hotel, Restaurant and Catering Law*, 4th edn, University of New South Wales Press, Sydney, 1988.

Thompson, C. & Mooney, M. 1998, Waiariki Institute of Technology, 'Is it all Rubbish? Incentives and Impediments for Waste Minimisation in the Accommodation Industry', paper at New Zealand Tourism and Hospitality Research Conference, 1 December 1998.

Vermeesch, R. & Lindgren, K. 1995, *Business Law of Australia*, 8th edn, Butterworths, Sydney.

Glossary

Terms used in the tourism and hospitality industry in Australia

A number of the terms and descriptions in this glossary have been drawn from the 'A–Z of Accommodation Terminology', of the Hong Kong Polytechnic Department of Hospitality Management.

à la carte a menu on which each item is priced separately

accommodation and taxi order a voucher issued by airlines to travellers to cover their costs while delayed on a flight; the voucher is redeemable by the airline at face value, and normally covers accommodation, breakfast, a main meal, and return taxi fare from the airport to the hotel

accommodation or locate a promise of a room for a guest—if not in that hotel, a commitment to find elsewhere

adjoining rooms two or more rooms side by side with connecting door(s) between the rooms

advance reservation chart chart used for the advance allocation of rooms to reservations

advertised tour any travel program for which a brochure has been prepared; more specifically, a tour which meets airline requirements for an inclusive tour number

AH&MA American Hotel and Motel Association

airline rate a reduced rate given to airline personnel negotiated between an individual airline and a hotel

alphabetical guest index an index listing alphabetically the names of all persons staying in the hotel

American plan a rate at a hotel including three full meals and room (that is, full board); resorts commonly use this plan

Apex advance purchase exclusion; used in purchasing air travel tickets

arrival and departure list a list of the expected arrivals and departures for a particular day, normally prepared the evening before

Association of Australian Conventions Bureaux an organisation comprised of convention and visitors' bureaux from around Australia

Australian Automobile Association a peak industry body made up of state and territory motoring associations

Australian Federation of Travel Agents a trade association formed in 1957 to represent the interests of retail travel agents

Australian Hotels Association an association representing the interests of more than 6000 hotels and resorts around Australia—ranging from suburban pubs to five-star properties

Australian Liquor, Hospitality and Miscellaneous Workers Union a union of workers covering employees in businesses in the hospitality and tourism industries—including hotels, motels, restaurants, cafés, and general tourism enterprises

Australian Tourist Commission government-backed organisation aimed at increasing the number of overseas visitors to Australia and maximising the benefits brought to Australia by such visitors

average daily rate a measure of hotel performance obtained by dividing total room sales revenue by total rooms sold

average guest check a measure of food-service performance obtained by dividing total food-sales revenue by total number of guests

average rate average income per room; usually calculated on a monthly basis

back of house support areas of a hotel or motel (usually not in direct contact with public)—such as housekeeping, laundry, and maintenance

back to back name given to tours and group bookings that follow one after the other on the same day; as one group books out, another takes its place, causing rooms to be continually booked throughout the tour season

banquet upmarket function usually involving a large number of people, and conducted formally

bed-occupancy list the housekeeper's list of persons occupying rooms or beds at a given time; another term for **housekeeper report**

bed sheet list of guests showing who is in each room; usually used by medium-sized hotels, and usually filled out each evening by the duty receptionist; some forms have three columns—showing arrivals, guests in-house, and departures

bedroom book the simplest room-status system, showing who is occupying each room; it can also be used for reservations; commonly found in smaller hotels/motels

bistro a small bar or restaurant serving food and beverages, usually with some form of entertainment

black list a record authorised by the management containing the names and addresses of persons not welcome in the establishment

block-booking term used for a reservation made for several people for the same period—for example, a group of business representatives, a group of club members, or a group of conference delegates

bonding insurance taken out on people who handle large sums of cash; bonding is a protection against dishonest staff

booking diary a book in which reservations and allied information is recorded under day of arrival

booking reservations made for rooms or functions

brought forward the outstanding total of a guest's account 'brought forward' from the previous day's business

brush-up tidying a room after a guest has checked out, making the bed and, and replacing bathroom supplies

buffet a large selection of food usually offered on a sideboard or similar table for self-service

bus boy US term describing a person who clears the table in a restaurant after each course

cabana a room adjacent to pool area, with or without sleeping facilities, usually separate from hotel's main building

cafeteria an inexpensive restaurant or snackbar, usually self-service

call list a daily list of room numbers giving times at which guests require calls; sometimes also includes arrangements for morning tea and newspapers; updated by either reception or the hall porter

cancellation notification that a guest with a reservation no longer requires a room; usually refers to a situation in which the reservation is cancelled in time for the room to be reallocated

captain a person who takes food orders and is in charge of the waiters serving a section (station) of a restaurant

caravan park commercial open-air accommodation establishment at which caravans can be rented by travellers or sites can be hired on which travellers can place their own caravans

carried forward the outstanding amount on an account, carried onto the next day or month's business

cash bar a bar at which guests pay cash for drinks

cash discount an allowance made by a supplier to a debtor for paying an invoice within a specified short period

cashier's office a separate section of the front office for receipt of payment of guests' accounts; also deals with foreign currency and the custody of goods for safe keeping

casino area within a ship, hotel, or resort which is licensed for gambling activities

CBO central booking office; *see also* centralised reservations

centralised reservations an office unattached to any one company, booking accommodation for all the hotels in a group or marketing consortia

chain two or more operations which belong to the same organisation (for example, Holiday Inns, Hilton, and so on)

charge voucher a bill giving details of the amount to be charged to a guest's account showing room number, item charged, price, and department concerned; the guest should be asked to sign the voucher before submitting it to the cashier

check-in the process of a guest registering and giving name and other relevant details upon arrival at the hotel

check-out the process of a guest settling his/her account and departing the hotel

chef de brigade reception shift leader; also known as chief receptionist

CHRIE an organisation founded 1946 as a non-profit association for schools, colleges, and universities, offering programs in hotel and restaurant management, food-services management, and culinary arts

CIP commercially important person; a client who has influence over a large amount of business

city ledger the record of the accounts of guests who deal with the hotel on a credit basis

classification the assignment of properties to a category of service provision

cleaners persons who clean the corridors and areas other than the guests' bedrooms; responsible to the housekeeping department

closed dates dates on which nothing can be rented because the house is full

club an establishment providing food, drink, and sometimes entertainment, overnight accommodation, and other facilities and services for members (but not for the general public)

coach a bus, single- or double-decker, used for long distances or for sightseeing

coachline a company that runs coach services

cocktail reception early evening function, not always followed by dinner

coffee shop a shop offering coffee, tea, and sometimes snacks, often on a 24-hour basis

commercial hotel a hotel located near business sectors, major highways, and airports; guests are usually transient business people, conventioneers, or short-term travellers

commercial rate rate agreed upon by a company and a hotel for all individuals connected with the contracting company

commission discount or payment made to a company or agent, such as a travel agent, for introducing business to the hotel or other hospitality establishment

communicating rooms rooms set side by side with a door between, allowing private access to both rooms without the use of a public corridor

'comp' complimentary use; no charges made

computer reservations system a computer system linking airlines, hotels, travel agencies, and so on; *see also* **global distribution systems**

computer terminal a device for entering data into a computer, or receiving its output; a terminal is linked to the main computer and is located in such places as reservations, reception, restaurants, and so on

concierge uniformed staff member who arranges special services for guests including transport, luggage, and so on; also refers to the area, situated in the front hall, in which porters carry out their duties in the hotel

conference rate the rate charged to a conference organiser or company for the use of the hotel's conference facilities, bedrooms, and meal outlets

confirmation a written or verbal agreement on a previously provisional arrangement (such as a reservation for accommodation)

confirmed reservation a provisional booking confirmed orally or in writing (the latter being preferred); usually involves some definite agreement regarding payment (for example, a credit card) and usually involves a 6 p.m. check-in deadline

connecting rooms two or more rooms with private connecting doors allowing access between rooms without going into the corridor

consumer price index (CPI) a measure of inflation used in Australia

continental breakfast a morning meal consisting of juice, toast, bread roll, coffee (or tea); in some countries, a continental breakfast consists of coffee and bread roll only

continental plan room and continental breakfast only; commonly called 'bed and breakfast'

continuation bill the second page of a guest's account; a follow-on to a bill

contract a legally binding agreement between two parties

contractors companies that have arrangements to provide specified services for the hotel

control office an office carrying out the duty of control with in a business; the office responsible for prevention and detection of fraud, theft, and so on

control a check made on all accounts to ensure that charges are correct; a system for preventing and detecting fraud, theft, and so on

convention centre a specialised facility designed to accommodate large gatherings of people for a range of purposes including conferences, events, and exhibitions

convention a business or professional meeting in a specific location

conventional chart a reservation chart showing room numbers, type of room, guests' names, lengths of stay, and so on; there is usually one chart for each month

corkage an amount charged to a customer who brings his or her own liquor into a restaurant; the term refers to a charge for opening the bottle (that is, removing the cork)

corporate rate the room rate charged to business

cot a baby's bed

coup a term used by casino staff to describe a round of games (for example, in roulette)

coupon a slip of paper presented by a guest on arrival at the hotel, giving information concerning a reservation made through a travel agent

courier the porter of the hotel who carries out duties outside the hotel, such as meeting the guests at the airport or station

couvert a place setting at a table for one person ('cover')

CPI consumer price index; a measure of inflation used in Australia

credit note a note sent by a supplier to a purchaser when goods have been returned for one reason or another

credit transaction a commercial arrangement in which goods are bought and sold with payment being made/received at a later date

croupier a casino employee who conducts a game of roulette

cruise ship a vessel with onboard accommodation, restaurants, gym, swimming pool, and other recreational activities designed for travellers to enjoy the experience of travelling on the ship, rather than seeking a definite travel destination

culture a shared set of values, attitudes, customs, and achievements among a group of people

curtailment a booking which has been made for longer than the guest actually requires the room

customer service the provision of necessities and preferences required by a customer; usually infers the provision of such services in a manner that meets the customer's expectations of quality

cut-off date designated day when a buyer must confirm, release, or add to a commitment for services; the final date for arrangements to be definitely made

day let a room let out for use during the day only, usually until 5 p.m.; often for business meetings; also known as 'day use'; *see also* **day rate**

day rate a room rate for **day let** (*see above*); usually one-half regular rate of room; sometimes called a 'use rate'

de luxe finest, luxurious style

deadline the date by which time a provisional booking must be confirmed

debtor a person who owes money to the business

debtors' ledger the ledger in which a record of all debtors to the business is kept; otherwise known as the sales ledger

demographics characteristics of a population

density chart a reservation chart showing the total available number of each type of room for each night; it does not show details concerning individual bookings

deposit reservation a reservation for which a hotel has received cash payment in advance for at least the first night's lodging, and for which the hotel is obliged to hold the room regardless of the guest's arrival time; the hotel should pre-register such a guest

deposit payment received in advance of services rendered; this does not necessarily constitute a contract, but is an act of good faith

Des Skal Clubs Association an organisation that aims to develop friendship and common purpose among members of the tourism industry, and to foster goodwill among the peoples of the world through tourism

destination the place to which a person is going; the intended end of a journey

DG distinguished guest

Diners Club the name of a particular credit card company

dining room general-purpose food-service area for all meals

dinner a main meal, usually served from approximately 6 p.m. to 11 p.m. (although times vary according to the establishment)

dispense bar bar from which waiters provide service of drinks to restaurant guests

DL double-locked; a term used to indicate that the room is locked by the guest from the inside and that the housekeeper is unable to enter the room

DNA did not arrive

DNS did not stay; for various reasons, a guest sometimes desires to move out almost immediately after being shown the room

domestic independent travel prepaid, unescorted tour within a country, designed to the specification of an individual client or clients

doorman the member of the uniformed staff whose place of duty is outside the main entrance to the hotel; (a term that is not gender-specific term is not yet in common use)

double-bedded room a room for two persons with one large bed

double occupancy a room occupied by two persons at one time

due out guests who are expected to depart from the hotel on a given day or during a given time period; *see also* **check-out**

dumb waiter a small food lift or trolley

duplex a two-storey suite (parlour and one or more bedrooms) connected by a stairway

duty manager a member of the management staff who is responsible for service to, and personal contact with, the guests

duty-free (shop) a building in a city, or an area within a ship, resort, hotel, or airport, where goods are purchased without tax by international visitors and residents travelling to international destinations

E & OE errors and omissions excepted

early departure the departure of a guest before the expected departure date; *see also* **curtailment**

electronic key a computer-controlled system of electronic reception and security; when new arrivals check-in, the computer issues a plastic key with a new combination to the room; the combination is thus changed every time that the room is resold; master and submaster keys are issued on the same system to staff concerned

embezzlement the theft of money by a trusted employee, by manipulating the accounts

employee a person working for an employer in return for wages or salary

employer the owner; the person for whom staff work in exchange for wages

EMT early morning tea; room service to guests' rooms or apartments between 5 a.m. and 9 a.m.

English breakfast a full breakfast consisting of a hot beverage, bread, fruit juice, cereal, and a cooked dish

environmental analysis examination of the impact of a development upon its environment

escorted tour a tour which uses the services of a tour manager or tour escort

ethnocentrism a belief or attitude that one's own culture is superior to others

expatriate a resident of a country who remains a citizen of another

family rate special rates for families who have children under a certain age staying in their parents' room; also known as 'family plan'

family service plated main dish with self-service vegetables

fast-food outlet a limited-menu retail outlet offering quick service (usually over a counter) with the option of the purchaser taking the food away for consumption elsewhere

FIT free independent travel (or traveller)

flat rate specific room rate for a group, agreed by the hotel and group in advance

float a small amount of money entrusted to the cashier for the purpose of giving change and making small payments

floor limit a maximum amount that a hotel is allowed to accept on any one credit card per payment; above this, authorisation from the credit card company is necessary; aso known as sanction limit

floor service the service of food and beverages to guests in their rooms (also known as 'room service'); the term is also used to refer to the area set aside on each floor for this purpose

floor supervisor staff member responsible for operations within a specific area

flowchart a chart showing the order of activity required to carry out a task quickly and efficiently

franchise agreement to use the brand and systems of an existing business

front desk area where guest checks into hotel, where keys can be kept, and where information is dispensed

front of house entire public area of a hotel

front-office cashier person who adds up all charges made to a room and collects money on the departure of the guests who occupied it

front office the offices of the hotel which are situated in or near the front hall and in direct contact with the guests

full board *see* **American Plan**

full comp fully complimentary; entirely free; no charges made for the room, meals taken in the hotel, telephone, valet, or any other items

function list a list of functions in the hotel, prepared once a week by the sales or reception office

function a booking made in the hotel for a conference, wedding reception, or similar; a special event booked for multiple numbers, often with a given theme

GDP gross domestic product; the sum total of the production of economic goods and services within a country

general manager the manager in overall charge of the hotel

GIT group inclusive tour; a package tour

global distribution systems linked reservation systems

globalisation the linkage of world economies and relationships

grand master the key that will open all locks in the hotel; it should be kept by the hotel manager

Green Globe a world travel and tourism council initiative to help environmental awareness and management in the tourism industry

grill room food-service operation featuring a limited à la carte selection from the grill

gross domestic product the sum total of the production of economic goods and services within a country; often abbreviated to GDP

group rate a specific rate agreed for a group of people who will all be arriving together

guaranteed booking a booking for which payment is assured and which is therefore held indefinitely; sometimes also referred to as 'guaranteed payment reservations'

guéridon service meal prepared from sidetable or trolley, and served to guest with skill

guest charge anything put on a guest's bill—purchases, room service, telephone, and so on

guest folio guest account on which all details and **guest charges** are recorded

guest house a small establishment (often owner-managed) providing accommodation, food, and beverages to residents only

guest list a list of all guests in a hotel, giving their room number and any other relevant details; same as **house list**

guest relations the interreaction between hotel staff with their guests

guest's record card a card for each guest, listing the dates stayed in the hotel and other relevant details; also known as the 'guest history card'

held luggage guest's property held in lieu of payment for accommodation

high season the period of time when demand for accommodation is highest and when prices are usually highest; also known as 'the peak season'

horizontal integration a policy of a hospitality enterprise that offers service across the range of market segments; arrangements for the smooth interaction and working together of elements of a similar status in an organisation

hospitality in a business sense, a commercial contract to enter into a service relationship which involves supplying the amenities, comforts, conveniences, social interactions, and experiences of shelter and entertainment that a guest/customer values

host bar private room bar where drinks are prepaid by a sponsor; also known as a 'sponsored bar' or an 'open bar'

hotel booking agent a person who books accommodation at hotels on behalf of customers

hotel register a book in which all details of guests are entered when checking into a hotel; an alternative to the use of registration forms

hotel 'an establishment, especially of a comfortable or luxurious kind where paying visitors are provided with accommodation, meals, and other services' (*Oxford English Dictionary*); the word is used to describe a range of accommodation properties, but in the traditional usage a 'hotel' is defined as a place offering sleeping accommodation for hire to travellers and transients, and including services such as food, beverage, and entertainment along with other facilities and services

hotelier an owner, innkeeper, or manager of a hotel

house count number of rooms rented on a particular date

house list a list of all guests in a hotel, giving their room number and any other relevant details; same as **guest list**

housekeeper report the housekeeper's list of persons occupying rooms or beds at a given time; another term for **bed-occupancy list**

imprest system a procedure used with the petty-cash book by which a **float** of money is set aside for payments of petty cash; the credit columns are analysed, the book is balanced at intervals, and the amounts are transferred to the ledger; the amount spent is reimbursed, bringing the balance up to the original sum

imprinter the machine used to imprint details from a credit card onto a voucher

inbound tour operator a firm that organises travel and tourism products, usually by arranging services to groups of people arriving from elsewhere

incentive travel bonuses or incentives for employees, provided by a company to its deserving employees in the form of travel tickets, accommodation, and meals

incident book a book in which incidents of significance (problems, disputes, and so on) are noted and logged; the contents of such a book is passed on to the following shift to be noted and, if necessary, acted upon

industry sectors categories of various service areas, such as lodging services, travel services, tourism services, and so on

inspected the designation given to a room after it has been thoroughly checked by a supervisor or housekeeper

institutional food services operations that provide meals within certain accommodation enterprises (including the food services of schools, hospitals, jails, military barracks, and so on)

International Hotel Code an international code used for reserving hotel accommodation, thereby overcoming language difficulties

invoice a business document made out by a supplier to a buyer stating all details and prices of goods sold to the buyer (and usually indicating payment that is therefore due to the supplier)

junior suite a single large room with a partition separating the bedroom furnishings from the sitting area

key-and-mail rack a rack holding the keys, in room number order, with a slot for each room where the guest's mail and messages can be held for collection

key card a card issued to a guest upon checking into the hotel, showing the room number, rate, and other details; for security reasons, the card should be produced every time the guest requests the room key

kiosk a shop in the lobby of the hotel; this can be owned by the hotel or, more usually, rented to an outside company

lead time the length of time taken to achieve something; in hospitality, the time from when a booking is made until the date of arrival

ledger card a card used in a mechanised accounting system on which the details of an account is recorded

leisure free or unoccupied time to be spent as a person desires

liquidity the financial status of an organisation with reference to the potential for readily converting its assets into cash

lobby the entrance hall of the hotel

lost property book a record of personal property found (usually left behind by guests) at the hotel; the record is usually kept by the head housekeeper; if goods are reclaimed the details of when and by whom must be entered in the book

low season the quietest period at the hotel when prices are at their lowest

luggage register a record of all dealings concerning guests' luggage; usually kept by the concierge, this should record the number of articles handled, by whom, from where the luggage was taken, and to where it was taken

mail-advice note a form notifying a guest that a letter or parcel is awaiting collection

mail-forwarding book a book or form on which details of mail-handling are recorded; the details should be in chronological or alphabetical order and should record full details of guest's name, forwarding address, and the length of time for which this address is valid

make-up the changing of linen on beds, and cleaning of bedroom and bathroom, while a guest is registered in the room

management contract an agreement between the owner of a property and a company whereby the latter has full responsibility for the operation of the property or service

market feasibility study an investigation of all the financial consequences and the target market for a new hospitality project

market niche a specialised area of a defined market

market segments subcategories of hotel guests (such as business, tour group, and so on)

marrying-up the bringing together of the duplicate(s) and original copy of a voucher; the top copy, the original, is sent to the cashier who, having charged the guest, sends vouchers to the control office at the end of the day; the duplicates are sent to the control office by the departments from which the charge originated; the control clerk then checks that the copies of the voucher agree, and have been charged correctly; in most hotels the vouchers are kept with the guest's account until departure

master bill the main account on which items to be charged to a company, or a particular person, are recorded; otherwise known as a 'main account'; (charges not covered on the master bill are entered on an 'extra account')

master key the key that will open all bedrooms in the hotel

Meetings Industry Association of Australia a national, independent, non-profit body dedicated to fostering professionalism and excellence in all aspects of meeting management

menu list of dishes available in the food-service units; the term is also used to refer to the card on which the list is printed, or to the dishes themselves

mise en place a term used by the kitchen and restaurant staff, referring to the preparation of the food

monthly occupancy report a report of the rooms let and number of sleepers in a hotel for the month

motel a roadside accommodation property catering primarily for motorists; also known as motor hotel, motor inn, or motor lodge

nature attraction naturally occurring structures, plants, or animals that attract tourists

net rate a rate offered to travel agents after commission has been deducted

theme park a purpose-built complex designed with the intention of providing visitors with an atmosphere of another place and/or time, usually concentrating on one dominant theme

tidy-up to straighten and clean a room after a guest's departure when full service has been provided earlier

timers timing devices, located near the switchboard, used to remind the operator that certain wake-up calls are required to guests' rooms

tour wholesaler a firm which combines tourism services produced by other businesses into a single service

Tourism Training Australia a non-profit organisation established by the tourism industry to identify the training needs of the industry and to take action to meet those needs

Tourist Information Centre a centre providing information on events and attractions in the local district

tour a party of persons travelling and staying together

transferred to ledger the transfer of guest's account to a ledger to be paid at a later date; the account is credited on the machine or tab and debited in the sales or outstanding accounts ledger

travel agent an intermediary who derives financial gain (in the form of a commission) by linking suppliers of tourism services with consumers through the provision of reservations, ticketing, and other services

traveller's cheque a cheque, worth a stated amount, that can be cashed or used in payment when in a foreign country; the customer must sign the cheque(s) in the presence of the issuing cashier and, again, in the presence of the paying cashier

turn-away the refusal of walk-in business because rooms are not available

turnkey agreement an arrangement whereby a hotel owner hands over full control of the hotel to a management company

turnover rate a measure of the labour performance of a business obtained by dividing the number of employees who are replaced by the total number of employees in the business (usually expressed as a percentage per year)

twin double a room with two double beds for two, three, or four persons; sometimes called a 'family room'

twin one room with two separate beds

vacant and ready a room that is unoccupied, cleaned, and ready to be sold

vertical integration the linked ownership of all providers of services within the tourism package—that is, airlines, bus operators, and hotel operators

VIP very important person

visitor's disbursement a docket made out by the hotel cashier when money is paid out on behalf of a guest and charged to that guest's account; also known as 'VPO' ('visitors paid out')

voucher a bill giving details of the amount to be charged to a guest's account showing room number, item charged, price, and department concerned; the guest should be asked to sign the voucher in each instance

walk-in a guest who comes to the hotel without prior reservation seeking accommodation for the night; also known as 'chance' guests

walking a guest the turning away of guests who hold confirmed, guaranteed, or pre-paid reservations (due to lack of available rooms); usually involves the paying of guest's accommodation (or part thereof) at another hotel

reception board a board situated in the reception office giving an up-to-date record of the rooms in the hotel, showing the situation of each room at that moment (but not indicating the past or future room status)

reception the section of the front office handling the checking-in of guests and the status of the rooms

refund money paid back to a guest because the guest has paid too much or because the hotel is offering a discount for some other reason; (the paying cashier must ensure that the guest signs a refund voucher)

release time time at which a reservation held for a guest (who has failed to arrive) can be released for sale to another guest

report sheet a sheet completed by room attendants showing vacant and occupied rooms, and the number of sleepers in each room; completed once or twice a day, these sheets form the basis of the housekeeper's report

reservation chart chart showing all rooms let in a hotel over a certain period of time, and the availability of vacant rooms; *see also* **density chart** and **conventional chart**

reservation form a form made out by the receptionist or reservation clerk when taking a booking from a customer containing all relevant information about the prospective guest(s) and accommodation requirements

resort area a district frequented by tourists and excursionists, which provides a range of leisure opportunities and accommodation types

Restaurant and Catering Association an association that supports individual restaurants and catering services

restaurant cashier's report a summary of restaurant sales made by the cashier; having recorded all sales in duplicate as they occur, the cashier uses the duplicates to compile and balance a summary sheet which analyses and summarises all sales

restaurant an establishment at which meals are served to the general public

reverse-charge call a telephone call connected by the operator in which the charges are paid for by the receiver of the call

RNA registered but not assigned; refers to the practice whereby a guest arriving early in the day (when no rooms are available) is asked to register, deposit luggage, and return to the hotel for room assignment later in the day

roll-away a wheeled bed placed temporarily in a guest room; also known as a 'z' bed

room card a card giving the history of each room over a period of time; this usually shows the name of each guest who has occupied the room, when the room was occupied, and for how long, together with any other relevant details

room occupancy percentage a performance measure of a hotel obtained by dividing total rooms available by rooms occupied

room removals list a list giving the changes of room status for the day; this might be a separate list or a list shown on the arrival and departure list

room state the status of any given room at any moment—occupied, vacant, out of order ('off'), or reserved

rooms division all departments involved with accommodation at the hotel

run-of-the-house rate an agreed rate generally priced at an average between minimum and maximum for group accommodations for all available rooms except suites

safe deposit a facility offered to guests for the storage of valuable property; also known as 'safe custody'

security the department which is in charge of protecting employees an from thefts and vandalism

segmentation the subdivision of the hospitality market into identifiable and the development of hospitality services specifically for those different of the market

service charge additional charges on a bill for services rendered

shift leader a member of front office staff in charge of a particular employees

shoulder period a mid price time between the high and low seasons

single a room with one bed for one person

skips people who leave the hotel without paying their bills; also known as outs'

sleep out a guest who rented a room but did not sleep in it

sleeper a person occupying sleeping accommodation in the hotel

Societe Des Clefs D'Or an international society to which only élite members concierge department may belong; members wear a badge of crossed keys o lapel of their coats

sommelier a wine waiter

split shift a shift in which employees work two periods in a day with a rest b in between

staffing ratio a measure of levels of employment by which the number of members is expressed as a proportion of the number of beds, or number rooms, or number of guests; used to compare one property with another or time period with another

stay-on a guest who makes a booking for more than one night; the term is appli to the guest after the first night has passed; also known as a 'stay'

stay-over a guest who was expected to check-out on a certain day but wł remains in the hotel beyond the stated day of departure

stop–go chart a chart in the reservation office showing at a glance whether spac is available

studio a sitting room that may be converted into a bedroom, or vice versa; some times called an 'executive room'

submaster key a key that opens all bedrooms on one floor only; also known as a 'floor master'

suite a unit that contains a separate living space as well as bed and bathrooms

sundries miscellaneous items (such as taxis, hairdressing, and laundry) charged to a guest's account

table d'hôte a set menu at a set price (usually with a limited choice of dishes for each course)

take or place a regular guest who makes reservations at short notice, and who is offered accommodation should a cancellation be made; if not, the hotel will reserve accommodation for the guest at another similar hotel in the area (prefer- ably within the same company)

tariff the price list giving the charges of the hotel

tavern licensed premises having no accommodation but providing bottle sales, bar service, and counter meals

TBC to be confirmed

telephone call sheet (or book) a list of charges to be added to guests' accounts for telephone calls made through the hotel operator

wash factor the number of rooms which are reduced during the period of **lead time**; this factor is forecast as a percentage by the front office manager; the term usually applies to group bookings

weekly rate a special rate given by some hotels for people staying for a week or longer; sometimes applied by charging for six nights with the seventh being free ('on the house'); commonly found in resort hotels

Who's Who a reference book giving details concerning prominent persons in society

World Tourism Organization the principal collator and publisher of global statistics on tourist activities

yield management a process of calculating the best mix of rates and occupancy percentages to obtain the maximum profit out of an operation; the term is commonly used in hotel and airline operations

youth hostel a type of budget accommodation at which bathroom and toilet facilities are often shared and only basic services are provided

Index